SOS – Secrets of Opening Surprises 14

Published by New In Chess, Alkmaar, The Netherlands
www.newinchess.com

Cover design: Steven Boland
Drawing on frontcover: Zander Dekker
Translation Chapter 7: Ken Neat
Production: Joop de Groot
Proofreading: René Olthof

ISBN: 978-90-5691-366-3

SECRETS OF OPENING SURPRISES

14

Edited by

JEROEN BOSCH

Contributing authors

Simon Williams

Alexander Finkel

Dimitri Reinderman

Sinisa Drazic

Igor Lysyj

Maurits Wind

Arthur Kogan

Matthieu Cornette

Max Illingworth

Jeroen Bosch

2012 New In Chess – The Netherlands

Contents

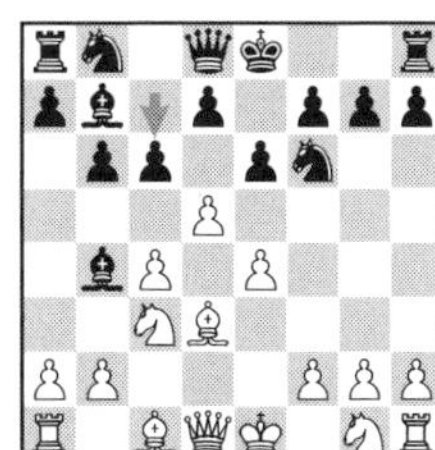

Novelty in the Queen's Grünfeld

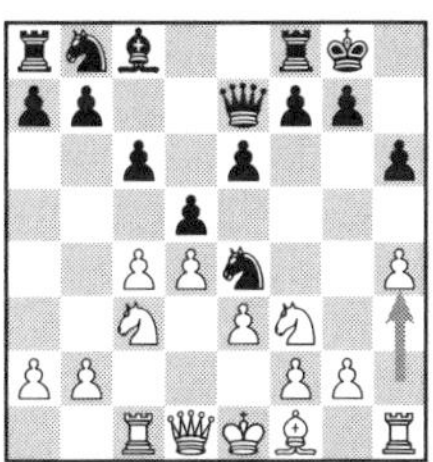

Let's play 10.h4!?

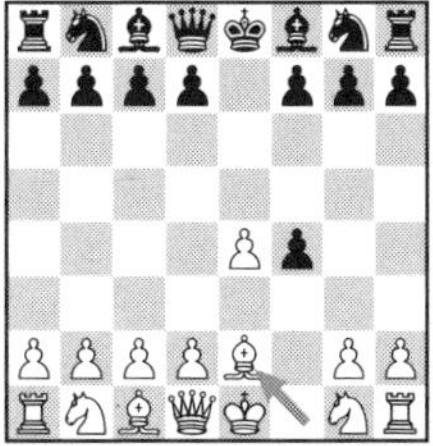

1.e4 e5 2.f4 exf4 3.♗e2!?

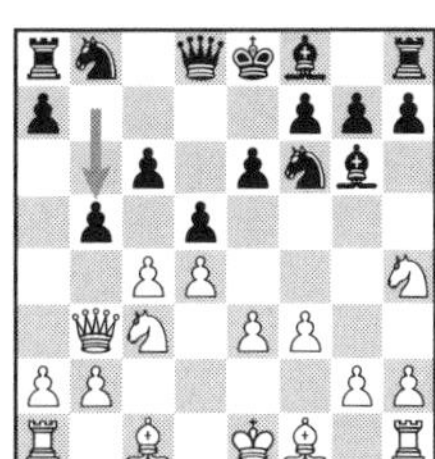

Let's play 8...b5!?

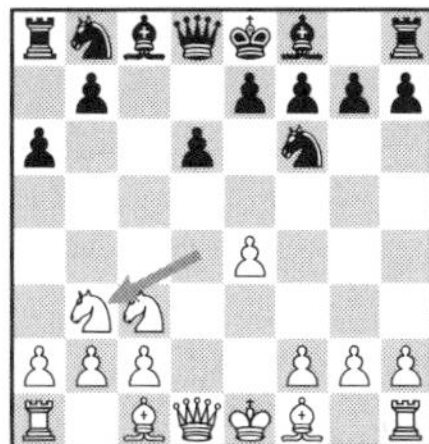

A voluntary retreat: 6.♘b3

CHAPTER 6 - page 47

Sinisa Drazic

A King's Indian Surprise

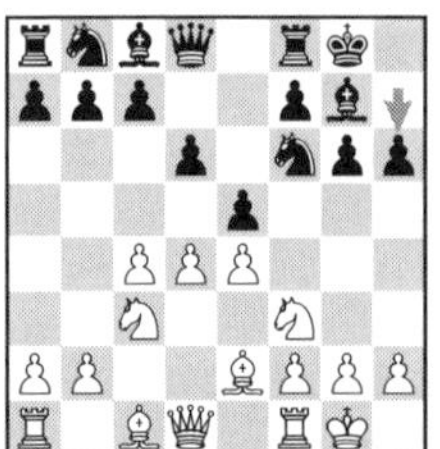

7...h6!? in the main line

CHAPTER 7 - page 55

Igor Lysyj

Queen's Indian: Chernyshov's Line

4.a3 ♗b7 5.♘c3 ♘e4!?

CHAPTER 8 - page 64

Jeroen Bosch

An Unusual Taimanov

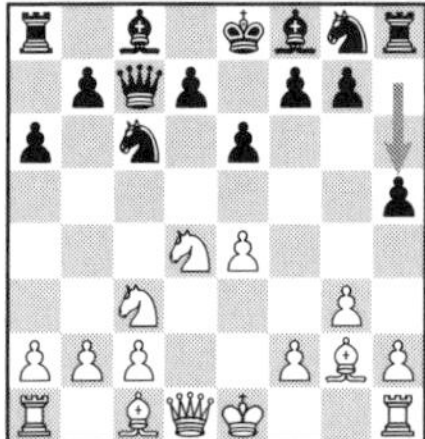

7...h5!?

CHAPTER 9 - page 70

Maurits Wind

The Mayet Defence

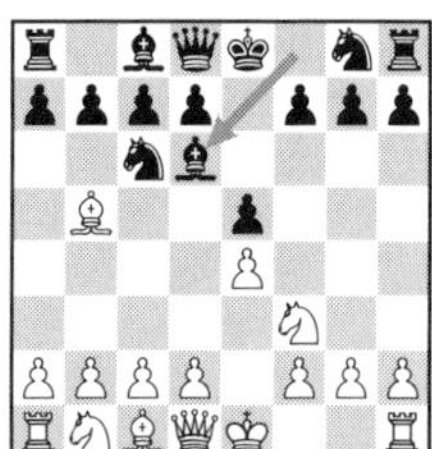

Spanish with 3...♗d6

CHAPTER 10 - page 81

Arthur Kogan

English Opening: Early Inspiration

1.c4 e5 2.a3!?

CHAPTER 11 - page 88

Alexander Finkel

Caro-Kann Advanced: an SOS Trend

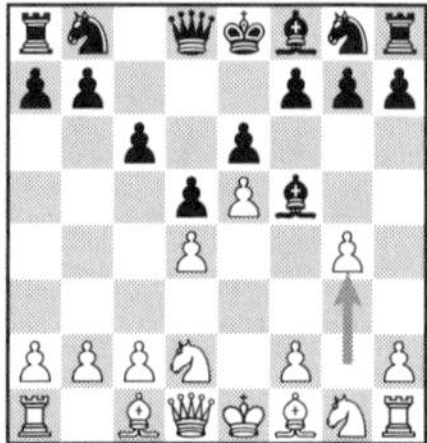

1.e4 c6 2.d4 d5 3.e5 ♗f5 4.♘d2 e6 5.g4!?

CHAPTER 12 - page 97

Matthieu Cornette

Grünfeld Fianchetto: a New Idea

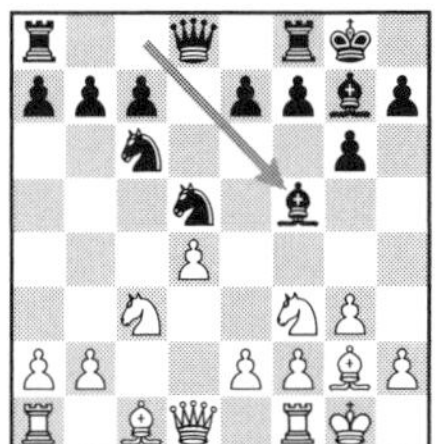

Avoiding the main line with 8...♗f5!?

CHAPTER 13 - page 104

Max Illingworth

Sicilian: the Illingworth Gambit

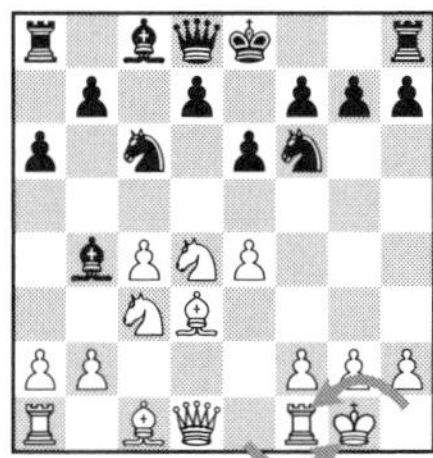

Sacrificing a piece with 8.0-0!

CHAPTER 14 - page 114

Jeroen Bosch

Avoiding the King's Indian Sämisch

1.d4 ♘f6 2.c4 g6 3.f3 ♘c6!?

CHAPTER 15 - page 120

Sinisa Drazic

Sicilian: the Bücker-Welling Variation

1.e4 c5 2.♘f3 h6!?

CHAPTER 16 - page 130

Jeroen Bosch

Fianchetto in the Alekhine Four Pawns

The less explored 5...g6!?

CHAPTER 17 - page 137

Arthur Kogan

King's Gambit – a Patzer Check

1.e4 e5 2.f4 ♕h4+!?

Chapter 1

Jeroen Bosch

The SOS Files

Svidler Improves Upon Smyslov

SOS-5, Chapter 10, p.80

In SOS-5 I wrote on two sidelines in the Ruy Lopez Exchange: 5...♗e6 and 5...♕e7. Both moves are playable at the highest level. In the Russian team competition Peter Svidler adopted an interesting novelty against Alexander Motylev in an old Smyslov favourite of the Ruy Lopez Exchange.

□ **Alexander Motylev**
■ **Peter Svidler**
Olginka tch-RUS Premier 2011

1.e4 e5 2.♘f3 ♘c6 3.♗b5 a6 4.♗xc6 dxc6 5.0-0 ♕e7!?

Smyslov's move, Black protects the e-pawn and prepares ... ♗g4 and queenside castling. He will often start a pawn storm on the kingside.

In the same article in SOS-5 I also investigated 5...♗e6!?, a move that was later adopted by such formidable players as Carlsen and Caruana. After 6.♘xe5 ♕d4 7.♘f3 ♕xe4 8.♘g5 ♕f5 (Carlsen preferred 8...♕g6 9.♘xe6 fxe6 10.d3 0-0-0 11.♕e2 ♗d6 12.♘d2 ♘f6 13.♘e4 ♘xe4 14.♕xe4 ♕xe4 15.dxe4 and the ending was equal in Naiditsch-Carlsen, Sarajevo 2006) 9.♘xe6 fxe6 10.d3 ♘f6 11.♘d2 0-0-0 12.♘c4 e5 13.♕e2 e4 14.dxe4 ♘xe4 15.♗e3 ♗d6 16.♖ad1 ♖he8 and Black had a pleasant position in Nisipeanu-Caruana, Plovdiv 2010.

6.d4

White almost invariably plays in the centre. Black obtained an excellent game after 6.♘a3 ♗g4 7.♘c4 f6 8.♘e3 ♗h5 9.♘f5?! ♕d7 10.d3 0-0-0 11.♗e3 ♗g4 12.♘g3 h5! 13.h3 ♗e6 (even sharper than 13...h4!?, which is also preferable for Black) 14.d4 ♕f7 15.♕c1 g5! (Black has a very strong attack and is not in the least bothered by the fact that his pieces on the kingside are still not developed) 16.dxe5 g4 17.♘d4 gxh3 18.♘xe6 ♕xe6 19.♖d1 ♖e8! 20.gxh3 ♕xh3 21.♕d2 fxe5 and Black won in S.Kasparov-Ris, Heraklion 2011.

6...exd4 7.♕xd4 ♗g4

Losing a tempo with 7...♕f6 as played by Igor Zaitsev and Bulgarian Champion Julian Radulski is a serious alternative.

8.♗f4 ♘f6

This is a more or less novel approach (there has been one earlier game where Black refrained from taking on f3). Black traditionally uses the opportunity to fracture White's kingside with 8...♗xf3 9.gxf3 ♘f6. However, after 10.♘c3 ♘h5 11.♗g3 White is 'clearly' slightly better, and has indeed scored significantly better than Black from this position (+4, =2).

9.♘c3

9.♘bd2 ♘h5 10.♗g5 ♕d6 11.h3 ♕xd4 12.♘xd4 ♗d7 13.g4 h6! 14.♗e3 ♘f6 15.c4 0-0-0 as in Gorin-Sarwinski, Koszalin 1998, looks quite alright for Black, especially when compared to all these Berlin endings where Black's king is still stuck in the centre around this time.

9...Nh5 10.Qe3!?

Giving up the bishop for a lead in development. The alternatives do not seem to promise much:

– 10.Bg5 Qd6 or even 10...f6 11.e5!? Qb4 12.exf6 Qxd4 13.Nxd4 Nxf6.

– 10.Be3 Bxf3 11.gxf3 Qe6 and compared to 8...Bxf3 9.gxf3 Nf6 10.Nc3 Nh5 11.Bg3! it is disadvantageous for White that his bishop is placed on e3 here. Black is comfortable.

– 10.Bg3 Nxg3 11.hxg3 is preferable for Black.

10...Nxf4 11.Qxf4

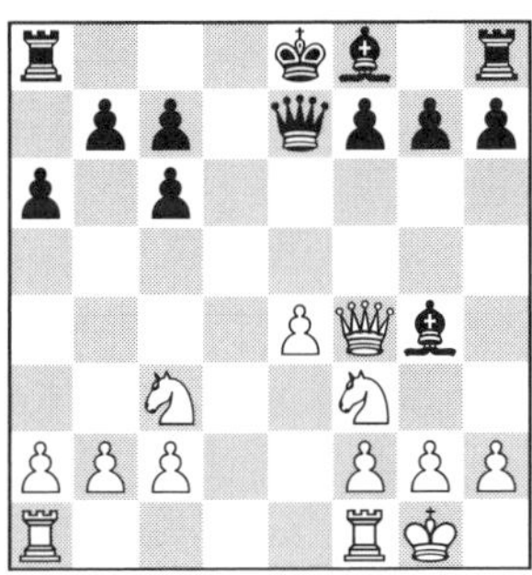

11...h5! 12.e5

12.Rad1 g6, when Black will be able to finally develop his kingside: 12.Ne5 g5!? 13.Qg3 Be6 is pleasant for Black.

12...0-0-0 12...g6. **13.Rad1 Re8**

Still aiming for complicated play. Meanwhile Black is completely OK after 13... Rxd1 14.Rxd1 g5!.

14.Rfe1 g5

Smyslov's original idea behind 5...Qe7! Black has done everything according to plan: ...Bg4, castling queenside, gaining space on the kingside.

15.Qe3

Very subtle. Motylev lures Black's king to b8 before sacrificing the exchange by taking on g5. Judging from the course of the game this is quite significant.

15...Kb8 16.Qxg5!?

White is in trouble and this positional exchange sacrifice is an interesting defensive measure.

16...Qxg5 17.Nxg5 Bxd1 18.Rxd1 Bg7 19.f4 19.Nxf7? Rhf8 20.Ng5 Bxe5 ought to win for Black. **19...f6**

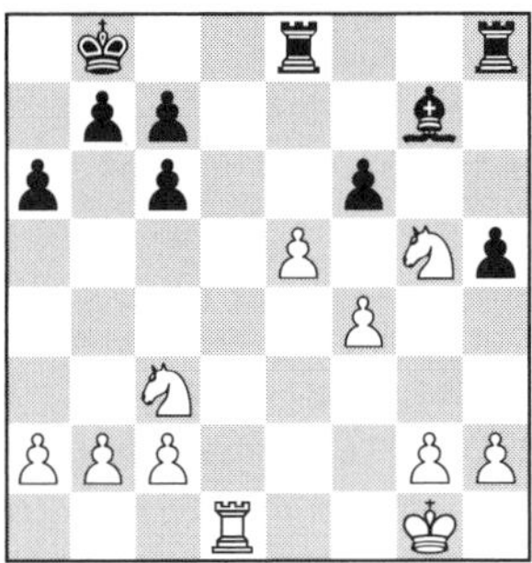

20.Nge4!

20.exf6 Bxf6 and although White has two potential passed pawns on the kingside, his compensation for the exchange is insufficient. Black has too many open files for his rooks. That's why Motylev tries to keep the position as closed as possible (favouring his knights and annoying the oppponent's rooks).

20...Rhf8 21.Rf1 Re7!? 22.g3 fxe5 23.f5 Ref7

Now with the king on c8 Black would simply win the f5 pawn (remember 15.Qe3 and 16.Qxg5). Now, however, White still has:

24.Nc5! Kc8 Only White can win after 24...Rxf5 25.Nd7+ Kc8 26.Nxf8 Rxf1+ 27.Kxf1 Bxf8 28.Ne4.

25.Ne6 Rg8 26.Ng5 Rd7 27.Nce4

White has excellent positional compensation for the exchange. The players agreed to a draw.

Chess is Fun

SOS-5, Chapter 4, p.38

Russian grandmaster Boris Savchenko has a rather interesting style. In the opening he is not just willing to experiment, no, he is prepared to take extreme risks. In the Russian Championship (Higher League) he took up the 'mundane' Zviagintsev Sicilian. Have fun!

□ **Boris Savchenko**
■ **Ivan Bukavshin**
Taganrog 2011

1.e4

To illustrate Savchenko's preferences in the opening: 1.c4 ♘f6 2.d4 g6 3.♘c3 ♗g7 4.h4!? d6 5.h5?! ♘xh5 6.e4 e5 7.d5 ♘f6 8.♗e2 h5 9.♘f3 a5 and White had very little for the pawn in the last round game of the Higher League, Savchenko-Inarkiev, Taganrog 2011.

1...c5 2.♘a3

You may recall that it was in the 2005 Russian Super Final that Zviagintsev sprang this move on the unsuspecting Alexander Khalifman, who promptly burst out laughing. White had the final laugh when he won on move 37. In the six years since this first outing the knight move has been played in some 500 documented games...!

Another weird Savchenko game came about after 2.b3. See SOS-9, Chapter 16, p.123, for Arthur Kogan's take on 2.b3. I can assure the reader that Kogan did not consider Black's next move! 2...h5 3.♗b2 ♘c6 4.♘f3 d5 5.exd5 ♕xd5 6.♘c3 ♕d8 7.♗b5 ♖h6 8.0-0 a6 9.♗xc6+ ♖xc6 10.♘e5 ♖h6, Paichadze-Savchenko, Aix-les-Bains ch-EUR 2011. White has a tremendous position of course, but he lost – see also New In Chess Yearbook 99 (pp. 14-15) for notes on the game.

2...♘c6 3.♗b5 ♘a5

This reminds us of course of our SOS versus the Rossolimo: 1.e4 c5 2.♘f3 ♘c6 3.♗b5 ♘a5 – see SOS-4, Chapter 15, p.111. Black prevents the doubling of his pawns and prepares to hit the bishop with ...a6.

4.♗a4

A novel approach. Previously the sedate 4.c3 a6 5.♗e2 ♘f6 6.d3 had been tested twice.

4...♕b6 5.c3

Also tempting is 5.♘f3 ♕b4?! 6.c4 ♘xc4 7.♘xc4 (7.♘b5!?) 7...♕xc4 8.d3 ♕b4+ 9.♗d2 with a huge edge in development.

5...♕g6 6.♕f3

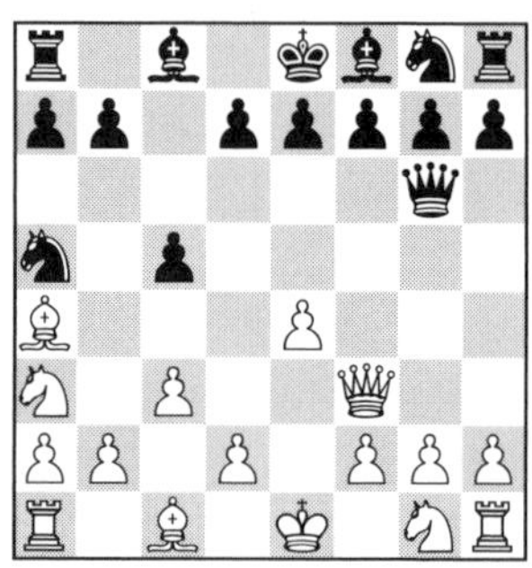

6...♘c6 7.♘c4

7.♘b5 ♘e5 is OK for Black (7...♔d8 is not bad either): 8.♕f5 ♕xf5 9.exf5 ♔d8 10.d4 ♘d3+ 11.♔e2 ♘xc1+ 12.♖xc1 a6 13.♘a3 b5 14.♗c2 cxd4 15.cxd4 ♗b7 16.♘f3.

7...♕e6?! 8.♘e3

8.d3 d5 9.♘a5! ♗d7 10.♗xc6 ♗xc6 11.♘xc6 bxc6 is slightly better for White.

8...♘e5 9.♕e2 c4 10.f3

This looks odd, but Black was intending to meet 10.♗c2 with 10...♘f6 (not 10...♘d3+ 11.♗xd3 cxd3 12.♕xd3 ♘f6 13.f3) 11.♘f3 ♘d3+ 12.♗xd3 cxd3 13.♕xd3 ♕xe4, when White should be slightly better.

10...♕a6! 11.♗c2 ♘f6 12.b3! b5

12...♘d3+ 13.♔f1 ♘xc1 14.♖xc1 ♕xa2 15.♕xc4 favours White.

13.f4 ♘g6
Like it or not, it was more consistent to play 13...♘d3+ 14.♗xd3 cxd3 15.♕xd3 ♗b7 16.e5 ♘e4 with some compensation.
14.e5 ♘xf4 15.♕f3 Here we see why White wanted to provoke ...b5.
15...♘6d5

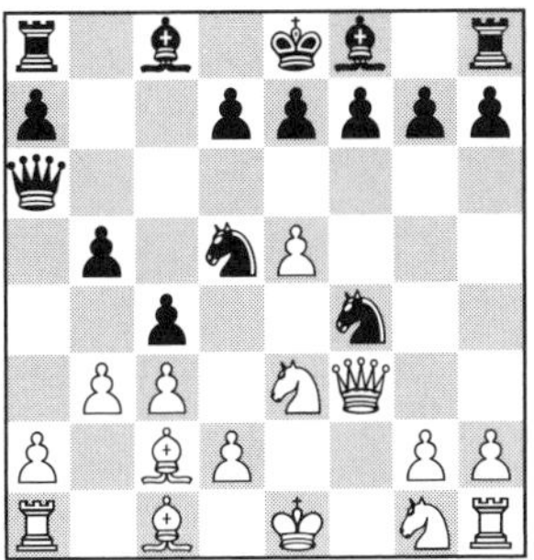

16.♘h3!
This wins material. 16.g3? ♘xe3 17.dxe3 ♗b7 18.♗e4? ♘d3+; 16.♗e4 e6.
16...♘xe3
White is much better after 16...♘xh3 17.♘xd5 ♘g5 18.♕g4 (18.♘c7+ ♔d8 19.♕xa8 ♔xc7 20.♕d5 e6 21.♕d4) 18...♘e6 19.bxc4 bxc4 20.♖b1.
17.dxe3 ♗b7! 18.♕xf4 ♗xg2 19.♖g1
Winning a piece, but things remain messy. 19.♗e4!? ♗xh1 20.♗xh1 ♖c8 21.b4±.
19...♗xh3 20.♕f3! ♖c8 21.♕xh3 g6 22.e4 ♗g7 23.♗f4 0-0

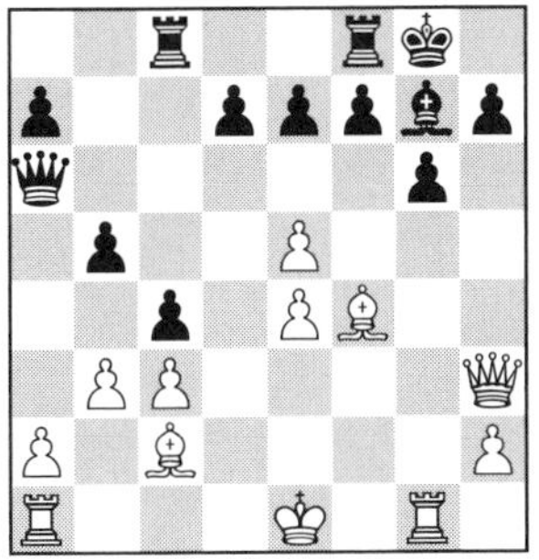

Black has two pawns for the piece, and White's king is hardly safe. Still, White has an edge. With his next move he logically attempts to close files in order to consolidate (and find a safe haven for his king).
24.b4 ♕a3!? 25.♗c1!? ♕a6 26.♗h6 ♗xe5 Raising his bet to a rook. The best chance was perhaps to return with the queen to a3. **27.♗xf8 ♖xf8 28.♖g5!?**
A nice consolidating move was 28.a3, with the point of 28...♕f6 29.0-0-0! ♗xc3 30.♖gf1 ♕g7 31.♖xd7.
28...♗f6?! After the natural 28...♕f6 White would have returned material with 29.♖xe5! ♕xe5 30.0-0-0.
29.♕g3 Strong was 29.♖d5 d6 30.a4!.
29...♕b6 30.a4? 30.♖d5; 30.0-0-0. **30...bxa4?** 30...♗xg5 31.♕xg5 a5! would have messed things up to a considerable extent.
31.♖xa4 e6? 32.♖ga5
Now White is clearly winning. Black resigned on move 49.

Reading SOS Brings Success

SOS-13, Chapter 7, p.61

Regarding the next game, White must have read Alexander Finkel's article in SOS-13 carefully, while his opponent left SOS-theory on move 16, only to resign 7 moves later (in a position where he should have played on!).

□ **David Klein**
■ **Peter Poobalasingam**
Haarlem 2011

1.e4 e6 2.d4 d5 3.♘c3 ♗b4 4.♘e2 dxe4 5.a3 ♗xc3+
5...♗e7 6.g4 was a companion article of Finkel. See SOS-12, Chapter 4, p.34.
6.♘xc3 ♘c6 7.♗b5
The best move according to Finkel.

7.d5 exd5 8.Qxd5 has been played by Solodovnichenko. After 8...Be6 (Finkel argues that Black equalizes after 8...Nge7 9.Qxd8+ Nxd8 10.Nxe4 Bf5) 9.Qxe4 Nf6 10.Qh4 Qd4 11.Bg5 Qe5+ 12.Be2 Nd4?! (12...0-0-0) 13.0-0-0!

– 13...0-0-0 14.Bd3 h6 15.Bxf6 Qxf6!N (15...gxf6) 16.Qxf6 gxf6 17.Ne4 (17.Rhe1±; 17.Rd2±) 17...Bd5 (17...f5 18.Nc5±) 18.f3 (18.Rhe1) 18...Bxe4 19.fxe4 White has a slight edge. After 19...Rd6 20.Rhf1 Black erred with 20...Kd8?, when 21.Bc4 cemented White's edge in Solodovnichenko-Edouard, Mulhouse 2011.
– Wrong is 13...Nxe2+? 14.Nxe2 Qxe2 15.Bxf6 gxf6 16.Rhe1 Qa6 17.Qxf6 0-0 (not 17...Rg8 when 18.Re3! wins as Black cannot prevent 19. Rde1 and taking on e6) 18.Re5 Rfe8 19.Rd3+–, Solodovnichenko.

7...Ne7 8.Bg5 f6 9.Be3 f5?!

Finkel devotes the bulk of his article to the stronger 9...0-0 but also covers the text.

10.Qh5+ g6 11.Qh6 Kf7 12.0-0-0 Nd5 13.Nxd5 exd5 14.Bf4 Qf8

14...Bd7 15.Bxc6 Bxc6 16.Be5 Qf8 17.Qh3 is indicated as clearly favourable for White by Finkel.

15.Qh4

15.Qh3 from Pilnik-Czerniak, Buenos Aires 1941, makes a lot of sense too.

15...Qe7 16.Qg3

16...Bd7

You could call this a novelty, but it does not change the evaluation: Black faces an unpleasant struggle for a draw.

16...Be6 17.h4 (17.Bxc6!?) 17...h5 18.Bxc7 Rhc8 19.Bd6 Qd8 20.Kb1 favoured White in Nataf-Apicella, Marseille 2001. See SOS-13.

17.Bxc7 Retrieving the pawn, whilst preserving a dark-squared edge. **17...Nxd4 18.Rxd4 Bxb5 19.Rxd5 Rhc8**

19...Rac8 should be met by 20.Bd6 (20.Ba5!?; 20.Qb3 Qe6 21.Qxb5 Rxc7 22.Rhd1±) 20...Qd7 21.Kb1 (for now 21.Re5 meets with the equalizer 21...Rhe8).

20.Bd6 Qd7

21.Re5!?

This cheeky move wins the game in a few moves. Again 21.Kb1 is enough for an edge.

21...Re8?

21...♗d3 22.♖e7+ ♕xe7 23.♗xe7 ♖xc2+ 24.♔b1 ♔xe7 25.♕e5+ ♔f7 26.♔a1 and when you are a computer you will be able to draw this fairly easy I suppose. But for humans Black's position is still rather unpleasant.
White wins after 21...♔g8? 22.♖e7 ♕c6 23.c3 ♖e8 24.♖c7 ♕b6 25.♕h4 or 21...♕xd6?? 22.♖xf5+ ♔e7 23.♖f7+.
22.♕b3+! ♔f6 23.♕xb5!?
And Black resigned, undoubtedly overlooking that he does not lose a piece, because of 23...♕xd6 24.♖xe8 a6! when White is better but nevertheless will have to work quite hard for a full point!
Objectively White had to play 23.♖d1! ♗c6 24.♕g3 with a very strong attack.

The Queen's Grünfeld Line

SOS-6, Chapter 11, p.88

If you want to leave the beaten track fairly soon, but still aim for typical 'Indian' complexity, then the Queen's Grünfeld Line (as Arthur Kogan dubbed it in SOS-6) might be up your alley. In the 2011 Dutch Championship Ivan Sokolov employed it to defeat the early leader Wouter Spoelman.

□ **Wouter Spoelman**
■ **Ivan Sokolov**
Boxtel ch-NED 2011

1.d4 ♘f6 2.c4 b6 3.♘c3 ♗b7 4.♕c2
Earlier this year Sokolov had encountered 4.♗g5, when a transposition to the Nimzo/Queen's Indian is possible. 4...e6 5.e3 h6 6.♗h4 ♗b4 7.♘e2 (7.♘f3) 7...0-0 8.f3 d5 9.cxd5 exd5 10.a3 ♗d6 11.♗f2 ♖e8 12.♘g3 c5 13.♗e2 ♘bd7 14.0-0 a6 15.♘f5 ♗f8 16.♕c2 g6 17.♘g3 ♖c8 18.♖ad1 h5! and Black was better in Bratanov-Sokolov, Mulhouse 2011.
For 4.d5 and the winner of the SOS Prize see the end of this chapter!
4...d5 5.cxd5 ♘xd5 6.e4 ♘xc3 7.bxc3 g6 8.♘f3 ♗g7 9.♗c4
If you consider taking up this line in your (surprise) repertoire, then the next fragment is well worth studying: 9.♗e2 0-0 10.0-0 ♘d7 11.a4 e5 12.♗b2 ♖e8 13.♗d3 exd4! 14.cxd4 c5 (14...♘c5!? 15.dxc5 ♗xb2 16.♖ae1! ♗a3∓) 15.d5 c4 16.♗xc4 ♗xb2 17.♕xb2 ♖xe4 18.♗b5 ♘c5 and Black is slightly better, Bukic-Planinec, Skopje 1971.
9...0-0 10.0-0 ♘d7 11.♗f4

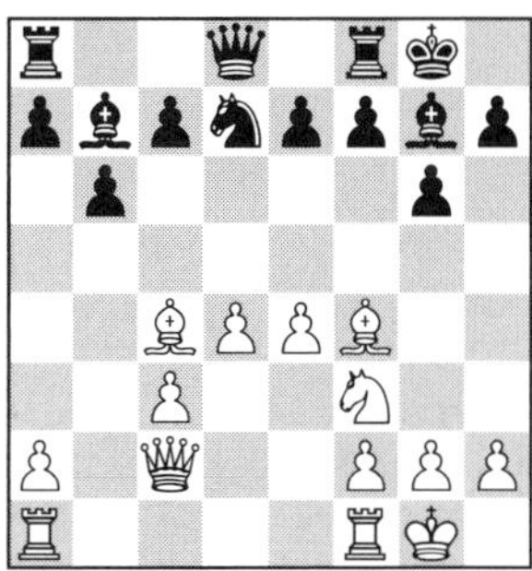

11...e5! 12.dxe5
More testing was 12.♗g5 ♕e8 13.♖fe1 (13.♖ae1) 13...exd4 14.cxd4 c5 15.♖ad1.
12...♕e7 13.♖ad1
Play is equal after 13.e6 fxe6 14.♗g5.
13...♘xe5 14.♘xe5 ♗xe5 15.♗xe5 ♕xe5 Material is equal, but Black's pawn structure is slightly superior, which is why the second player may already entertain some hope of achieving more than a comfortable draw.
16.♗d5 c6 17.f4 ♕e7 18.♗b3 ♖ad8 19.e5 ♗c8!
Well-played. Rather than opening the long diagonal for the bishop, Sokolov transfers the bishop to neutralize White's counterplay.
20.♖xd8 ♖xd8 21.♖d1 ♔g7!
21...♕c5+ 22.♔h1 ♖xd1+ 23.♕xd1 ♕xc3

is only a draw after 24.♕d8+ ♔g7 25.♕f6+ ♔h6 with a perpetual.

22.♖xd8 ♕xd8 23.♕d1 ♕e7

23...♕xd1+ 24.♗xd1 ♗e6 25.a3 is a draw.

24.♕d4 c5 25.♕e4 h5 26.♗d5 b5 27.♗c6?! a6 Black is slightly better.

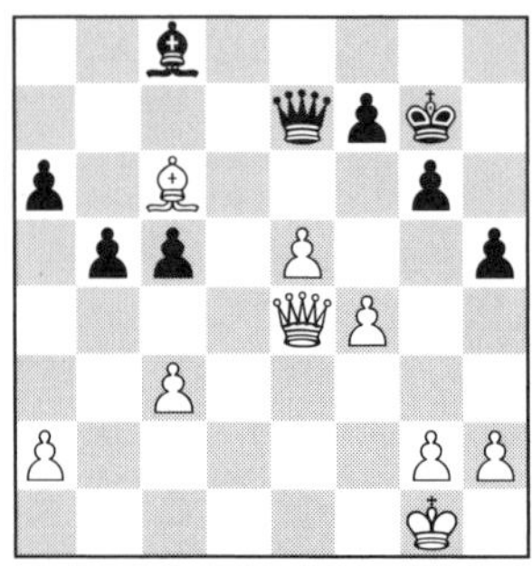

28.a3? c4 29.♕d4 ♗e6 30.a4

White cannot keep out the opponent's queen with 30.♕d6, as Black has 30...♕a7+ 31.♔f1 ♕e3.

30...b4 31.cxb4 ♕xb4 32.♔f2 a5?!

Stronger was 32...♕a3. **33.♔e3??**

A blunder which allows mate in two. White had to play 33.♔e2, when he is much worse but perhaps not yet losing.

33...♕e1+

And White resigned, as he is mated after 34.♔f3 ♗g4+.

Novelty Wins SOS Prize

SOS-6, Chapter 11, p.88

We received an interesting letter from one of our Irish SOS readers, Colin Menzies. Colin came up with a strong novelty in the Queen's Grünfeld Line, the main point of Black's play involving a piece sacrifice (albeit for three pawns) which promises Black an excellent game. The whole idea is convincing enough for the SOS Prize!

1.d4 ♘f6 2.c4 b6 3.♘c3 ♗b7 4.d5

With this ambitious line White aims to 'suffocate' the bishop. **4...e6 5.e4**

Colin agrees with SOS author Arthur Kogan that the prophylactic 5.a3 is stronger. However, he also writes that most players are out of book by now, so that roughly two-thirds of his opponents play 5.e4.

After 5.a3 Black has 5...♗d6!?, when 6.e4 is met by 6...♗e5!.

5...♗b4 6.♗d3

White has an imposing centre, and Black will have to find counterplay soon.

Colin also gives the following alternatives:

– 6.♗g5 h6 7.♗xf6 ♕xf6 8.♕f3 ♗xc3+ 9.bxc3 ♘a6∓ with a big hole on c5. (9...♕e7 is also good)

– 6.e5 ♘e4 7.♘e2 0-0 8.a3 ♘xc3 9.bxc3 (9.♘xc3 ♗xc3+ 10.bxc3 exd5 11.cxd5 d6) 9...♗c5∓ with a lead in development.

6...c6!

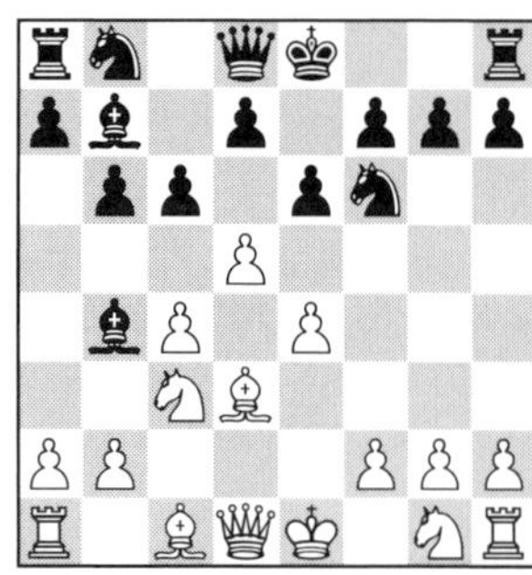

A good novelty that requires calculation (or preparation), as 7.e5 now seems strong. Colin writes that he first played this move in the 2008 Bunratty congress. Somehow, the game has not entered the databases, so we can still present it as a novelty! Colin found the move over the board, and writes that: 'This line still comes up quite often for me online (mostly blitz). If White plays 'natural moves' with a vague plan of holding a strong centre, he can quite easily end up facing this line. With best play from White,

Black has no trouble achieving equality (at the very least), which I believe is the real value of this move, and probably means the Advance Variation without a3 is a bad idea in general for White.' His score from this position is about 65% from 20 games.

6...b5 was recommended by Arthur Kogan in SOS-6. Kogan warmly supports Black's cause after 7.cxb5 exd5 8.e5 d4. However, instead of 8.e5, White should play 9.exd5 which seems to promise an advantage.

A good alternative is 6...exd5 7.cxd5 c6 (as played by Dizdarevic against Iotov at Plovdiv 2010) but this does not offer White any dangerous temptations and equalizes.

7.e5?!

Again I would like to quote Colin at length: 'I think this move is an error, as it leads to Black getting three pawns for a piece (at the very least) and a very comfortable position. No one expects a knight sac so early, which is where the SOS factor comes in, I guess! Of course White doesn't have to play e5, but in that case Black gets a very playable position without much effort, because the pressure on d5 means White cannot hold on to his extended centre. Most of the following variations illustrate that Black simply exchanges on d5 and castles, with clear equality (in fact White has to be slightly more careful, or he can be left with a horrible pawn structure).'

– 7.♘f3 cxd5 8.exd5 0-0 9.dxe6 dxe6 is slightly better for Black.

– 7.♘e2 cxd5 8.cxd5 exd5 9.exd5 and now Black should accept the pawn on offer: 9...♘xd5 10.0-0 ♘xc3 11.♘xc3 0-0 and White has just about enough compensation for the pawn.

– 7.dxe6 dxe6 8.♘f3 ♘bd7 9.♕e2 (9.♕c2? ♘c5∓; 9.e5?! ♘c5) is about equal.

7...cxd5! 8.exf6

White must accept the sacrifice.

8...♕xf6

9.♗d2

– 9.♔f1 is the best move, as it protects g2 and moves out of the pin: 9...dxc4 10.♗c2 (10.♗xc4? ♗xc3 11.bxc3 ♕xc3 is a double attack) 10...♗xc3 11.bxc3 ♕xc3 12.♗d2 ♕f6 13.♘e2 d5 and while things still look unclear, Black seems to be more comfortable.

– 9.♘e2? d4∓ 10.♕b3 (10.a3 dxc3 11.axb4 cxb2) 10...♗a5 11.0-0 dxc3 12.bxc3 ♘a6 13.♗e3 0-0 14.c5 ♘xc5 15.♗xc5 ♕g5! 16.♘g3 ♕xc5 and Black won in the stem game Rea-Menzies, Bunratty Challengers 2008.

– 9.♕c2? d4∓.

9...dxc4 The threat on g2 is why the whole variation works. **10.♗f1 d5**

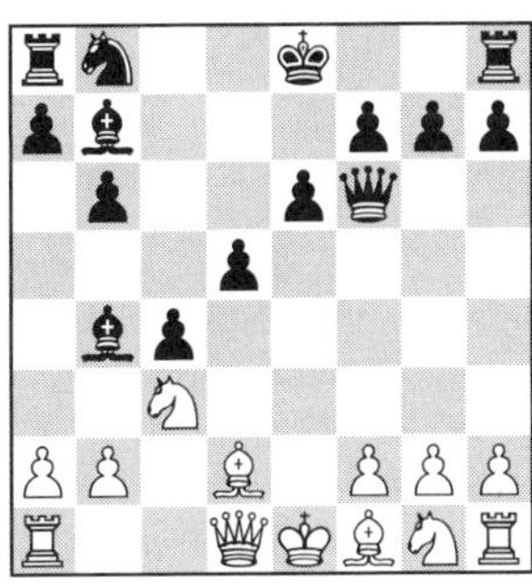

And with three pawns for the piece, and a dominating centre, Black has the better chances.

CHAPTER 2

Jeroen Bosch

SOS in the Lasker Defence

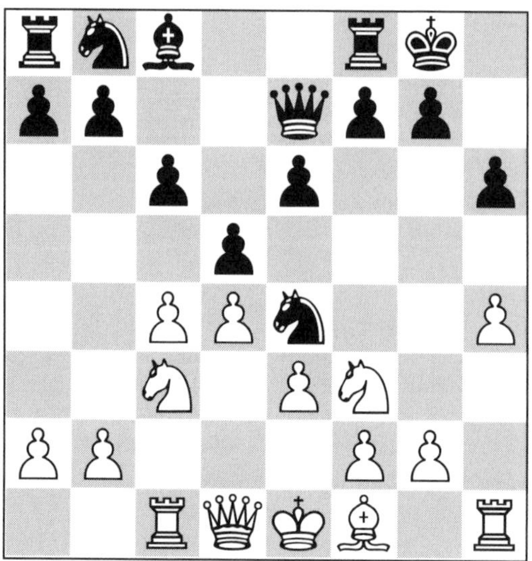

Let's play 10.h4!?

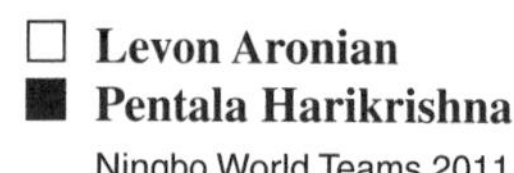

□ **Levon Aronian**
■ **Pentala Harikrishna**
Ningbo World Teams 2011

The Lasker Defence of the Queen's Gambit is quite fashionable these days. As so often in chess the World Champion is setting the standard. Anand used this rock-solid line of the second World Champion to successfully defend his title against Veselin Topalov. Not only did he win the 12th and final game of their 2010 World Championship's match, but later in the year he also repeated the line in Nanjing to score another devastating win against the Bulgarian.

Former World Champion Vladimir Kramnik is of course another major adherent of Lasker's simplifying manoeuvre. The summer of 2011 may have warmed the hearts of 1.d4 devotees though, as Levon Aronian came up with a remarkable idea that so far has brought White great opening results. In great SOS style Aronian goes h4 and g4 where previously players only considered such mundane matters as development and castling. Enjoy!

1.d4 ♘f6 2.c4 e6 3.♘f3 d5 4.♘c3 ♗e7 5.♗g5 h6 6.♗h4 0-0 7.e3 ♘e4

This is known as Lasker's Defence. Black aims to exchange two pairs of minor pieces, thereby relieving his game. As he has no weaknesses he aims to equalize in the early middlegame, often by means of ...dxc4 and ...e5 or ...c5.

8.♗xe7 ♕xe7 9.♖c1

9.cxd5 ♘xc3 10.bxc3 exd5 is another main line in the Lasker.

9...c6

This is thought to be more accurate than the immediate 9...♘xc3 10.♖xc3 c6, although play usually transposes. Interestingly, Aronian's idea had been anticipated in this position by Dutch grandmaster Jan Werle (albeit in a rapid game).

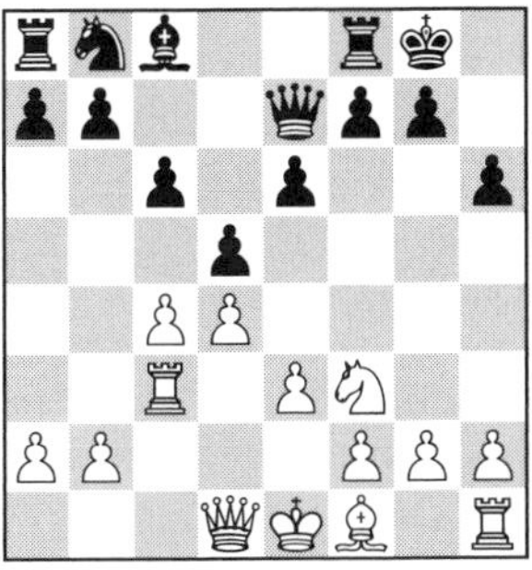

11.g4!? – White argues that the pawn on h6 is a clear target with Black already castled on the kingside. Moreover, after the exchange on c3 Black has no minor pieces developed just yet, so how is he ever going to profit from the 'weakening' g4? Indeed, there is no break in the centre available in reply to this audacious flank attack. 11...♘d7 12.♖g1 (12.h4 looks even better, and could in fact transpose to our main game, if Harikrishna had taken on c3 on move 11) 12...g6?! 13.g5 h5 (13...hxg5 14.♘xg5, when 14...e5 15.cxd5 cxd5 16.dxe5 looks a little better for White, while 14...♘f6 15.h4 e5 or 14...♔g7 may be better) 14.cxd5 exd5 15.♗e2. Black has ended up in a position where he has no pawn breaks (...f6 or ...c5) without damaging his structure, Werle-Van der Werf, Leeuwarden rapid 2009.

10.h4

Within the SOS-series we have often remarked that moves like h4 and g4 in the opening are the hallmark of modern chess. However, no one had actually dared (or perhaps even thought of) playing it in this respectable Queen's Gambit position.

However, once you are clever enough (or crazy enough?) to have come up with the idea, it may strike you that Black is not exactly in a great position to take advantage of this flank attack with the prescribed break in the centre. He simply has too little control over the central squares at the moment (the price of playing twice with the same piece in the opening and exchanging off his good bishop).

Indeed, had the opening been a Sicilian, where Black had castled kingside and had weakened his king with ...h6, then I think that we all would have started to embark on a flank attack. So hats off for Aronian for this original opening idea in SOS-style. And while we are at it, we might as well wonder if 10.g4 isn't playable as well?

The answer is not exactly blowing in the wind. In his 2011 first round World Cup match, Austrian GM Markus Ragger twice played this move versus Alekseev. Two draws were the result, but in both games Ragger was comfortably placed, to say the very least: 10...♖d8 (10...♘d7 11.h4 was played in Ragger-Alekseev, Khanty-Mansiysk 2011, a game with the regular FIDE tempo. Play transposes to the comments on move 11 in our main game. Note that 10…f5!? 11.gxf5 ♕f6 was a blitz game Halkias-D.Fridman, Warsaw 2010) 11.♖g1 (11.h4 c5 12.cxd5 exd5! was Black's main idea. Play is unclear, as Black has counterplay too: 13.g5 ♘c6 14.gxh6 ♕f6!) 11... c5 (the idea behind placing the rook on d8. Alekseev aims for counterplay in the centre) 12.cxd5 ♘xc3?! (12...exd5 has to be investigated too, of course. White could continue 13.g5!?, when 13...hxg5?! – 13... ♘xg5 14.♘xg5 hxg5 15.♕h5!?; 13...♘xc3 14.♖xc3 hxg5 15.♘xg5 – 14.♘xe4 dxe4 15.♘xg5 favours White greatly, as 15...cxd4 is met by 16.♗c4!) 13.♖xc3 cxd4 (13...♖xd5 14.♕c2!; 13...exd5? 14.♖xc5) 14.♘xd4 exd5. White has a structural edge but he has to take care of his king in the centre, or so it seems. Ragger, in fact, demonstrates that it is Black's king who has all the worries: 15.g5! (very energetic!) 15...hxg5 16.♕h5 g4 (16...f6 17.♗d3 just wins for White)

17.♖xc8 (a powerful sacrifice, but not the best one! Chess engines will prove that White is winning after 17.♗d3 g6 18.♗xg6! fxg6 19.♕xg6+ ♕g7 20.♕h5!! – this type of quiet move is difficult for humans to find. Black has no satisfactory defence against the threat of 21.♖xc8 and 22.♖xg4. The main line is 20...♘c6 21.♘xc6 bxc6 22.♖xc6 ♔f8 23.♖g6 and queen and rook join in a winning attack) 17...♖xc8 18.♕xg4 (and here 18.♗d3! was still good enough for a winning position after 18...♕b4+ – 18...g6 19.♗xg6 fxg6 20.♖xg4+– – 19.♔d1 ♘c6 20.♕xg4 ♔f8 21.♕xg7+ ♔e7 22.♕g5+) 18...♕f8 19.♘e6! (19.♘f5 ♘c6 20.♕h5 g6 21.♖xg6+ fxg6 22.♕xg6+ ♔h8 23.♕h5+ is a draw) 19...♖c1+! (19...fxe6 20.♕xe6+ ♔h8 21.♖g5 ♕b4+ 22.♔d1 wins for White) 20.♔d2 fxe6 21.♕xe6+ ♕f7 22.♕xf7+ ♔xf7 23.♔xc1 and White is a pawn up but did not win in Ragger-Alekseev, FIDE World Cup 2011 rapid.

– The boring 10.♗e2 ♘xc3 11.♖xc3 dxc4 12.♗xc4 ♘d7 is the main line, where White has not exactly been able to prove anything lately.

10...♘d7

Mikhail Golubev's 10...♖d8 is interesting. The idea is to transpose to our comments on Ragger-Alekseev above after 11.g4 c5 12.cxd5 exd5. Still, White does not have to lunge forward now. I would propose 11.♕c2!?.

11.g4

This position may also be reached via the move 10.g4 ♘d7 11.h4, as was the case in the Ragger-Alekseev mentioned game in the previous comment. Black is now at crossroads.

11...e5

In principle the logical strike in the centre.

● 11...f5 12.gxf5 exf5 (12...♖xf5 deserves attention, although I would not mind playing the position after 13.♗d3; 13.♘xe4 dxe4 14.♘d2 e5! 15.d5 ♘c5 is unclear but seems fine for Black) 13.cxd5 ♘xc3 14.♖xc3 cxd5 15.♕b3 ♕e4 (sharp, but otherwise White just has a sound structure and better development. 15...♘f6 16.♘e5 must be better for White) 16.♗e2 ♘f6 17.♖g1 f4 18.♖c7

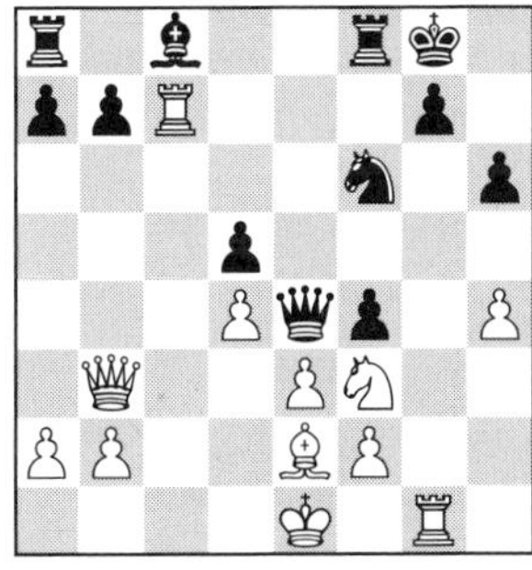

and now:

– 18...♘e8? 19.♘d2! ♕h7 (19...♕f5 20.♖e7) 20.♕xd5+ ♔h8 21.♖e7 ♗f5 22.e4 ♗g6 23.h5 ♘f6 24.♕xb7 ♖ab8 25.hxg6 ♖xb7 26.♖xb7! ♕g8 27.♗c4 and Black resigned after a few more moves in Sambuev-Martchenko, Montreal 2011.

– 18...♗d7 19.♘e5 fxe3 was best, when play is unclear after 20.♕xe3 ♕b1+.

– 18...♕b1+? 19.♗d1 and Black has no satisfactory defence against the attack on g7: 19...♗d7 (19...♖f7 20.♖xf7 ♔xf7 21.♘e5+ ♔g8 22.♕b4+–) 20.♘e5 ♖ad8 21.♖xb7 fxe3 22.fxe3 ♕e4 23.♗f3 ♕xh4+ 24.♔e2, winning material.

● 11...♘d6!? 12.c5 (12.cxd5 exd5 would open the e-file in Black's favour, while the knight on d6 is extremely well-placed. However, play is still interesting after 13.g5; 12.g5!? is a worthwhile try as 12...♘xc4 13.♗xc4 dxc4 14.gxh6 gxh6 15.♘d2 favours White) 12...♘e8 13.g5 e5! 14.gxh6 gxh6 15.♖g1+ ♘g7 (White keeps an edge after both 15...♔h8 16.dxe5 ♘xe5 17.♕d4 f6 18.♕f4 and 15...♔h7 16.dxe5 ♘xe5 17.♘xe5 ♕xe5 18.♗d3+) 16.♗h3 (only equal seems 16.dxe5 ♘xe5 17.♘xe5 ♕xe5 18.♕d4 ♕xd4 19.exd4 ♗f5) 16...f5 (stronger than 16...e4 17.♗xd7! ♗xd7 18.♘e5) 17.dxe5 ♘xe5 18.♘xe5 draw agreed in view of the equal ending after 18...♕xe5 19.♕d4 ♕xd4 20.exd4 f4. Ragger-Alekseev, Khanty-Mansiysk 2011.

● 11...♘xc3 12.♖xc3 seems like a concession, but may actually transpose to the game, while it is also relevant in view of the (less accurate) move order 9...♘xc3 10.♖xc3 c6 11.g4!? ♘d7 12.h4. 12...e5 (play is also sharp after 12...dxc4 13.♗xc4 – 13.g5!? – 13...b5 14.♗e2 – 14.♗d3 e5 with counterplay – 14...♗b7 15.g5) 13.cxd5 cxd5 14.g5 and we have transposed to the main game.

12.cxd5 ♘xc3

Black finally has to exchange the knights.

12...cxd5 13.♘xd5 ♕d6 and Black has no compensation for the pawn.

12...exd4 13.♕xd4 ♘xc3 14.♖xc3 cxd5 15.g5! with a superior position.

13.♖xc3 cxd5

13...♘b6 is met by the intermediate move 14.d6! ♕xd6 15.♘xe5 ♕d5 16.♖g1 ♕xa2 17.g5! with a strong attack.

13...♘f6 14.d6 ♕xd6 15.♘xe5 also looks worse for Black.

14.g5

Everything according to plan! White has made contact with the enemy, while his position in the centre is still stable.

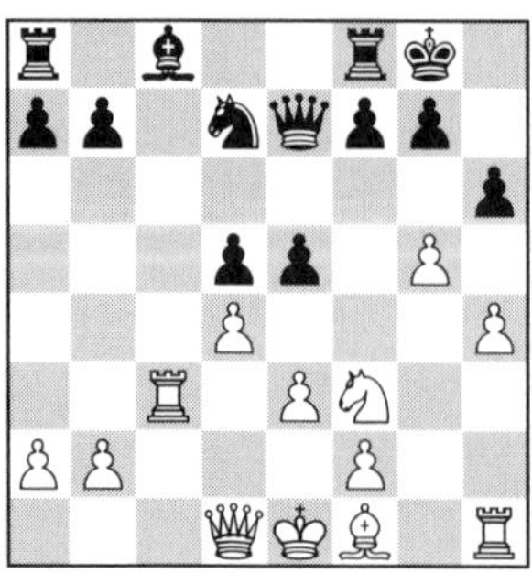

14...h5

Harikrishna understandably wants to keep all files on the kingside closed. However, pawn h5 is a further weakness, and even optically it is clear that White's opening has been a success.

● A few weeks later at the Summer Universiade in China Kravtsiv played 14...hxg5 15.hxg5 e4, which looks extremely risky because of the opening of the h-file.

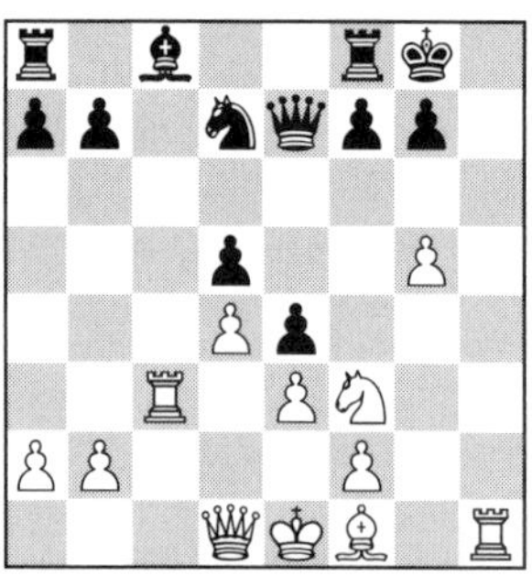

– Wang Hao now continued 16.♘d2?!, forcing Black to take the g-pawn, when the game went 16...♕xg5 17.♖h5 ♕g1 18.♖h3 (not 18.♖xd5 ♘f6, when Black is better) 18...♘f6 19.♖g3 ♕h1 but failed to obtain sufficient compensation. It was obvious that Black was better after the continuation 20.♘b3 b6 21.♔d2 ♗g4 22.♕c1 ♖ac8 23.♗a6 ♕xc1+ 24.♘xc1 ♖xc3 25.bxc3 ♖b8, Wang Hao-Kravtsiv, Shenzhen 2011. In the end the eventual winner of the silver medal managed to draw with White.

– More logical is 16.♘e5!, when after 16...♘xe5 (16...♕xg5 17.♖xc8 ♖axc8 – 17...♖fxc8? 18.♖h8++– – 18.♘xd7 favours White) White can take advantage of the open h-file with 17.♕h5 f6 (17...♘f3+? 18.♔d1 f6 19.g6) 18.g6 (18.gxf6 ♘f3+ 19.♕xf3 ♕xf6 20.♕xf6 ♖xf6 is an unpleasant ending for Black) 18...♘xg6 19.♕xg6 with a strong attack. After 19...♗d7 20.♕h7+ ♔f7 21.♖g1 ♖g8 22.♕h5+ ♔f8 23.♕xd5 White has retrieved his pawn with a better position.

● 14...e4 15.♘d2 hxg5 can be answered by 16.♕h5 and this must be the reason why Kravtsiv first took on g5 before playing ...e4. White will retrieve the pawn and keeps a slight edge.

15.♗b5!?

The simple 15.♗e2 is also worth considering.

15...exd4

Black sees an opportunity to exchange queens and goes for it, but in the ending White's plus is indisputable.

Stronger is 15...e4 16.♗xd7 (16.♘d2 ♘b6! 17.♕xh5 a6 18.♗e2 ♗f5 and White has won a pawn, but this is a pyrrhic victory as the quality of Black's position has considerably increased over the last few moves) 16...♗xd7 17.♘e5 ♖ac8 18.♕xh5 ♖xc3 19.bxc3 and now after 19...♗f5 Black certainly has compensation for the pawn, although I would still prefer White.

16.♕xd4 ♕e4 17.♕xe4 dxe4 18.♘d2 ♘e5

18...f5 keeps the pawn but places another pawn on a light square.

19.♘xe4 ♗e6 20.f4! ♗d5

White has a distinct endgame plus after 20...♘g4 21.♘c5 ♗xa2 22.♔e2.

21.fxe5 ♗xe4

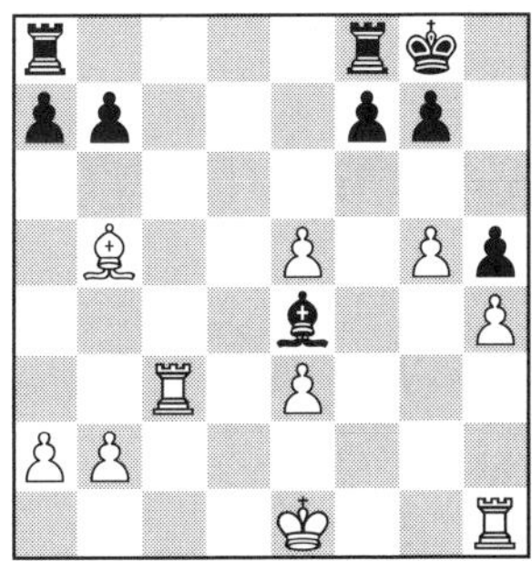

22.0-0!

Aronian follows Richard Reti's dictum that one should only castle once there is no better move available.

22...♗d5

After the exchange of rooks with 22...♖ac8 23.♖xc8 (23.♗c4!?) 23...♖xc8 White has 24.e6! fxe6 25.♗d7 to keep his edge.

23.♗d7 ♖fd8 24.♖c7

Black is virtually stalemated, and has to wait when and where he will be dealt the final blow.

24...a5?!

White should win after 24...♗xa2 25.g6! fxg6 26.e6.

25.a4 ♖a6 26.♖f4!

26.♖d1?! is a self-pin and there is no point in allowing the rook ending after 26...♗e6 27.g6! ♗xd7 28.gxf7+ ♔xf7 29.♖dxd7+ ♖xd7 30.♖xd7+ ♔f8 31.♖xb7 ♖g6+! 32.♔f2 ♖g4 when 33.b4! should still win.

26...♖f8 27.♖d4

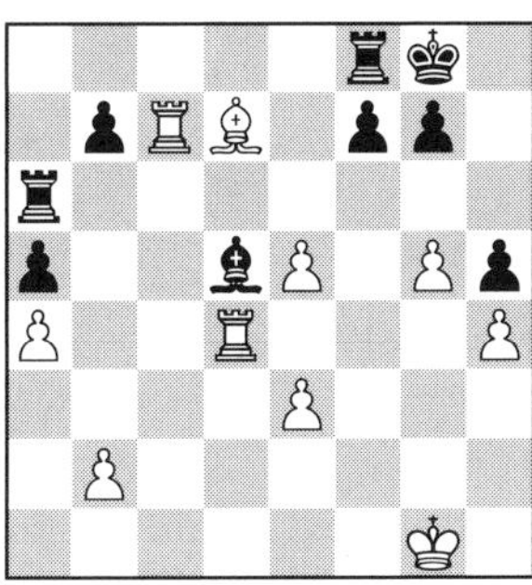

Now the bishop has to leave its optimal square, after which all is clear.

27...♗c6 27...♗e6 28.♖xb7. **28.e6 fxe6 29.♗xe6+ ♔h8 30.♗f7 ♖b6 31.b3 ♗f3 32.g6 ♖c6 33.♖xc6 bxc6 34.e4 ♗e2 35.e5**

A fantastic win after a completely novel idea in an age-old main line of the Queen's Gambit Declined.

CHAPTER 3

Simon Williams

King's Gambit: Tartakower Variation

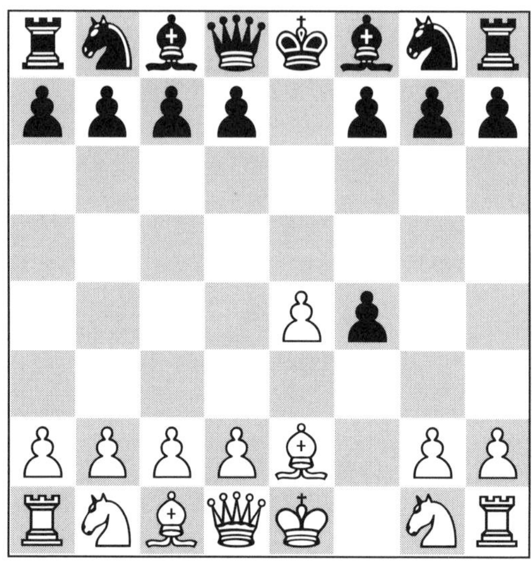

1.e4 e5 2.f4 exf4 3.♗e2!?

□ **Henry Edward Bird**
■ **Leon Weiss**
Bradford 1888

1.e4 e5 2.f4 exf4 3.♗e2

According to Y.Estrin and I.B.Glazkov, in their book *Play the King's Gambit*, 'This continuation was first suggested by the well-known Russian player Petroff in the 1840s'. Petroff is more well known for figuring out a rather boring reply to 1.e4, but if he did come up with 3.♗e2 then credit where credit is due!

This 'little bishop gambit' is a very interesting way of trying to take your opponent out of theory. The bishop is more passively placed on e2 compared to c4 but there are some benefits to placing the bishop on this square. For a start White can now often consider meeting ...♘f6 with e5. This lost a lot of its sting with a bishop on c4, as Black could reply with ...d5!. This reply is not possible now. White can now also play c4 in some variations, this is especially effective when Black reacts with 3...d5. Another obvious benefit is that White has delayed developing his knight to f3 so he does not have to worry about ...g5 and then ...g4. Do I believe that 3.♗e2 is sound? It certainly has great surprise value and that is what the SOS books are about. In general most gambit lines are now going out of fashion due to computer involvement but I believe that

3.♗e2!? has the potential to score some devastating wins. The problem with 3.♗e2!? is 3...f5!. If Black finds this move then White must be happy to aim for equality.

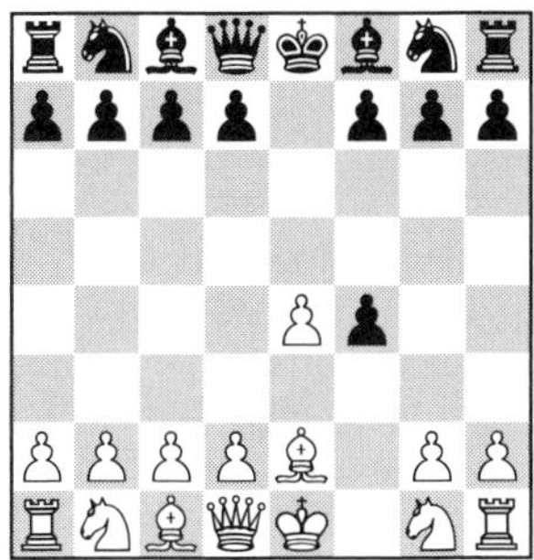

3...f5!

To start this chapter off we are going to look at some of the earliest games played in this variation. Two famous players, Henry Bird and Savielly Tartakower, were the first strong players to experiment with 3.♗e2. Alekhine mentioned that he believed 3... f5! to be a good reply to 3.♗e2 and it does certainly seem critical. In practical play 3...f5! is quite a rare guest and this move does look very odd, so I expect that only a well-prepared opponent would play in this manner. 3...f5! does seem like a good move though and it looks like White should aim for equality with 5.d4!?. That is one reason why this opening is best used as a surprise weapon!

● 3...♘e7 is interesting. Black aims to play ...d5 but by playing the knight to e7 and not f6 Black avoids the unpleasant move e5. Now 4.d4 d5 5.exd5 ♘xd5 6.♘f3 ♗b4+ 7.c3 ♗e7 8.0-0 0-0 9.c4 ♘e3 10.♗xe3 fxe3 11.♕d3 ♗f6 was slightly better for Black in Tartakower-Alekhine, New York 1924.

However, 4.♘f3! is correct, when the position would transpose to our next game after 4...d5 5.exd5 ♘xd5, which looks fine for White.

In the game Ree-Bok, Netherlands tt 2010/11, Black played 4...♘g6 instead, after 5.♘c3 c6 6.d4 d5 7.exd5 cxd5 8.0–0 ♘c6 9.♗d3 ♗e7 10.♘e2 ♗g4 11.c3 ♗d6 12.♕b3 ♘ce7 13.♕xb7 0–0 14.♕b3 ♕d7 15.♗d2 a tense situation had arisen, after 15...♗xf3 16.♖xf3 ♘h4 Ree correctly sacrificed the exchange with 17.♖xf4 ♗xf4 18.♘xf4 with about even chances.

● 3...d5 seems to be Black's most common reply to 3.♗e2. This move will be examined in more depth in the next game of this chapter. 4.exd5 ♘f6

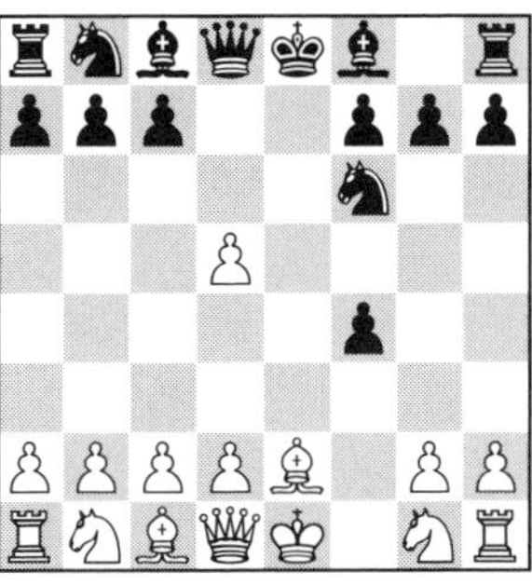

5.c4?! was Tartakower choice on a couple of occasions. This is not to be recommended though (I would stick to quick development with 5.♘f3!. which looks best and is examined later on in this chapter) 5...c6 6.d4 ♗b4+ (6...cxd5 7.♗xf4 dxc4 8.♗xc4 ♗b4+ 9.♘c3 0-0 10.♘e2 ♗g4 11.0-0 ♘bd7 12.♕b3 ♗xc3 13.bxc3 was slightly better for White in Tartakower-Bogoljubow, New York 1924) 7.♔f1 cxd5 8.♗xf4 dxc4 (8...0-0!?) 9.♗xb8 ♘d5! 10.♔f2 ♖xb8, with an already very good position for Black in Tartakower-Capablanca, New York 1924.

4.e5

4.exf5 looks dubious, as Black can reply 4...♕h4+ 5.♔f1 d5 and Black's position already looks good. Thoeng-Hector, Antwerp 1994, continued 6.♘c3 (6.g3?! fxg3 7.♔g2

gxh2 8.♖xh2 ♕g5+ 9.♔h1 is one amusing idea – White is relying on the open lines on the kingside to generate some play. A word of warning though: this does look very dodgy and I would only suggest that you even think about playing this line in a blitz game!) 6...c6 7.d4 ♗xf5 8.♘f3 ♕h6, when White was lacking any counterplay for the pawn.
4.d3?! seems to be a novelty as early as move 4! The position does look good for Black though, as long as he plays 4...♕h4+! 5.♔f1 fxe4 6.dxe4 ♗c5!, with a big advantage.
4...d6 It makes sense to immediately attack White's centre.

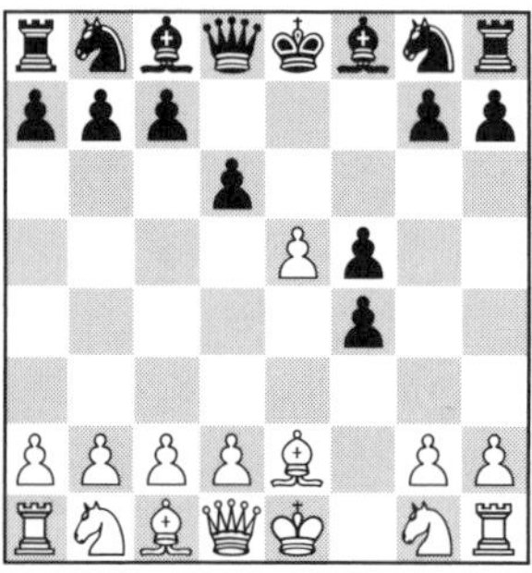

5.♘f3

– In an earlier game Bird tried capturing on d6. Bird-Zukertort, London 1886, continued 5.exd6 ♕h4+ Black is advised to play this before White has a chance to play ♘f3. 6.♔f1 ♗xd6 7.d4 ♘e7 8.♘f3 ♕f6 9.c4, funnily enough this transposes to the position after 10.c4 in the main game.
– 5.d4!? has been suggested in some places and it does remain an interesting choice. Mieses-Maroczy, Vienna 1903, continued 5...dxe5 6.dxe5 ♕h4+ (critical, as otherwise White would probably be able to capture his pawn back on f4 with a satisfactory position. 6...♕xd1+ is a rather dull way to play but it also looks like a safe way to equalise. In some cases Black could even claim an edge due to White's e-pawn. 7.♗xd1 ♘c6 8.♗xf4 ♘ge7 9.♘c3 looks roughly equal. Here 9...♘g6?! allows 10.♗h5) 7.♔f1 ♗c5 8.♘h3 ♗e3 9.♘c3 (9.♗xe3 fxe3 10.♗b5+ was suggested in *Play the King's Gambit*, but the authors stop analysing at this point! To be honest I do not really see the point to this move and it just looks like Black is doing well, for example: 10...c6 and now maybe White could try 11.♘c3!? but this looks inadequate: 11...cxb5 – 11...f4!? must also be good for Black – 12.♘xb5 ♕c4+ 13.♕e2 ♕xe2+ 14.♔xe2 ♘a6 White is lacking any compensation for the piece. Black is winning) 9...♗e6 (9...♘e7! looks more precise, as after 10.♘d5 – 10.♕d3!? – 10...♘xd5 11.♕xd5 ♘c6 Black has managed to keep his light-squared bishop, which does help plug up some holes) 10.♘d5 (10.♗xe3! looks even better, for example: 10...fxe3 11.♘b5 ♘a6 12.♕d4! ♕xd4 13.♘xd4 ♗c8 14.♗b5+ ♔e7 – 14...c6 15.♘xc6 – 15.♗xa6 bxa6 16.♘f4, when White should be a bit better) 10...♗xd5 11.♕xd5 ♘c6 12.♗c4 looked OK for White but Black should be able to improve his play earlier on, both 6...♕xd1+ and 9...♘e7 should be fine for Black.
5...dxe5 6.♘xe5

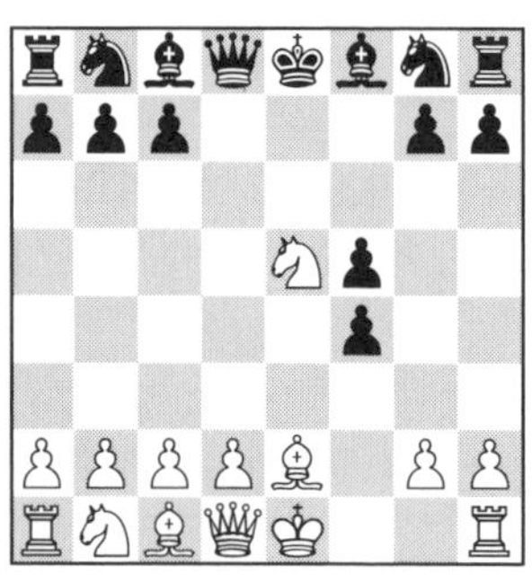

6...♕h4+
Critical and best.

7.♔f1

If White's king was castled here then he would have full compensation for the pawn. Unfortunately White's rook on h1 can not join in the game for a while, so the compensation looks a bit suspect.

7...♗d6 8.♘f3 ♕f6

Black could have also considered 8...♕h6!? so that the black knight can develop to f6, for example 9.d4 ♘f6 10.c4 c6 and Black is doing very well – he is a pawn up with good development!

9.d4 ♘e7 10.c4 c6 11.♘c3

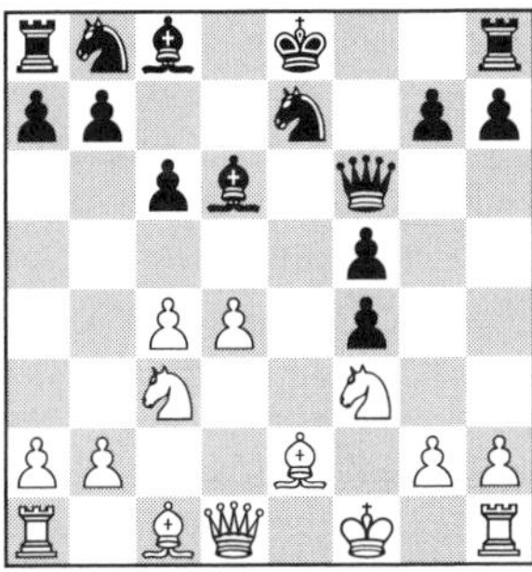

The position is rather unclear. White has some chances in the centre of the board but Black is well developed and has a dangerous pawn formation on the kingside. I would prefer to be Black but there is still a lot of play left in the position.

11...♘d7

Black could have played 11...g5!?, leading to a very messy position.

12.♗d2 ♕h6?

If Black wanted to place his queen here, then he should have done it on move 8.

Two more sensible moves were 12...0-0 and 12...g5.

13.c5!

White takes his chance to create some attacking play.

13...♗c7 14.♕b3

From b3 the queen takes up a dangerous position, pressurizing Black's queenside and kingside.

14...♘f6 15.♗c4 ♘e4

15...b5!? was worth considering, as after 16.cxb6 axb6 Black can consider playing ...♗a6 at some point which exchanges White's strong light-squared bishop off.

16.♖e1 ♘xd2+ 17.♘xd2 ♔d8 18.♘f3!

White has clearly outplayed his opponent in the early middlegame and he now has a very good position. Some ideas include ♘e5 and d5, opening up the centre.

18...b5

This move should have been played a long time ago!

19.♗e6 b4 20.d5!

Simple and good. White opens up Black's king.

20...bxc3 21.d6 ♖b8 22.dxe7+ ♔xe7

23.♗d7+?

White could have won a lot quicker with the fairly straightforward 23.♗g8+!, for example: 23...♔d8 (23...♔f6 24.♕e6+ ♗xe6 25.♖xe6 mate) 24.♖d1+! (24.♕f7? would be a mistake due to 24...♗a6+ and the black king can run away to the queenside) 24...♗d7 25.♕f7 ♔c8 26.♖xd7!, with a devastating attack.

23...♔d8 The bishop is immune: 23...♔xd7?? 24.♕f7+ ♔d8 25.♕e7 mate.

24.♕f7 ♗xd7

Or 24...♗a6+ 25.♔g1 ♗d6!? 26.cxd6 ♕xd6 27.♕xg7 cxb2 28.♔f2, and White is winning.

25.♖d1 ♔c8 26.♕xd7+ 26.♖xd7? allows Black to defend with 26...♖b7.

26...♔b7 27.♖d6! The rest is easy.

27...♕h5 28.♕xc6+ ♔c8 29.♕a6+ Black resigned.

□ **Klaus Bolding**
■ **Clement Houriez**
Val d'Isere ch-FRA 2004

1.e4 e5 2.f4 exf4 3.♗e2!? d5

A natural response to 3.♗e2!?. Black aims for quick development, figuring that White's bishop is rather passively placed on e2.

4.exd5 ♘f6

Black can also consider 4...♕xd5, which is often a good idea in similar lines of the King's Gambit, but here White has a pleasant development advantage after 5.♘f3 ♘c6 6.♘c3 ♕d8 7.d4 ♗d6 8.0-0.

5.♘f3!

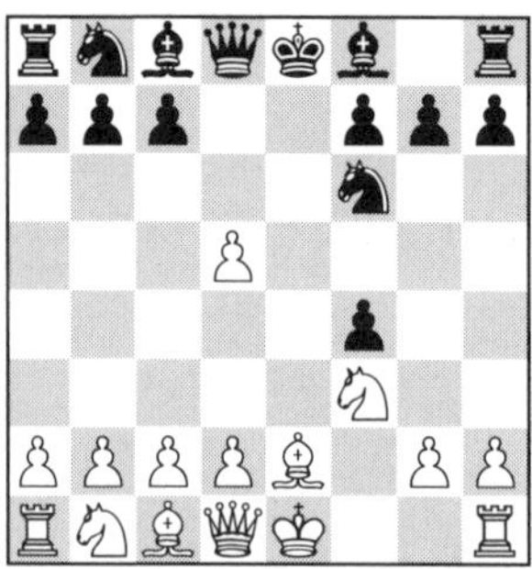

I would imagine that if you take the plunge and decide to play 3.♗e2!? then this position is one of the most likely positions that you could reach. It is also worth noting that this position is more commonly reached via the move order 1.e4 e5 2.f4 exf4 3.♘f3 d5 4.exd5 ♘f6 5.♗e2. It is important that you try to get to grips with what White should be trying to do here. The basic plan is to advance in the centre with c4 and d4, castle kingside and then recapture your pawn on f4. If you can achieve all this then you should be left with a superior position. This game is a model example of that!

5...♘xd5

● 5...♗e7 is another way in which Black could develop. Now amazingly I cannot find any games in my database where White has continued with 6.c4!?, which is the most logical move. Play could continue 6...0-0 7.0-0 c6 8.dxc6 ♘xc6 9.d4. White must have an advantage due to his strong centre. He can always play d5 if the d-pawn becomes attacked.

● 5...♗d6 makes a lot of sense. The bishop is more active on d6 compared to e7 and the bishop also guards the pawn on f4. On the downside, Black's bishop maybe a target to White's c-pawn: 6.c4 c6 (Black has to break up White's strong pawn centre) 7.dxc6 (the safest, even though 7.d4!? cxd5 8.c5 ♗c7 is interesting) 7...♘xc6 8.d4 and White should be doing quite well here due to his strong centre. Bricard-Ludewig, Mürren Mitropa Cup 1987, continued 8...0-0 9.0-0 a6 10.♘c3 ♗c7 11.♔h1 ♗g4 12.d5 ♗xf3 13.♗xf3 ♘e5 14.♗e2, with a big advantage for White.

6.c4 ♘f6

– 6...♘b4!? is an interesting idea, for example: 7.d4 ♗f5 and White can now continue in romantic fashion with 8.0-0!? (8.♘a3 is more conservative!), when he has decent compensation for the exchange after 8...♘c2 9.♗xf4 ♘xa1 10.♗d3 ♗xd3 11.♕xd3 ♘c6 12.♘c3 and Black has to find a safe place to hide the king. If he goes kingside then he must watch out for ♘g5!. And if 12...♗e7, then 13.♘d5.

– 6...♘b6 makes it possible for Black to play ...g5 in the future. Bergström-T.Ernst, Gausdal 1994, continued 7.d4

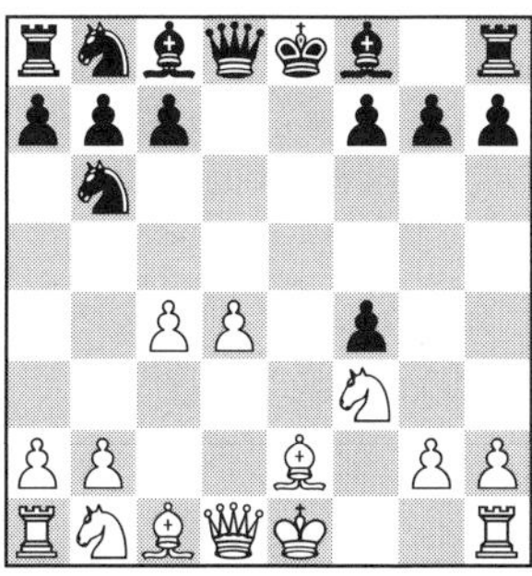

7...g5 (this move does save the pawn on f4 but Black's king is going to always feel a bit insecure now) 8.h4!? (a safer option would have been 8.0-0 ♗g7 9.c5) 8...f6 (8...g4! 9.♘e5 f3 10.gxf3 g3 looks good for Black) 9.hxg5 fxg5 10.♘e5 ♗g7 11.♗h5+ ♔f8 12.♕e2 ♗e6 and now White should have played 13.b3!, with good chances.

7.d4 I already like White's position here. White will win the pawn on f4 back and then he will be left with the superior centre.

7...♗b4+

7...♗d6 runs into 8.c5 ♗e7 9.♘c3!. This move makes it more difficult for Black to secure his knight on the d5-square. After 9... ♗e6 10.♗xf4 ♘c6 11.0-0 White has a space advantage but Black does have control of the d5-square. The position is roughly equal.

8.♘c3 ♘c6 9.♗xf4 White has a small advantage. **9...0-0 10.0-0**

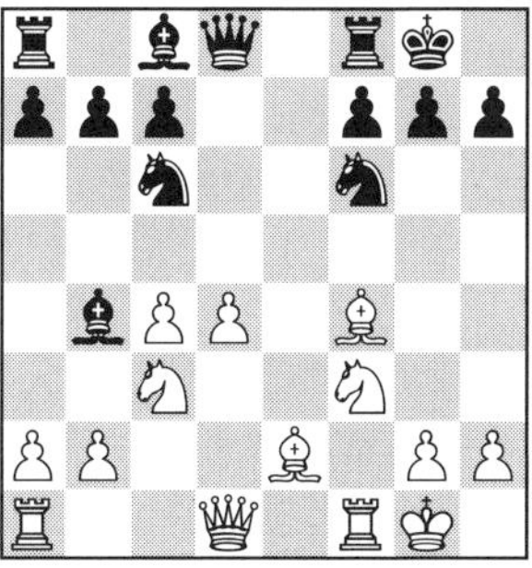

We can see just how useful White's d-pawn is. Black has to constantly be on guard for the d5 push. White's development is also very easy, he can continue with the simple plan of ♕d2 and ♖ad1/e1.

10...♘h5

A better plan would have been 10...♖e8, which aims to stop White from playing ♕d2. Play could continue 11.a3 ♗d6 (11...♗xc3 12.bxc3 leaves Black horribly weak on the dark squares) 12.♘e5!?, when White has a certain amount of pressure.

11.♗g5!

An obvious but strong move.

11...♗e7

11...f6 is a rather ugly move to play. White is better after 12.♗c1!, the safest square for the bishop. Black's pieces are misplaced, especially the knight on h5. White is also ready to play d5. Note that 12.♗e3 ♖e8 is annoying for White.

12.♗xe7

An even stronger possibility was 12.♗e3!. White no longer has to fear ...♖e8 and White's dark-squared bishop is superior to Black's, so he should keep these pieces on the board: 12...♘f6 (the knight was doing nothing on h5, by playing it to f6 Black can at least threaten ...♘g4) 13.d5 ♘b8 14.♕d2, and White has a big advantage.

12...♘xe7 13.♘g5!?

White aims for an immediate attack.

A more solid approach would have been 13.♕d2 ♘f6 14.♗d3 c6 15.♖f2, with a safe advantage. White has more space, a strong centre and better positioned pieces.

13...♘f6

Another interesting line would have been 13...♘f5 14.♕d2 (14.♘xh7 ♔xh7 15.♗xh5 g6 16.♗f3 ♘e3 17.♕d2 ♘xf1 18.♖xf1 is unclear, White certainly has compensation for the exchange but he still has to prove whether it is enough) 14...♘f6 15.d5 and White has the advantage.

14.♕d3

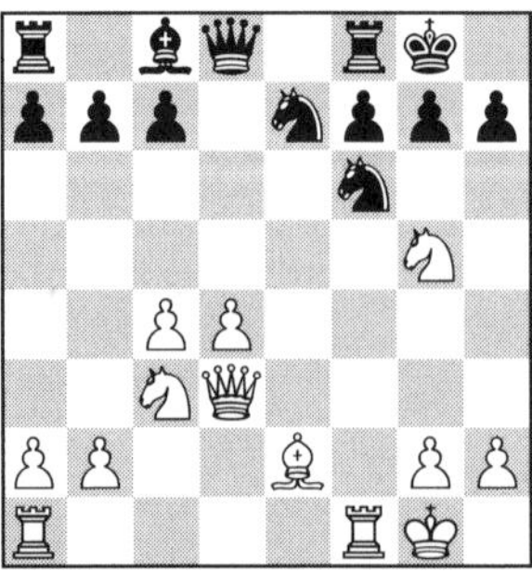

Route one tactics! White just wants to play ♖xf6 and ♕xh7 mate.

That is the way that you should play the King's Gambit, no messing about, aim straight for the king!

14...♘g6

14...♗f5!? was worth considering, for example: 15.♖xf5 ♘xf5 16.♕xf5 ♕xd4+ 17.♔h1 ♖fe8 and White has two minor pieces in exchange for a rook and pawn. A trade that is normally favourable.

Things are not so clear here though, as Black has good control of the d- and e-files.

15.h3 ♗d7 16.♖f2

White slowly increases the pressure on Black's position.

16...♗c6 17.♖af1 ♕e7

Black could have considered kicking White's knight on g5 away, for example 17...h6, when White has the interesting idea 18.♘xf7!?, when Black has to be careful: 18...♖xf7 (18...♔xf7? is a mistake due to 19.♗h5, which wins back the piece with interest) 19.d5 (19.♕xg6 ♕xd4 is fine for Black) 19...♘e5 20.♕g3 ♗xd5 21.♕xe5 ♗c6 22.c5 with the idea of playing ♗c4 22...♕e7 and Black is just about OK.

18.d5

This is good but White also had the interesting exchange sacrifice 18.♖xf6!?. This move looks very tempting, for example: 18...gxf6 19.♘ge4 f5 20.♖xf5 ♗xe4 21.♘xe4 f6 after which White has a dangerous initiative but Black can struggle on.

18...♗d7

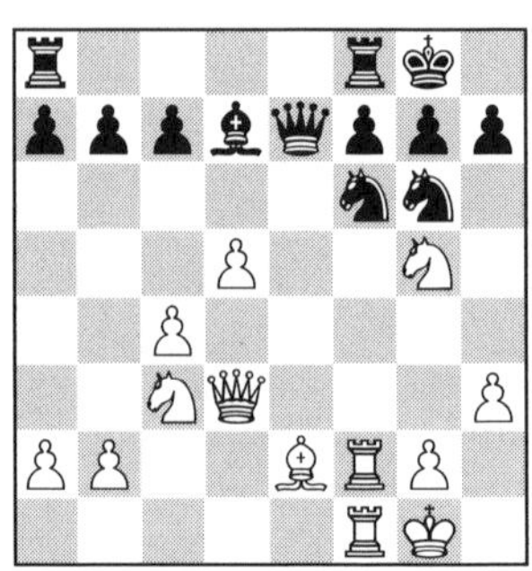

19.h4!?

Here come the reserves!

19.♕d4, placing f6 under more pressure, also makes a lot of sense, for example: 19...h6 20.♖xf6! hxg5 (20...gxf6? 21.♘ge4 is horrible for Black) 21.♖6f3 and White has a small advantage.

19...♘e5

19...♕e5 looks like an improvement. With this move Black is aiming to make it hard for White to play h5 due to ...♕xg5. White can still now play the exchange sacrifice on f6, for example 20.♖xf6!? gxf6 21.♘ge4 f5 22.♘c5 ♗c8 23.h5, with an unclear position.

20.♕c2

White decides to keep an eye on the h7-square. Another good choice would have been 20.♕g3!, when White is threatening ♘e6!.

Let's take a look: 20...♔h8 21.♘e6! fxe6 22.♕xe5 ♕c5 23.b4 ♕xb4 24.dxe6 ♗c6 25.e7 and Black's position has fallen apart. White should be winning here.

20...h6

21.♖xf6

An even stronger but hard plan to see was 21.d6!, with the idea of trying to play ♘d5 next. Play could continue 21...♕xd6 (21...cxd6?? 22.♘d5 ♘xd5 23.♕h7 mate) 22.♖d1 ♕c5 23.♘d5! hxg5 24.b4! and out of nowhere Black's queen is trapped in the middle of the board!

21...hxg5 22.♘e4

Again 22.d6 was interesting, when one crazy line goes 22...cxd6 23.♘d5 ♕d8 24.♖h6!? (madness!) 24...♘g6 25.♘f6+ (25.♖h5 keeps the game alive) 25...gxf6 26.♖xg6+ fxg6 27.♕xg6+ ♔h8 28.♕h6+, with a draw!

22...♖ae8?

Black crumbles in a difficult position. After this move the position is lost. Black should have tried 22...♘g6!, when he seems to be defending everything, for example: 23.hxg5 gxf6 24.gxf6 ♕e5 25.♕c1 ♔h7 26.♘g5+ ♔g8 27.♘e4 ♔h7 28.♘g5+ ♔g8 29.♘e4, with a draw.

23.♘xg5 The rest is easy.

23...g6 23...♘g6 24.♖xf7. **24.c5**

White's centre has been a success story!

24...♗f5

A desperate try. White's next move is rather easy to spot!

25.♖1xf5 gxf5 26.♕xf5 ♘g6 27.h5

27.d6! or even 27.♘e6! were even stronger possibilities.

27...♕xc5+ 28.♔h1 ♖xe2 29.♖xg6+ ♔h8 30.♕f6

Mate.

□ **Jon Arnason**
■ **Heikki Westerinen**
Brighton 1982

1.e4 e5 2.f4 exf4 3.♗e2 ♘c6

This rarely seen move is an interesting way of meeting White's opening. I do not believe that it is as good as 3 ...f5! but White still has to respond actively. We will look at all of Black's other sensible options in the next game.

4.d4

There cannot be too much wrong with this move. White places another pawn in the centre and attacks Black's pawn on f4.

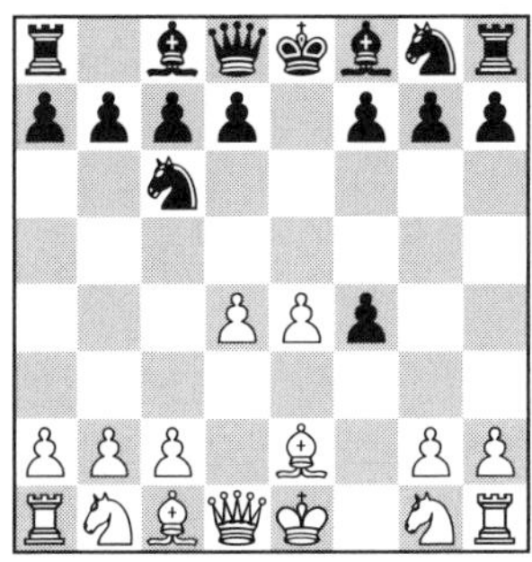

4...♘f6!?

Black aims for quick development and an attack against White's centre.

– 4...d5 is quite a common reply from Black. White should now continue 5.exd5 ♕xd5 6.♘f3.

This was played in Tartakower-Yates, New York 1924, which continued 6...♗g4 7.♘c3 ♗b4 8.0-0 ♗xc3 9.bxc3 ♘ge7 10.♗xf4, when White was already better due to his strong dark-squared bishop, which is placing c7 under attack.

– 4...g5 has been played twice leading to a typical King's Gambit type of struture. The last encounter continued 5.h4 (5.♘c3!? is worth considering, for example: 5...♗g7 6.d5 ♘e5 7.d6!, when White has decent attacking chances) 5...♗g7 6.c3 h6 7.g3?! (this is a bit too optimistic. White should have played 7.hxg5 hxg5 8.♖xh8 ♗xh8 9.♗d3, when the queen can move over to h5 with some counterplay) 7...fxg3 8.hxg5 hxg5 9.♖xh8 ♗xh8 10.♕d3 d6 11.♕xg3 ♗f6 12.♗e3 g4, J.Nabuurs-Pruijssers, Groningen 2009.

5.♗f3

This seems sensible but there is another option: 5.♘f3!? has yet to be tried, but it looks like an interesting choice, for example: 5...♘xe4 6.d5 ♘e7 (6...♘e5!? is wild! 7.♕d4! – 7.♘xe5? ♕h4+ 8.g3 fxg3 is winning for Black – 7...♘xf3+ 8.♗xf3, with a roughly equal position) 7.♕d4 f5 8.♘c3 ♘xc3 9.♕xc3 and White has compensation in exchange for the pawn, as Black has some untangling to do. Practical examples are needed! 9...♘xd5 is greedy here: 10.♕e5+ ♘e7 11.♘d4! d6? 12.♗h5+.

5...d5 6.e5 ♘e4 7.♗xf4

This position looks about equal to me. White has won his pawn back, but Black has some very active pieces. If I had to face this variation then I would seriously consider White's other option 5.♘f3, which looks like a lot of fun!

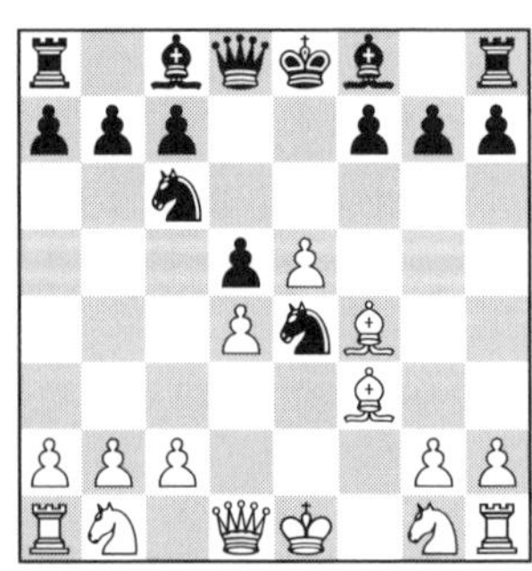

7...♗e6 8.♘e2 ♗e7 9.0-0

Perhaps White should have tried 9.c4!?, for example: 9...0-0 10.cxd5 ♗xd5 11.0-0 f6! 12.exf6 ♘xf6 13.♘bc3 ♗xf3 14.♖xf3, with an even game.

9...♘g5 10.♘d2 ♘xf3+ 11.♘xf3 f5

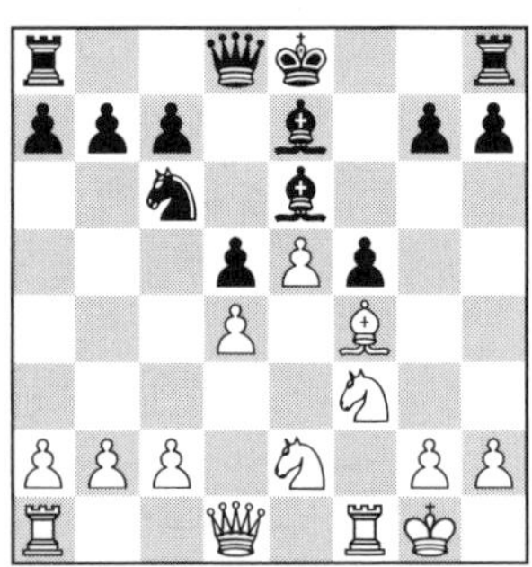

The position has become quite closed, which is a bit untypical for a King's Gambit. I cannot see how either side can really claim an advantage here.

12.exf6 White decides to keep some lines open. 12.♕d2 was a safer option.

12...♗xf6 13.♘g3 0-0 14.♘h5?! 14.c3 is more logical. **14...♗g4 15.♘xf6+ ♕xf6 16.♗xc7 ♗xf3 17.♖xf3 ♕xd4+ 18.♕xd4 ♘xd4 19.♖xf8+ ♖xf8**

The dust has settled and we have a reached a fairly equal ending. If anyone can claim an advantage then it must be Black, as his knight is more active compared to White's bishop.

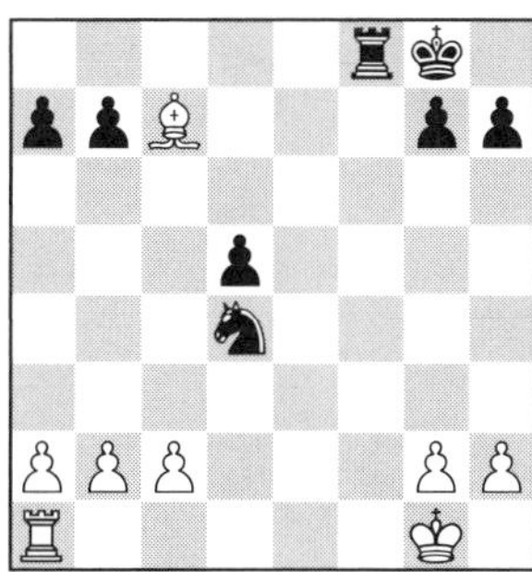

20.♖d1?!

20.c3 may have been a slight improvement. In general White should aim to keep the rooks on the board as the combination of rook and bishop work very well together. 20...♘e2+ 21.♔h1 ♖c8 22.♗e5 ♖e8 is a draw.

20...♘xc2 21.♖xd5 ♘e3 22.♖d8 ♖xd8 23.♗xd8 ♘d1!

White now has some problems defending his queenside pawns.

24.b4 ♔f7 25.♔f1 ♔e6?!

This move is OK but I would have wanted to stop White from playing ♔e2, for example: 25...♘c3! 26.a3 ♔e6 (White now has a very hard defensive job as Black's king will reach c4, on top of this his queenside pawns are fixed on the same colour square as his bishop) 27.♔f2 ♔d5 28.♗e7 b5! and Black should win this ending.

26.♔e2!

White's king can now come over to the rescue of his queenside.

26...♘c3+ 27.♔d3 ♘xa2 28.♔c4 ♘c1

Even though Black has won a pawn he has allowed White's king to become very active when he did not need to.

29.♗g5 ♘e2 30.♗e3 Black's knight is also in some danger. The game now ended. **30...♔f5 31.♗xa7 ♘f4 32.g3 ♘e6 33.♔b5 ♘c7+ 34.♔b6 ♘d5+ 35.♔c5 ♘xb4** Simplifying into a drawn position. **36.♔xb4 ♔g4 37.♔b5 ♔h3 38.♗b8** Draw.

□ **Willem Bor**
■ **Luc Henris**

Belgium tt 2000/01

1.e4 e5 2.f4 exf4 3.♗e2

In this, the last game, we will take a look at any other possibilities that Black might try.

3...♕h4+

In general this move should help White, as he can gain a tempo with ♘f3 at a later point. The misplacement of his king is not such a big deal.

● 3...h6 is one rather greedy approach. Black simply wants to play ...g5, holding onto his extra pawn. 4.d4 g5

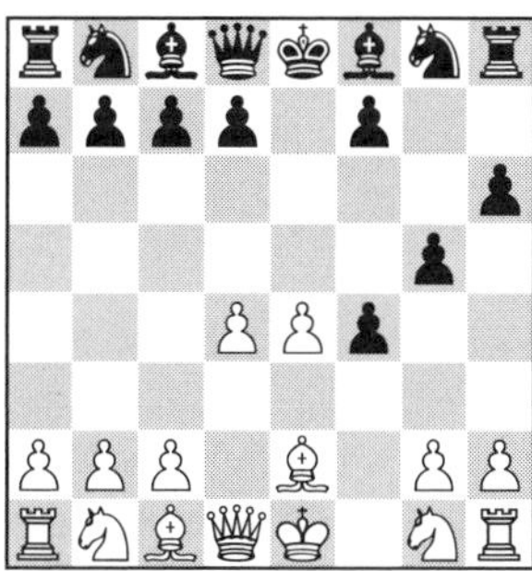

5.h4 (White can also play without this move, which does not seem to help him too much. For example, 5.♘c3!? looks like a good alternative. The idea is to play g3 next: 5...♗g7 6.g3! d5! 7.exd5 fxg3 8.hxg3 ♘e7 9.♗f3, with an unclear position) 5...♗g7 6.g3!? fxg3 7.hxg5 hxg5 8.♖xh8 ♗xh8 9.♗e3 d6 (9...d5! looks more dynamic) 10.♘c3 ♘c6 11.♕d2 g4 12.0-0-0 ♗d7 13.♘d5 ♘ce7 14.♗g5 f6 15.♗xf6 ♗xf6 16.♘xf6+ ♘xf6 17.♕f4 ♘eg8 18.e5 was chaos in N.Littlewood-Zwaig, Tel Aviv ol 1964.

● White should hardly fear 3...♗e7, for example: 4.d4 ♗h4+ 5.♔f1 ♘f6, Mazuchowski-Thomas, Lansing 1997, and here I would have seriously considered playing 6.g3!? (6.♘c3 is the safe option, which must be OK for White) 6...fxg3 7.hxg3 ♘xe4 (7...♗xg3 8.♕d3! traps Black's bishop!) 8.gxh4 ♘g3+ 9.♔g2 ♘xh1 10.♘f3, when I like the look of White's position!

● 3...♘e7 leads back into 1.e4 e5 2.f4 exf4 3.♗e2 d5 4.exd5 ♘f6 5.♘f3! after 4.♘f3 d5 5.exd5 ♘xd5.

4.♔f1 d6

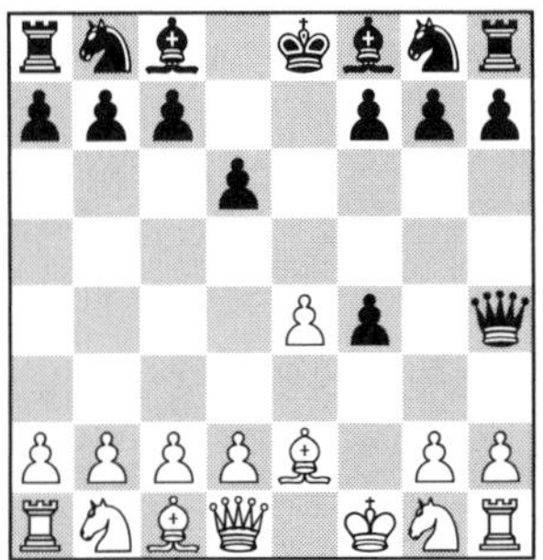

5.d4

White has scored 3/3 with this move. It is often worth delaying ♘f3 until later on, but another move worthy of consideration was 5.♘c3!?. White tries to take advantage of the c7-square now that Black's queen has moved away. This is the move that I would play. After 5...♘f6 6.♘f3 ♕h6 7.d4 White must be happy with the outcome of the opening, if not then do not play the King's Gambit! White has a strong centre and a good development. Play could continue 7...♗e7 (7...♘c6 8.e5 ♘h5 9.♘d5 ♔d8 – we have been following Kammer-Stockmann, Germany tt 1997/98, and now White should have played 10.♖g1!, with the idea of playing g4 again, when White would be better) 8.e5 dxe5 9.dxe5 ♘h5 10.♖g1 0-0 11.g4!, with an unbalanced game.

5...g5!

This is the most critical choice. Black holds onto his extra pawn on f4.

5...♘e7 6.♘f3 ♕h6 7.h4!? (in order to stop ...g5 and prepare g3 without allowing ...♕/♗h3+), with an unbalanced game.

6.♘c3

Rather than playing a plan with ♘f3 White has another idea in mind...

6...♘e7

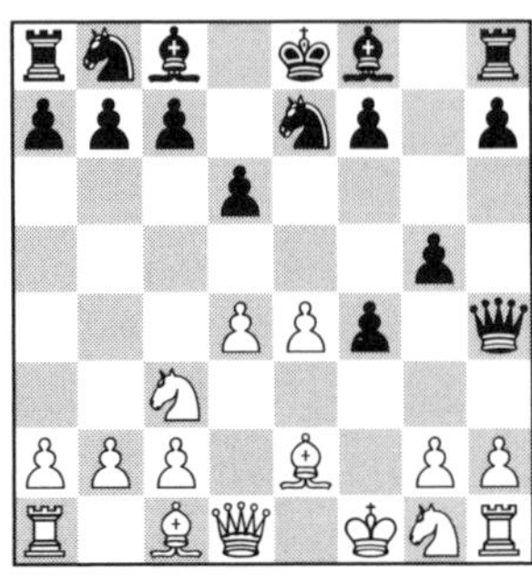

7.g3?!

I like this plan and I have tried a similar idea in the King's Gambit against David Howell, but it is also very double-edged. After the position opens up, White's king could be in more danger compared to Black's and that seems to be the case here.

7.♘f3 is also possible and it may be stronger, for example: 7...♕h6 8.h4 g4 9.♘h2 ♕xh4 10.♔g1 ♕g5 11.♘xg4 ♖g8 12.e5 ♗xg4 13.♘e4, with a mess!

7...♕h6 7...fxg3?! looks far too risky. White should reply 8.♔g2! ♕h6 9.hxg3, with a strong attack.

8.gxf4 gxf4 9.♕d3 ♗d7?!

This is just too passive. Black should have played 9...♖g8, followed up with ...♘bc6, when Black's position is to be preferred.

10.♘d5 ♘xd5 11.exd5 ♗e7 12.♕e4 ♕g6 13.♗d3 c6

Black still has a slight advantage here but he quickly goes wrong.

14.♕xf4 ♕h5 15.♘f3

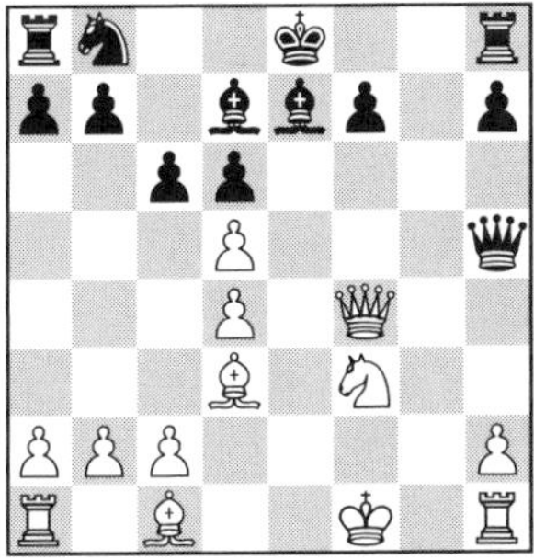

15...♖g8?!

15...♕xd5 was simple and good. Black might as well keep his pawn advantage. White can keep fighting though, for example: 16.♗d2 ♘a6 17.♖e1 ♗e6 18.c4 ♕h5 19.♔e2!?.

16.♖g1 ♗h3+ 17.♔f2 ♖xg1 18.♔xg1

White is OK now, as his king has reached safety. The position is dynamically equal.

18...cxd5 19.♗e3 ♘d7 19...♘c6 was a more active square for the knight. **20.♖e1** White's playing a bit too carelessly. He should be in a rush to do something, because in the game Black is able to gain a dangerous initiative on the kingside. 20.♘g5!?

20...0-0-0 21.♗f2 ♖g8+ 22.♗g3

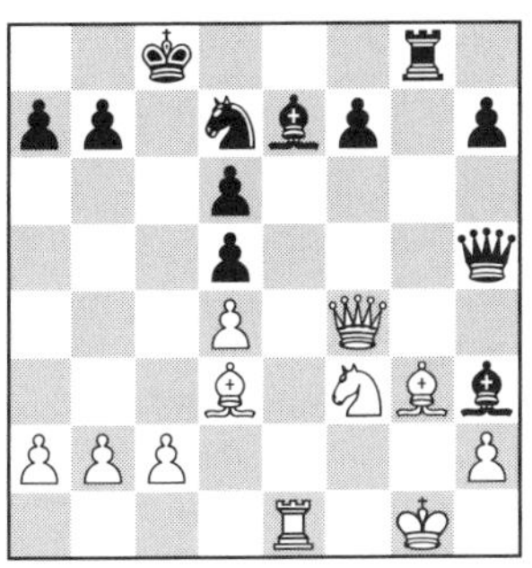

22...♖g4 22...♗e6! was simple and strong. Black is now ready to play ...♘f6 and ...♖g4. White's king is certainly in more danger than Black's!

23.♕e3 ♗d8 24.♘d2 ♖xd4?

A mistake which White misses!

24...♗g5! 25.♕e8+ ♔c7 26.♗b5 ♖xg3+! 27.hxg3 ♗xd2 is clearly better for Black.

25.♔h1?

White could capture the rook! For example: 25.♕xd4 ♗b6 26.♖e8+ ♔c7 27.♗xd6+! ♔c6 (27...♔xd6 28.♘c4+ ♔c7 29.♘xb6 is good for White) 28.♖c8+ ♔xd6 29.♘c4+ ♔e7 30.♘xb6 White is better.

25...♗b6 26.♕e7

Black is back on top again!

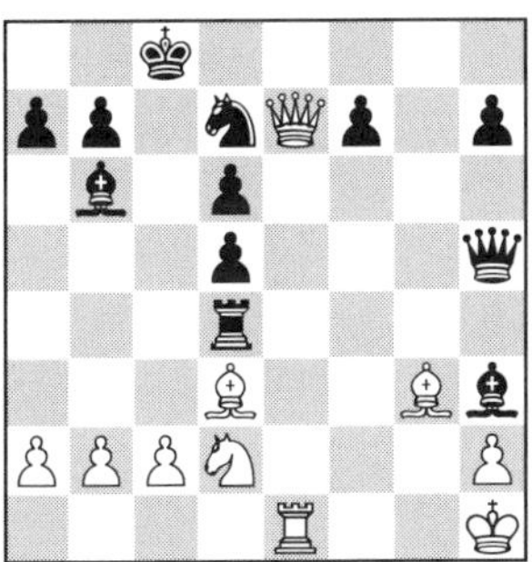

26...♕h6?! 26...♗f5! was clearly better for Black. **27.♘f3** Equal now! **27...♖g4?? 28.♗f5**

Winning for White! This game was clearly not perfect by any means, but it was a good old scrap. Earlier on White should have considered playing either 5.♘c3 or 7.♘f3.

Anyway I hope my article has inspired you to give 'The little bishop's gambit' a go in the odd game. It is quite annoying that Black has the move 3...f5 available to him, but even then he has to find that move and it hardly looks logical!

CHAPTER 4

Alexander Finkel

An Opening Bomb in the Slav

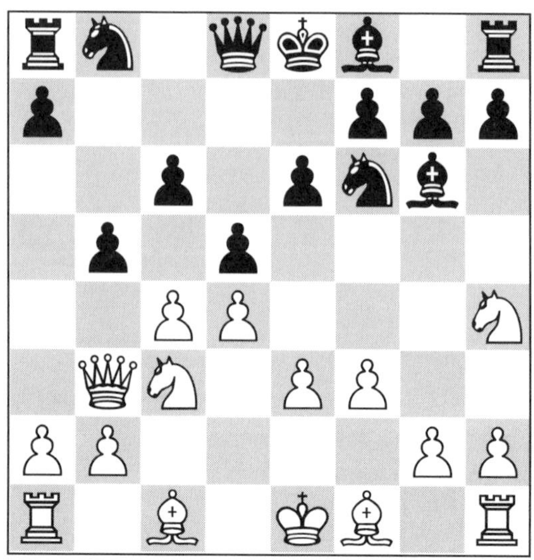

Let's play 8...b5!?

Nowadays the Slav Defence is one of the most popular openings versus 1.d4, while the 4.e3 ♗f5 5.♘c3 e6 6.♘h4 line is enjoying an enormous popularity between players from club level to the top grandmasters in the world. For that reason it is extremely surprising and exciting to find a virgin soil in the field of countless theoretical variations! It's hard to think of a more unexpected and yet sound idea than 8...b5!? in the position arising after 8.♕b3. No wonder it was brought into practice by one of the most creative and unconventional players, the Swedish GM Tiger Hillarp Persson, who is capable to look at a position from quite a different angle than most other players.

Thus far 8...b5!? has served Black fairly well: Black holds a respectable plus 1 score out of nine games played with this move, losing only two. One may ask: if Black is doing so great after 8...b5!? why hasn't it been picked up by more players and become a popular reply to 8.♕b3? Well... apparently it's not all just honey for Black! First of all Black should be ready to play a pawn down if White accepts a gift. He does get long-term compensation and a good chance to seize the initiative if White stumbles on the way (and it is very easy to do so), but a pawn is a pawn.

Another, probably even more irritating, issue is dealing with 9.c5!?. In that case

Black should either accept defending a slightly worse position after 9...♘bd7 10.a4 a6 11.♘xg6 hxg6 12.♕a3 ♖b8 13.axb5 axb5 14.♕a5 or to opt for the highly risky 9...a5, allowing White to get a dangerous initiative by a typical knight sacrifice on b5. Although both of these line are perfectly playable (as you will learn from the illustrative games), none is offering comfortable equality. On the positive side, dealing with 8...b5!? is never easy for White so I would say that employing this opening bomb may well be very rewarding!

☐ **Yury Kuzubov**
■ **Tiger Hillarp Persson**
Helsingor 2009

1.d4 d5 2.c4 c6 3.♘f3 ♘f6 4.e3 ♗f5 5.♘c3 e6 6.♘h4 ♗e4 7.f3 ♗g6 8.♕b3 b5!?

An extremely interesting continuation, forcing White to think independently from the very first moves. White is facing a tough choice, as he needs to define the pawn structure for the rest of the game – a decision most players prefer to make based on home preparation and some good advice from a silicon friend!

9.cxd5?!

It's amazing that none of the players confronted with 8...b5 (in the nine games played thus far) dared to accept the pawn sacrifice, although it is definitely the most critical continuation.

I believe that if White is willing to refute 8...b5 he's got to take the pawn: 9.cxb5 c5 (Black's idea makes sense due to the position of White's f3 pawn), and now:

– 10.g3!? (probably the most challenging move) 10...♗h5!? (otherwise White would take on g6 followed by ♗g2 and 0-0) 11.♕d1 ♗d6 12.♘g2 ♘bd7 13.♗e2 ♖c8 14.0-0 0-0 15.♘f4 and White keeps the slightly better chances, although Black has clear compensation.

– After the immediate capture on g6 White would need to make some concessions in order to complete his development, as his kingside proves to be quite vulnerable: 10.♘xg6 hxg6 11.g3

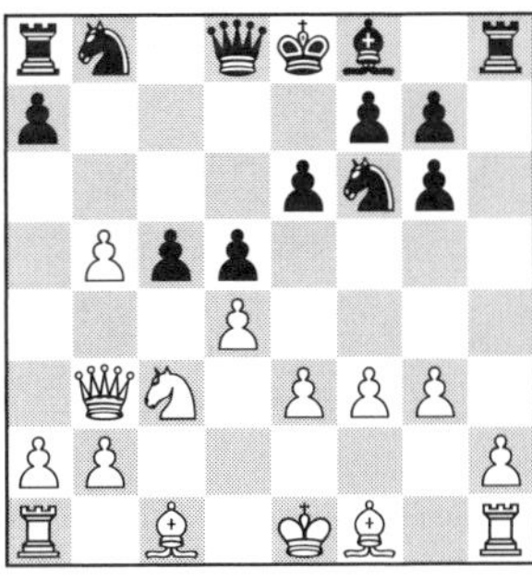

11...♗d6! (of course not 11...♘bd7?! 12.♗g2 ♗d6 13.0-0 0-0 14.a4 ♖c8 15.a5, with a huge edge for White) 12.♔f2 (a very interesting position arises after 12.dxc5 ♗xg3+ 13.♔e2 ♘bd7 14.c6 ♘e5 15.♗g2 ♗xh2 and Black has serious counterchances due to ...♘h5, followed by ...♕h4 ideas; 12.♗g2 ♖xh2!) 12...♘bd7 13.♗g2 ♕c7 14.♗d2 (14.♘e2 g5! also looks great for Black) 14...cxd4 15.exd4 ♘b6 (or even 15...♖xh2!? 16.♘e2 ♖xh1 17.♖xh1 ♘b6), with excellent compensation for the pawn.

9.c5!? is another challenging move, which will be explored further.

9...exd5

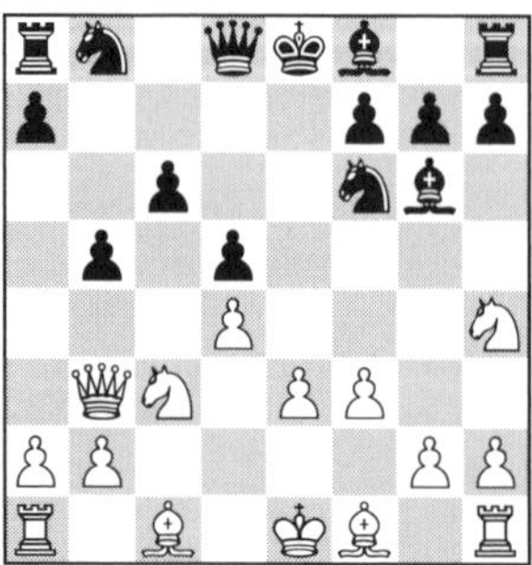

10.♘xg6

Sooner or later this move has to be played.

– 10.g3 ♗e7 (or 10...♗d6 11.♗d2 a5 12.a4 b4 13.♘d1 ♘bd7 14.♘f2 ♕b6 15.♗h3 0-0 16.g4 ♖ad8 with good play in Delemarre-Vogel, Netherlands 2008/09) 11.♗h3 0-0 12.0-0 a5 13.♘xg6 hxg6 14.♗d2 a4 15.♕c2 ♕b6 16.♖ac1 ♘a6, Saric-Ragger, Zadar 2009.

– 10.a4 b4 11.♘e2 ♗d6 12.♘xg6?! (12.g3) 12...hxg6 13.♗d2 ♘bd7 14.♕d1 ♘h5 15.♔f2 c5∓, Lund-Hector, Denmark 2008/09.

10...hxg6 11.♗d2 a5 12.a4

Black got a fantastic attacking position after 12.0-0-0 ♗e7 13.g4 ♘a6 14.♕c2 a4 15.h4 ♘b4 16.♕b1 a3 17.b3 ♕d6∓, Giri-Hillarp Persson, Wijk aan Zee 2009.

Perhaps 12.♘e2!? is a better try.

12...b4 13.♘e2 ♘bd7 14.♕d3 c5!

One doesn't need to be a grandmaster to realize that Black is doing great!

15.b3 ♕c7

Another, equally good option was 15...♗d6!? 16.♖c1 ♖c8 17.g3 ♕c7 18.e4 0-0! 19.♗g2 (19.e5? ♗xe5 20.dxe5 ♘xe5 21.♕e3 d4–+) 19...c4 20.♕c2 ♖fe8!∓ intending 21.e5 ♗xe5 22.dxe5 ♘xe5 23.0-0 ♕b6+ 24.♔h1 ♘d3–+.

16.♖c1

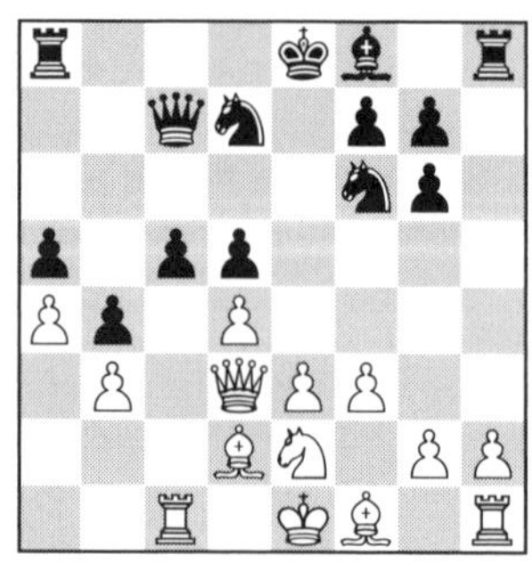

16...♖c8?!

I don't see why Black should refrain from taking on h2: 16...♖xh2!? 17.♖xh2 ♕xh2 18.dxc5 ♘xc5 19.♕b5+ ♘fd7 20.♘d4 ♕d6∓.

17.e4 c4

Very serious attention deserved the odd looking 17...dxe4!? 18.fxe4 ♕d8 when White's centre is under serious pressure, but it's too much even for such a creative player as Tiger!

18.♕c2

18.♕e3!? intending 18...c3 19.e5 cxd2+ (19...♘g8 20.e6 ♘df6 21.♘xc3 bxc3 22.♗b5+ ♔d8 23.♖xc3 ♕xc3 24.♗xc3 ♖xc3 25.♕e5 with an attack) 20.♔xd2 ♕b8 21.exf6+ ♔d8 22.fxg7 ♗xg7 23.g3±.

18...dxe4 19.♕xc4

19.fxe4 ♕b7!.

19...♕xc4 20.bxc4

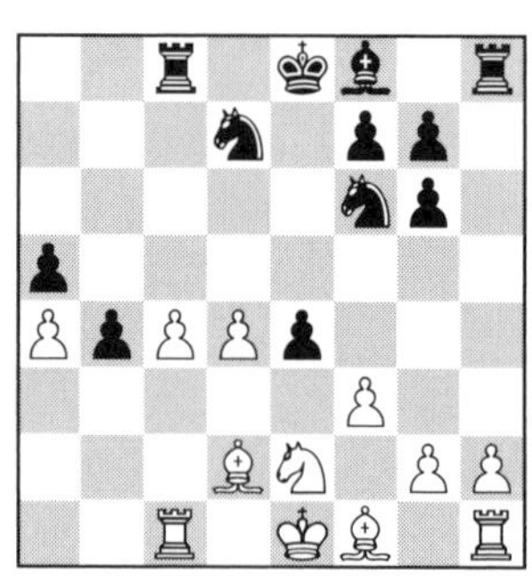

20...♘b6?!

The endgame is very complex, so Black has to play very precisely not to get himself in trouble.

The pawn on a5 desperately needs protection, so it made sense to bring the bishop to c7: 20...♗d6! 21.c5 ♗c7 22.♔f2 exf3 23.gxf3 ♘d5 when both sides have chances.

21.c5 ♘bd5

Not 21...♘xa4 22.♘g3!.

22.♔f2± ♗e7 23.g3 exf3 24.♔xf3

Black is deprived of active counterplay, so White just builds up the pressure.

24...0-0 25.♗h3 25.♖e1!? intending 25...♖fe8 26.♘c1. **25...♖cd8 26.♖he1 ♖fe8 27.♘f4 ♘c7 28.♖c4 g5 29.♘d3 ♘fd5 30.♘c1**

Even better was 30.♘e5 ♗f6 31.♘c6 ♖xe1 32.♗xe1 ♖e8 33.♗d2 b3 34.♖c1±.

30...g6 31.♘b3 f5 32.♔f2 32.g4 f4 33.♗f1 ♖a8 34.♖cc1 ♔g7 35.♖e4±.

32...♗f6 33.♖xe8+ ♖xe8 34.♗g2 ♔f7

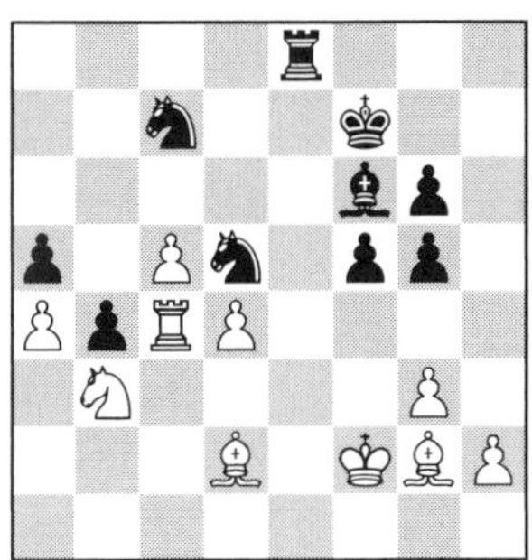

35.♖c1?

Throwing away the greater part of his advantage.

After the correct 35.♘xa5! g4 (perhaps White missed that after 35...♖a8 he can just take on b4: 36.♗xb4+–) 36.♘b3 ♖h8 37.♔g1 g5 38.a5± Black is on the ropes.

35...g4 36.♗f1 g5 37.♗c4 ♔g6 38.♖e1 ♖d8! 39.♖c1 ♘e7 40.♗e3 40.♘xa5 ♗xd4+ 41.♔e2 ♖h8 42.♔d3 ♗f2 43.♗xb4 ♖xh2 44.c6 ♘c8∓. **40...♘c6 41.♖d1 ♘d5 42.♗xd5 ♖xd5 43.♔e2 ♔f7 44.♔d3 ♘e5+ 45.♔c2 ♘c6 46.♗f2** 46.♔d3=. **46...♗g7 47.♖e1**

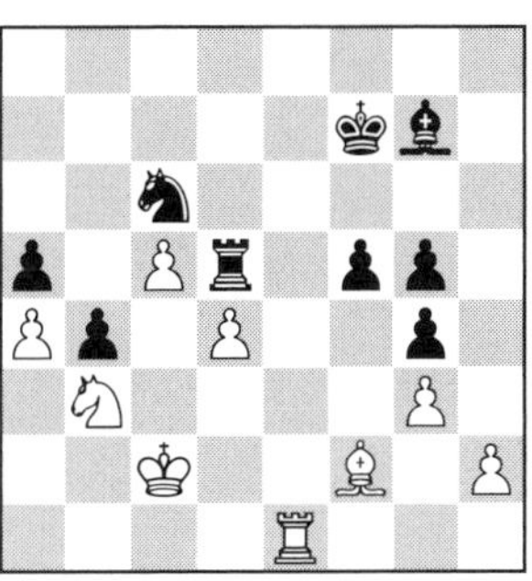

47...♗xd4? A blunder which eventually turned out to be the winning move!

47...f4?! 48.♔d3±; 47...♖d8! 48.♔d3 ♘e5+=.

48.♖d1 ♖xc5+ 49.♘xc5 ♗xf2 50.♘b3?

After the simple 50.♖f1! Black is helpless: 50...♗d4 51.♖xf5+ ♗f6 52.♘b3+–.

50...♔e6∓ 51.♔d3 ♘e5+ 52.♔e2 ♗b6 53.♖f1 ♘f3 54.♖c1? 54.♘d2!∓. **54...♔d5 55.♖c8 f4–+ 56.♖g8 ♔c4 57.♘d2+ ♘xd2 58.♔xd2 ♗e3+ 59.♔e2 b3 60.♖xg5**

And White resigned because of 60...♖xg5 b2 61.♖b5 ♔c3 62.gxf4 ♗xf4 63.♖b6 ♗xh2.

An excellent game by both players!

□ **Alexander Zubov**
■ **Alexander Lastin**
Moscow Open 2009

1.d4 d5 2.c4 c6 3.♘f3 ♘f6 4.e3 ♗f5 5.♘c3 e6 6.♘h4 ♗e4 7.f3 ♗g6 8.♕b3 b5 9.c5

This move is clearly more dangerous for Black than 9.cxd5, but it's most certainly not a refutation of the 8...b5 line.

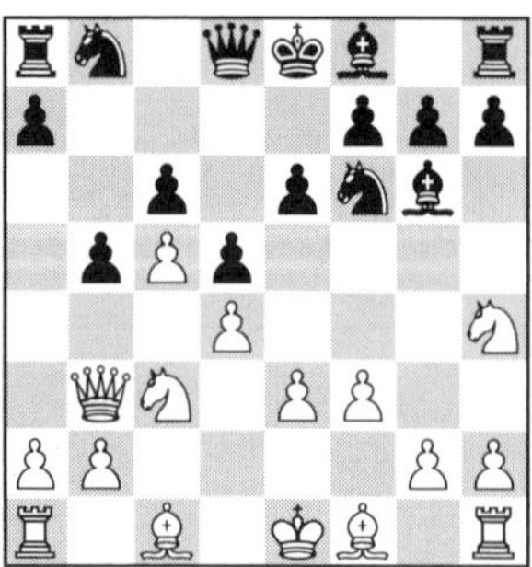

9...♘bd7

9...a5!? is covered in Schenk-Hector.

10.a4 a6 11.♕a3

Taking control of the a-file.

The immediate capture on g6 may just lead to a transposition in case Black reacts correctly to 12.♕a3: 11.♘xg6 hxg6 12.♕a3, and now:

– 12...♕b8? 13.axb5 cxb5 14.♘xb5 ♖xh2 15.♖xh2 ♕xh2 16.♕a5+–, Malakhov-Hector, Helsingor 2009.

– The position arising after 12...♖b8 is very important for the evaluation of the 8...b5 line, as Black can't safely avoid it (9...a5!? is a possible move, but it hardly applies to the term 'safely'!). After 13.axb5 axb5 14.♕a6 ♕c7 15.♕a5 ♕c8 16.♗d2 it is pretty obvious that White has the better chances due to the well established control over the a-file and the possibility to put pressure on c6 by ♘a2-b4. However, it's a perfectly playable position for Black.

11...♖b8 12.axb5 axb5

13.♕a5?!

Apparently White thought that he could take on g6 at any moment...

13.♘xg6 hxg6 14.♕a5 ♕c8 15.♗d2±.

13...♗c2!

Suddenly the white knight on h4 feels very uncomfortable!

14.♕xd8+ ♔xd8 15.g3?!

Another inaccuracy, after which White is on the defensive for the rest of the game.

It was better to play 15.f4, with equal chances, as it's too dangerous for Black to push ...b4:

– 15...b4 16.♘d1 ♗e7 (16...♘e4 17.♘f2 ♘xf2 18.♔xf2 ♔c7 19.♘f3 ♗e7 20.♖a7+ ♖b7 21.♖a6±) 17.♘f2 ♔c7 18.♗d3 ♗xd3 19.♖a7+ ♖b7 20.♖xb7+ ♔xb7 21.♘xd3 ♖a8 22.♘f3±.

– 15...♔c7 16.♖a7+ ♖b7 17.♖a8 ♖b8=.

15...g5!∓ 16.♘g2 b4 17.♘e2 g4?!

17...h5! 18.♗d2 (18.h3!?) 18...g4 19.♘h4 ♗h6 20.♘f4 ♗g5∓.

18.fxg4 ♘xg4 19.♘ef4

White is not willing to take any chances.

19.♗d2!? e5 20.♘c1 exd4 21.exd4 ♗g7 22.♗g5+ ♗f6 (22...♔e8 23.♘e2 ♘f8 24.♗f4±) 23.♗xf6+ ♘dxf6 24.h3 ♘h6 25.g4±.

19...e5 20.♗d3 b3!

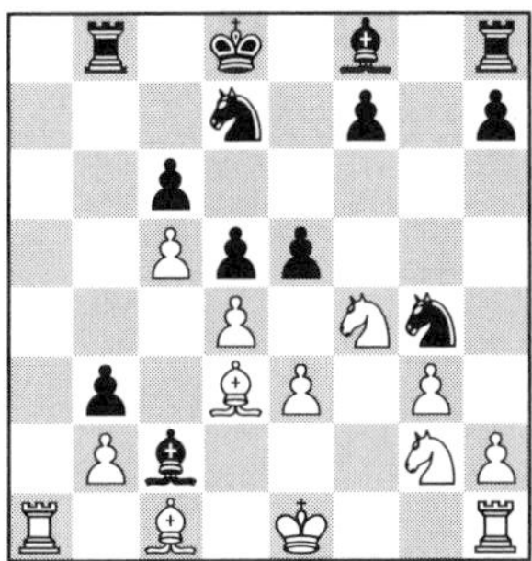

A strong move keeping things under control.

21.♗xc2 bxc2 22.♘e2 ♗h6 23.♖a3

The position is about equal, so both players seem to be quite happy to wrap up the game.

23.h3 ♘gf6 24.0-0 ♘e4 with counterplay.

23...exd4 24.♘xd4 ♘ge5 25.♖c3 ♗f8

25...♘f6!?.

26.0-0 ♗xc5 27.♖xc2 ♔c7 28.♗d2

½-½.

☐ **Andreas Schenk**
■ **Jonny Hector**
Germany Bundesliga 2009/10

1.d4 d5 2.c4 c6 3.♘f3 ♘f6 4.e3 ♗f5 5.♘c3 e6 6.♘h4 ♗e4 7.f3 ♗g6 8.♕b3 b5 9.c5 a5

A very risky move, inviting White to sacrifice the knight on b5, as he often does in certain lines of the Chebanenko Slav. The arising position is very complex and cannot be fully exhausted by variations, however it is pretty obvious that White gets excellent compensation for the sacrificed material. Nevertheless, the position is double-edged so White is no longer in the 'comfort zone' of risk-free play as in the main lines of the 4.e3 variation.

10.♘xb5

Apparently this bold move is White's best (not to say only) attempt to pose Black some problems in the opening.

After 10.♘xg6 hxg6 11.g3 ♗e7 12.♗g2 0-0 13.0-0 e5 14.♗d2 ♘bd7 15.♕c2 ♖e8 Black is very close to equality.

10...a4?!

Although the alternative looks quite scary I tend to believe it offers Black way more practical chances than the text-move: not many players would enjoy defending Black's position after 10...cxb5 11.♗xb5+ ♔e7 12.♗d2 (12.e4 a4 13.♕d3 ♘a6 14.♗d2 ♘c7) 12...♕c7 13.♕a4 (13.0-0 ♘c6 14.♗e1 ♖c8 15.♗g3 ♕b7 16.♘xg6+ hxg6 17.♕a4) 13...♗h5 14.e4, however things are far from being clear in that case.

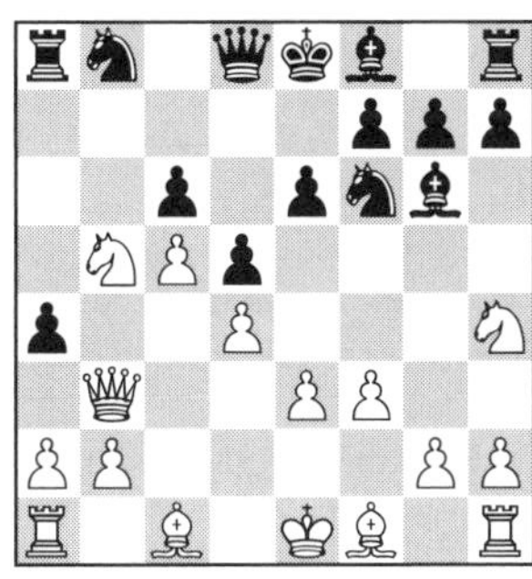

11.♕a3?!

After this move Black can be very happy

with the outcome of the opening. White had two promising alternatives at his disposal to secure his opening advantage.

– The safest is 11.♘d6+! ♗xd6 12.♕b7 ♘bd7 (12...♕a5+ 13.♗d2 ♖a7 14.♕c8+ ♕d8 15.♕xd8+ ♔xd8 16.cxd6 ♖b7 17.♘xg6 hxg6 18.♖b1±) 13.cxd6 c5 14.♕c7 0-0 (14...c4!?) 15.dxc5 ♕xc7 16.dxc7 ♘xc5 17.♘xg6 hxg6 18.♗d2 ♖fc8, with a very comfortable endgame.

– The more aggressive 11.♕c3!? looks just as attractive: 11...cxb5 12.♗xb5+ (forcing the black king to come to e7, since the white queen is no longer hanging on a3) 12...♔e7 13.b4! ♕c7 (13...axb3 14.axb3 ♖xa1 15.♕xa1 ♕c7 16.♘xg6+ hxg6 17.♗d2±) 14.0-0 ♘bd7 15.♘xg6+ hxg6 16.g3±.

11...cxb5 12.♘xg6 hxg6 13.♗xb5+ ♘bd7 14.♗d2 Not 14.♗xa4?? ♕a5+ 15.♗d2 ♕xa4–+. **14...♗e7 15.♗xa4**

15...0-0?

It's surprising that such a great attacking player as Hector ruins a very promising position by this passive move. The rook was very active over the h-file, so Black should have started active operations on the kingside right away.

15...♕c7! 16.b4 (16.♕b3 g5 17.♕c2 g4 18.0-0-0 0-0 19.b4 ♖fb8∓) 16...g5! 17.♗xd7+ ♔xd7 18.♕d3 ♖xh2∓.

16.♕b3 e5

It wasn't too late for 16...g5!?, with the idea to get some play on the kingside.

17.♕c2 exd4 18.exd4

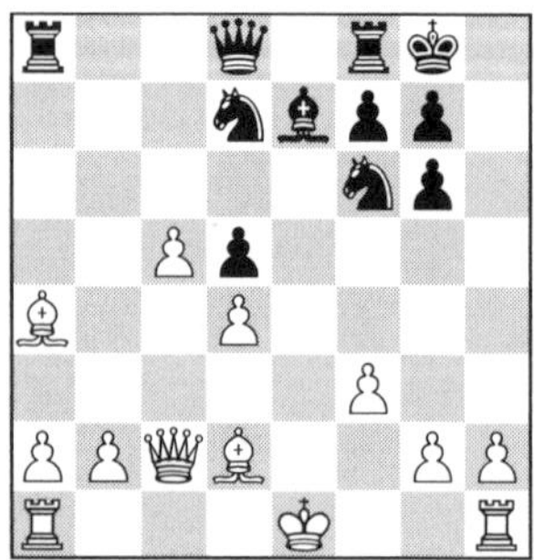

18...♗xc5?

The position wasn't calling for such drastic measures. After the more solid 18...♘h5!? 19.0-0 ♗f6 20.♗e3 ♖e8 21.♗f2 ♘f4 22.♗b5 White is definitely better but Black has his chances as well.

19.dxc5 ♕e7+

Nothing changes after 19...♘xc5 20.♕xc5 ♖xa4 21.0-0±.

20.♔d1 ♘xc5 21.♗b4! 21.♗b5? ♖fb8 22.a4? (22.♗e2 ♘b3–+) 22...♖xb5 23.axb5 ♖xa1+–+. **21...♖fc8 22.♖c1 ♕a7 23.♗xc5 ♖xc5** 23...♕xa4 24.♕xa4 ♖xa4 25.a3±. **24.♕xc5 ♕xa4+ 25.♖c2 ♕xa2 26.♔e2**

White emerged out of the mini-complications with a decisive advantage, but his technique let's him down.

26...♖b8?! 26...g5. **27.♖d1?** The simple 27.♕a3! ♕xa3 28.bxa3+– would probably force Black to resign. **27...♖xb2 28.♖xb2 ♕xb2+ 29.♔f1 g5 30.♕c8+** 30.h3 ♔h7 31.♕c1 ♕b5+ 32.♔g1 ♕a4 33.♕d2±. **30...♔h7 31.♕f5+ ♔h6 32.♖b1 ♕d4 33.♖e1**

For some reason White decided to call it a day, even though Black's defensive task is far from being easy! Draw.

CHAPTER 5

Dimitri Reinderman

Sicilian Najdorf: the 'Mejvik Variation'

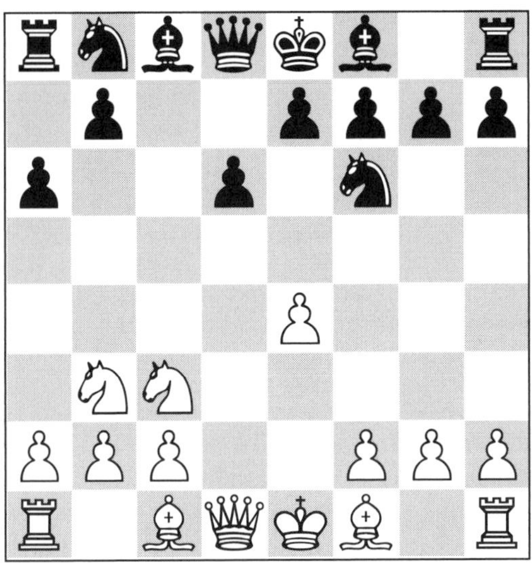

A voluntary retreat: 6.♘b3

If you want to surprise your Najdorf opponent on move 6, there are quite a few possibilities if you believe the database, which shows 30 different moves played by White. However, a lot of them are either main lines (even 6.h3 has been played and analysed a lot lately), pointless, or even losing material. To find a move which is both surprising and sound is not so easy, but recently the move 6.♘b3 came to my attention.

Let me first explain how I got to know this variation. I play an online browser game, Utopia, in which you have to cooperate with other players from your kingdom to fight other kingdoms. To communicate, we use IRC (the oldest chat network on internet) and so I found out that one of my kingdom mates, a Swedish student called Jacob Mejvik, was a chess player. He told me that amongst his companions he was known (or notorious) for playing a special variation of the Najdorf, the 'Mejvik Variation' 6.♘b3. And while I thought it had mainly curiosity value, I asked him to send his analysis of the move, part of which was done with the help of GM Grandelius.

In opening books (or in SOS articles) you'll often find that the opening/variation the author embraces is either better for White or at least equal for Black in all variations. Of course this is not really credible, especially in offbeat openings. Mejvik's analysis had the same flaw: either the final evaluation of variations was off the mark or superior moves for Black were not considered.

It is permissible to be (too) optimistic when analysing one's own pet variation, so I don't blame him. It can be a dilemma for an author though: should one be subjective (which often means not telling your readers the whole truth) or objective (which might mean you are not really promoting the opening/variation you write about)?

In case of SOS articles, best is probably to show 'model games' in which things go well, but also mention what happens in case of perfect play. Also, phrases like 'with chances for both sides' can both be good marketing and a correct objective evaluation.

Back to 6.♘b3. White does not have an advantage after this move, but that shouldn't dissuade you from playing this move, since it's hard enough to prove an advantage after moves like 6.♗g5 or 6.♗e3. The voluntary retreat 6.♘b3 can transpose to other variations, for example after 6....e5 7.♗e2 (or 7.a4, 7.♗e3, 7.g3 etc.; 7.♗g5 is a more unique case as after 6. ♗g5 the reply 6…e5 is rare). However, normally you will at least have gained some time on the clock.

There are also some variations which are only possible (or likely) to result via the 6.♘b3 move order. And while Black is equal with perfect play, it does give chances for both sides...

In the first game of this article, Novikov-Nepomniachtchi, Black plays the typical Najdorf move ...e5. Often in this formation the white bishop goes to e2, but Novikov places it on the more active square c4. White got a bind on the queenside and eventually won.

Kim-Tologontegin sees White attacking with g4-g5 after Black plays the Scheveningen move 6...e6. After inaccurate play by Black he got a bad position and White easily won.

In the end of the article I'll analyse some other possibilities. One of them is the exciting 6....b5 7.e5!? This you won't find in the database!

□ **Stanislav Novikov**
■ **Ian Nepomniachtchi**
Nojabrsk RUS-ch U20 2005

1.e4 c5 2.♘f3 d6 3.d4 cxd4 4.♘xd4 ♘f6 5.♘c3 a6 6.♘b3 ♘bd7

After 6...e5 there are lots of ways to get into regular variations. An interesting option is 7.♗g5 ♗e7 8.♕d2 ♗e6 9.0-0-0 ♘bd7 10.f3 b5 11.h4 0-0 12.♔b1 ♕c7 13.g4, with a sharp position in Galego-Nogueira, Bobadela Mestres 2002.

7.♗e3 e5

Although 6.♘b3 anticipated this move, it's still perfectly alright.

So does White have anything better than 8.♗e2 with a normal Najdorf position? Probably not, but while 8.♗c4 isn't better, at least it's different. Don't play it if you like your pair of bishops though.

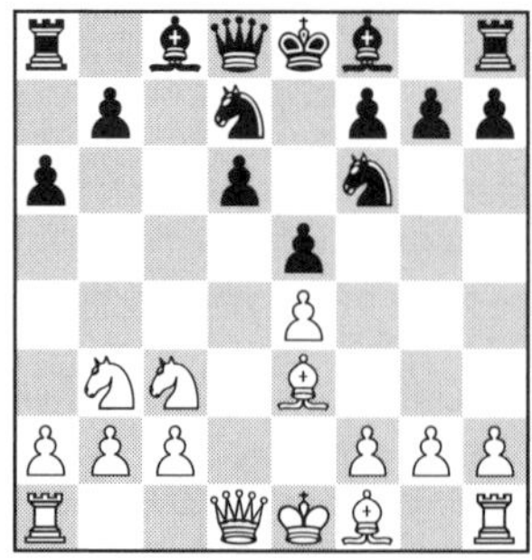

8.♗c4

Another high level game went 8.f3 b5?! (too early) 9.a4 b4 10.♘d5 ♘xd5 11.♕xd5 ♖b8 12.♗c4, with a nice position for White in Tiviakov-Gelfand, Elista 1998. The move order in this game was 6.♗e3 e5 7.♘b3 ♘bd7 and now 8.f3.

8...♗e7 8...b5 9.♗d5 ♘xd5 10.♘xd5 is a tiny bit better for White.

9.0-0 0-0 10.a4 ♘b6

This forces White to give up his dark-squared bishop, but in Sicilian structures with ...d6 and ...e5 White often does this voluntarily anyway.

If Black develops normally, 10...b6 11.f3 ♗b7 12.♕e2 looks better for White than the normal lines after 6.♗e2 e5.

11.♗xb6 ♕xb6 12.♘d5 ♘xd5 13.♗xd5

White dreams of exchanging the light-squared bishops and getting a knight to d5, but Black's chances on the kingside shouldn't be underestimated.

13...♔h8 14.♕d3 f5 15.a5 ♕c7 16.♖a4

16...f4

Interesting was 16...fxe4!? 17.♗xe4 ♗e6, when 18.♗xh7 d5 would appeal to Sveshnikov players.

17.♖c4 ♕d7 18.f3

White is better off without this move (which weakens the a7-g1 diagonal), and should have played 18.♘d2 ♗d8 19.b4.

18...♗d8 19.♖b4 ♖b8 20.♖a1 ♖f6 21.♘d2 b5 22.axb6 ♖xb6 23.♕b3 ♕a7 24.♖xb6 ♗xb6+ 25.♔h1

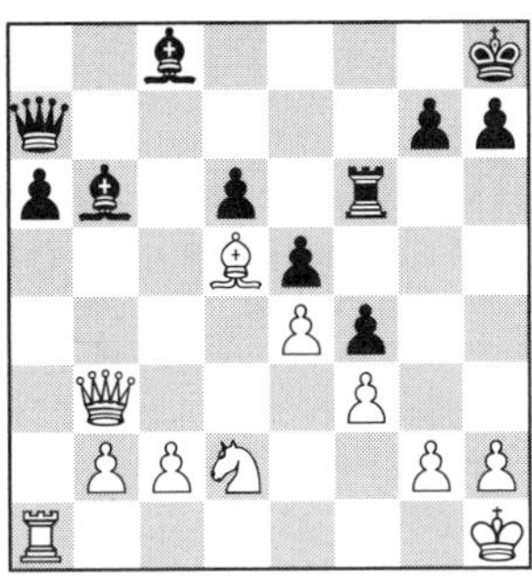

25...g5

Better is 25...♕c7 26.♕c4 ♕d8 followed by 27...♖h6 which forces the knight to f1 (otherwise mate in two!).

With the pawn on g5 the black queen can no longer gain easy access to square h4.

26.♕c4

Now White could have played 26.♘c4! ♗c5 27.♕a4 ♖f8 28.c3 with a clear advantage. Looking at the moves that follow now, it seems that both players were short of time.

26...♕d7 27.♕c6 ♕d8 28.♖a3 ♔g7 29.♖c3 ♖f8 30.♖d3 ♗c5 31.♘b3 ♗e3 32.♗c4 g4 33.♖xd6

33.♕xd6 is safer, after 33...♕xd6 34.♖xd6 gxf3 35.gxf3 ♖f6 36.♖xf6 ♔xf6 37.♔g2 Black has good drawing chances, but it's still a pawn.

33...♕h4 34.♕c7+ ♔h8 35.♖d1 g3

36.♕xe5+ ♖f6 37.♕e8+ ♔g7

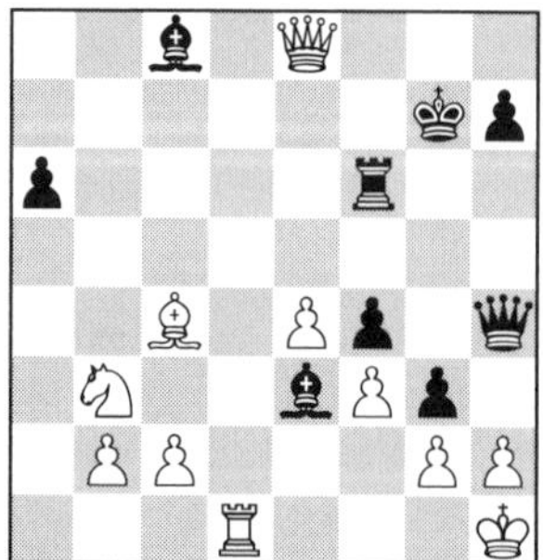

38.♖d7+

The only move; otherwise White loses.

38...♗xd7 39.♕xd7+ ♔h6 40.h3 ♕g5

If it wasn't for his king, White would be winning with two strong pawns for the exchange. But the king counts, and any check that Black gives will be close to mate.

41.♘d4 ♗xd4

A winning attempt. 41...♕a5 42.♘f5+ ♖xf5 43.♕e6+ is a perpetual.

42.♕xd4 ♖c6 43.e5 ♔h5 44.♗f7+ ♔h6 45.♗c4 ♖c8 46.♔g1 ♖d8 47.♗d5 ♔h5?!

Black could (and should) win a pawn here with 47...♖e8 48.e6 ♖d8 49.c4 ♕f5 50.♔f1 ♖b8 51.♗e4 ♕xe6, but the c-pawn should give White a draw.

48.♔f1

But now White can play for more than a draw. He moves his king to a safer position and his majesty will even turn out to be an attacking piece.

48...♕g6 49.♔e1 ♖d7 50.♔d2

Now White has a clear plan: c4, ♔c3 and push the pawns. It's not easy to defend against this plan, since the black queen has to defend her husband and the pawn on f4.

50...♕f5 51.c4 a5 52.♔c3 ♖e7 53.e6 ♔g5 54.c5 ♕f6

Endgames are losing for Black, but otherwise White will enter Black's position with his king.

55.c6 ♖c7 56.♔c4 ♕xd4+ 57.♔xd4 ♔f5

The wrong direction. The king should go to f6 (here or on the next moves).

58.b3 h6 59.h4 h5 60.♔c5 ♔e5 61.♗c4

This bishop will eventually go to d7, when one of the pawns will queen.

61...♖g7 62.♔b6 ♔d6 63.♗a6 ♖c7 64.♗b7 ♖g7 65.♗c8 ♖g8 66.♔b7 ♖f8 67.♗d7 ♖f5 68.c7

Black resigned.

□ **Alexey Kim**
■ **Semetery Tologontegin**
Voronezh 2006 (6)

1.e4 c5 2.♘f3 d6 3.d4 cxd4 4.♘xd4 ♘f6 5.♘c3 a6 6.♘b3 e6 7.♗e3 ♗e7 8.g4

In the Perenyi Attack (6.♗e3 e6 7.g4) Black can (and often does) win material with 7... e5 8.♘f5 g6, with a very sharp and interesting position.

Since there is no knight on d4, Black doesn't have this option in the game.

8...♘c6 9.g5 ♘d7 10.♕d2

Now the position looks like one from the Keres Attack. An early ♘b3 is not so common there, but the advantage is that White doesn't have to worry about ...Nxd4 anymore.

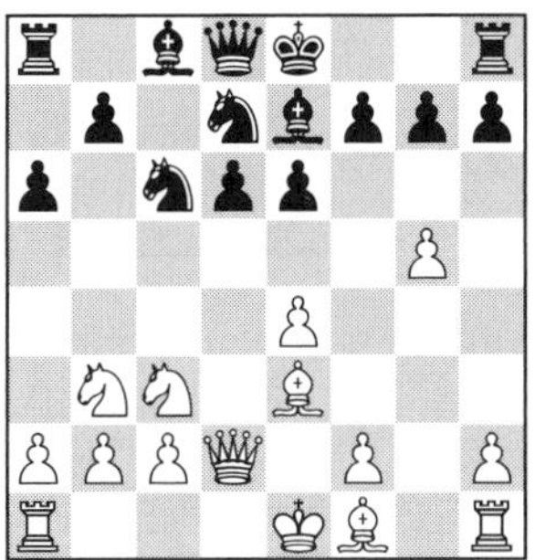

10...b5 11.0-0-0 0-0 12.f4 Nc5

Black is not afraid of Nxc5, since that brings a black pawn closer to White's king.

13.Bg2 b4?!

But now c5 becomes a weakness.

13...Na4 14.Nxa4 bxa4 15.Nd4 Nxd4 16.Qxd4 a3 17.b3 a5 would bring about a sharp position, with chances for both sides.

14.Nxc5! dxc5?!

14...bxc3 15.Qxc3 loses a pawn, but with open lines there's always some compensation. Now Black just gets a bad endgame.

15.Qxd8 Nxd8 16.Na4 Nb7 17.e5

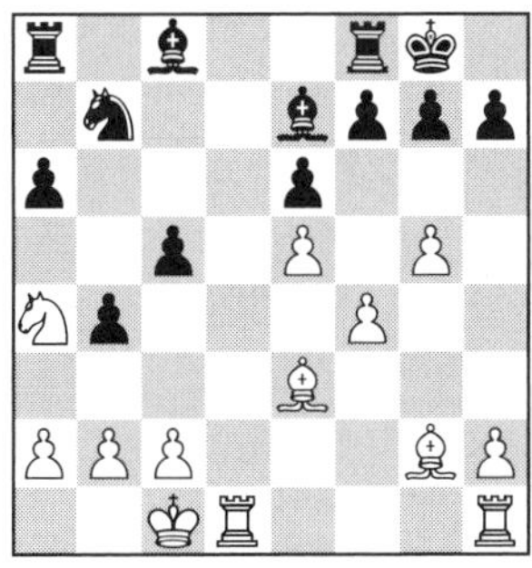

The difference in activity between the white and the black pieces is clear.

17...Rb8 18.Rhe1

This way White can take on b7 and c5 without leaving the rook hanging on h1.

18...Re8 19.Bc6

White is impatient and wants to capture the pawn right away.

Waiting with 19.b3! is even stronger. Since Black can't do anything, White has time to improve his position.

19...Rd8 20.Bxb7 Bxb7 21.Bxc5 Bc6?

After 21...Kf8 the win is not so easy, for example 22.Bxe7+ Kxe7 23.Nc5 Bf3! 24.Rxd8 Rxd8 25.Nxa6?! Rd4! gives Black counterplay.

22.Bxe7 Rxd1+ 23.Rxd1 Bxa4 24.Bxb4

With two pawns more the win is easy, even with opposite-coloured bishops on the board.

24...h5 25.Ba5 Kh7 26.b3 Bc6 27.Rd6 Rc8 28.Kd2 Kg6 29.Ke3 Kf5 30.c4 g6

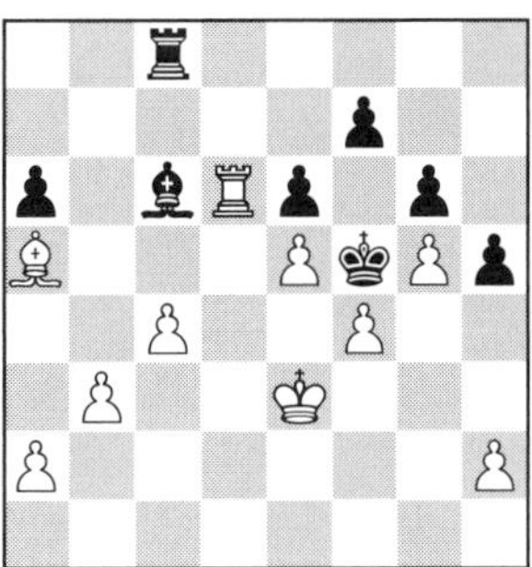

31.Rxc6

At first sight a bit odd, but it turns out to be a good practical decision. Black's king will stay on f5 and his rook cannot do anything active while White pushes his pawns.

31...Rxc6 32.h3 h4 33.Bd8 Rc8 34.Bb6 Rc6 35.c5 Rc8 36.b4 Rc6 37.a3 Rc8 38.a4 Rb8 39.Ba5

39.b5 axb5 40.axb5 Rb7 41.c6 Rxb6 42.c7 Rxb5 43.c8Q also wins.

39...Rc8 40.Kf3 Rc6 41.Bd8 Rc8

42.♗e7 ♖b8 43.c6 ♖b6 44.c7 ♖c6 45.♗d6 a5 46.bxa5 ♖c3+ 47.♔e2 ♔e4 48.♔d2 ♔d4 49.a6 ♖xh3 50.c8♕ ♖h1
Black resigned.

6...b5 and other moves

1.e4 c5 2.♘f3 d6 3.d4 cxd4 4.♘xd4 ♘f6 5.♘c3 a6 6.♘b3 b5
After 6...♘c6 I recommend 7.♗e3, to play 8.g4 after 7...e6.
Black also can switch to the Dragon with 6...g6. Probably best is to play the classical variation with 7.♗e2 and 8.0-0, but 7.e5!? isn't totally stupid.
There are also some games with 6...♕c7. Apart from developing, White can try 7.♘d5!?.

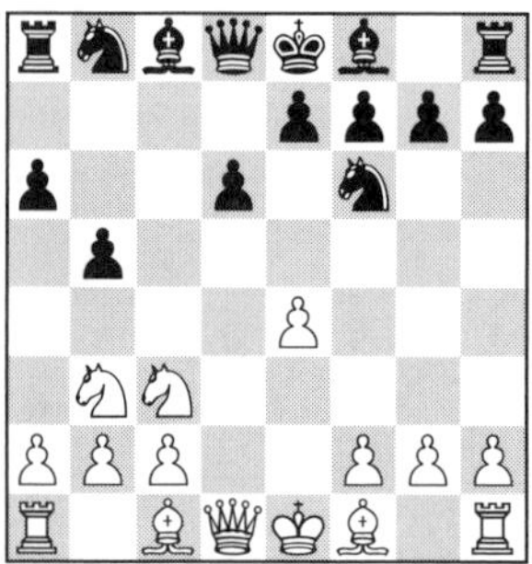

7.e5!?
Of course White can play some normal move, but this pawn sacrifice is more in 'SOS-style'. It doesn't give an advantage with correct play, but White can win the pawn back if he wants.
7...dxe5 8.♕f3 ♖a7 9.♗e3 ♗b7
Mejvik analyses 9...♖d7 10.♘c5 ♖d6 11.♕a8 as 'not as killing as I first thought', which is correct. White does have enough compensation for the pawn though, e.g. 11...♘bd7 12.a4 b4 13.♘3e4 ♘xe4 14.♘xe4 ♖g6 15.♘c5 ♘xc5 16.♗xc5 and White regains the pawn.
10.♕g3 ♖a8 11.♕xe5
It's actually possible not to take the pawn. Houdini says it's equal after 11.♖d1 ♘bd7 12.♘c5 ♗c6 13.♘xd7 ♘xd7 14.♗e2 e6 15.0-0 but it's a difficult position to play (for both sides probably).
11...♘bd7 12.♕g3

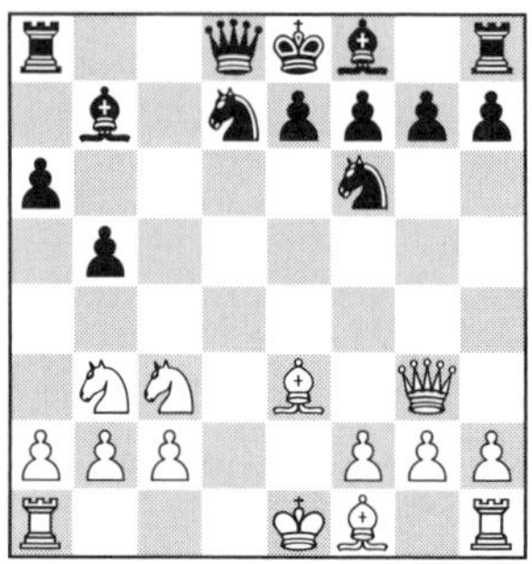

Black and White both have three pieces developed, the main difference is the position of the queen. White's queen is active (but could be vulnerable to attacks), Black's queen doesn't have a lot of squares to go to. She could go to b8, but ♘a5 might be annoying then. Maybe the best option is to play ...♖c8 and ...♕c7 (after developing the kingside or even right away).
12...e6
The most normal move, although 12...g6 and 12...♖c8 are also fine.
13.♖d1 ♖c8
Preventing 14.♘c5 and preparing ♕c7.
14.♗d3 ♕c7 15.♕xc7 ♖xc7 16.0-0
With an equal position.

CHAPTER 6

Sinisa Drazic

A King's Indian Surprise

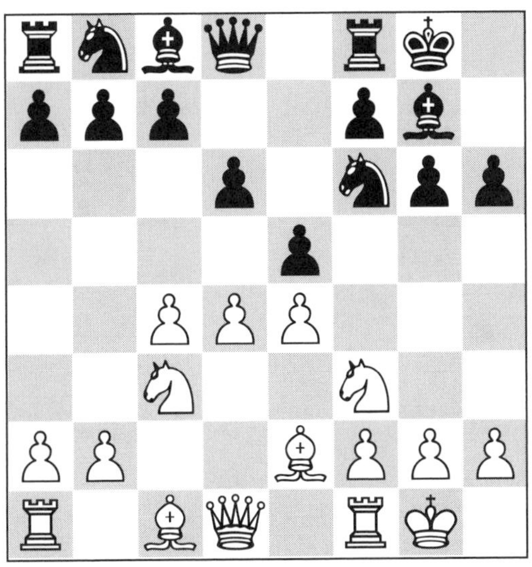

7...h6!? in the main line

I am an active tournament player, and therefore often confronted with the problem of what to play against my next opponent and how to surprise him. For, if you give me the choice between going into deep well-analysed variations, or playing something new and original, I will choose the second option. Computers have made opening preparation easier, but on the other hand there are now many young players who lack fundamental chess knowledge. For this reason, I like to force those players to think with their own heads, right from the start of the game! I want to play 'head to head', not against some version of Rybka.

The present subject is the result of my search for something new in the King's Indian. At one point I said to myself, why not play some useful move in an early stage of the game which would stop the lines with ♗g5. Also why not confuse my opponent? Indeed, some perfectionist will be nervous and try to refute my line with direct moves, which can give me some extra chances to play for the edge!

My results in this line have been good, but to be honest I usually play this line against players who are below my level. The move ...h6 has its good and its bad sides, and the games that I selected will demonstrate this.

In the first game of this article (and in the notes) I will explain some typical mistakes that Black can make in the King's Indian. Indeed, remember that the move 7...h6 may surprise your opponent, but the laws of chess do still apply!

□ **Guillermo Llanos**
■ **Anibal Aparicio**
Buenos Aires 1991

1.d4 ♘f6 2.c4 g6 3.♘c3 ♗g7 4.e4 0-0 5.♘f3 d6 6.♗e2 e5 7.0-0 h6

A very rare move indeed. The main idea is to get out of the standard positions of the King's Indian; to avoid ♗g5; and to be ready for d4-d5, when Black has ...♘h7 and ...f5 (which is a basic idea in the KID), before White is ready to stop this option (with say ♗e3 and ♕d2). The downside of an early ...h6 is that in some variations the move might not be necessary and could be a loss of tempo. However, it is rare that after such a semi-useful move White can count on a big advantage at such an early stage of the game!

8.♖b1

Unclear play arises after 8.d5 ♘h7 9.g3 ♗h3 10.♖e1 ♘d7.

And 8.♗e3 ♘g4 9.♗c1 ♘c6 10.d5 ♘e7 leads to a well-known and popular position. John Nunn was one of the top GMs to play this successfully as Black.

8...♘c6 9.d5

The only way to fight for an advantage and to justify ♖b1.

Usually after taking on e5, White cannot count on any advantage. This is the case here too! After 9.dxe5 dxe5 10.♗e3 (likewise 10.h3 ♕e7 11.♘d5 ♕d6 is equal, but not 11...♘xd5 12.cxd5 ♘d4 13.♘xd4 exd4 14.♗d3±) 10...♗g4 the chances are even.

9...♘e7 10.♘d2

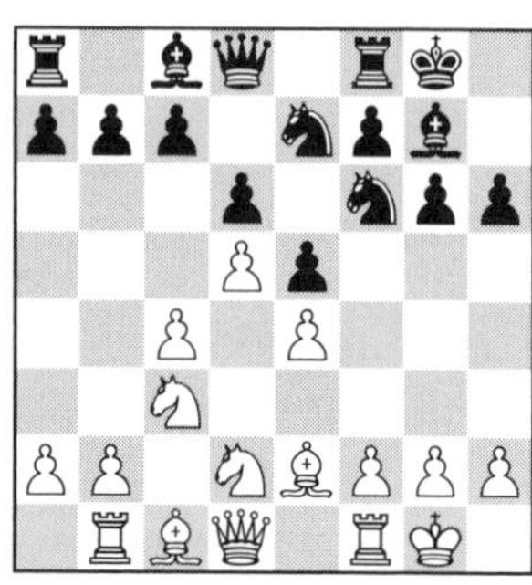

10...g5?!

A typical positional mistake. Better was 10...♘h7 or 10...♘d7 with 11...f5 to follow. After the text Black will be without counterplay!

– I also don't like 10...c5. (Why play ...c5, after White has already prepared b4 with ♖b1?) 11.a3 ♘e8 12.b4 b6 13.bxc5 bxc5 14.♘b3 ♔h7 (14...f5 15.♗d2 ♘f6 16.f3±) 15.♗d2 f5 16.f3 f4 17.♘a4 g5 18.♗a5 ♕d7 19.♘axc5. Of course. White rightly sacrifices a piece and he is now almost winning! 19...dxc5 20.♘xc5 ♕d6 21.♘d3± Ellers-Pasalic, Leipzig 1995.

– 10...a5 11.a3 ♘d7 (I like 11...♘h7 12.b4 axb4 13.axb4 f5 with a full struggle ahead) 12.b4 axb4 13.axb4 f5 14.♕c2 f4?! (this is a positional mistake. Now White can exchange the light-squared bishop after which he is simply better because of the fact that the black bishop on c8 is one of the most dangerous pieces in the KID! Of course, 14...♘f6 was a much better solution, keeping the option ...f5-f4 and many others!) 15.♗g4± ♘f6 16.♗xc8 ♖xc8 17.c5 g5 18.f3 g4 19.♘c4 h5 20.♗a3 ♘e8 21.♕e2 ♘g6 22.♔h1 ♕g5 23.♖bc1 ♖f6 24.b5 and White's play on the queenside is much faster, Kojoukhar-Pasalic, Germany 1995.

11.♖e1 ♘d7 12.♗g4

A typical reaction. Black has a bad position and will have no chances anymore to organize a strong attack!

12...a5 13.♘f1 f5 14.♗xf5 ♘xf5 15.exf5 ♖xf5 16.♘e4 ♖f7 17.♘fg3 b6 18.♕h5 ♘f6 19.♘xf6+ ♕xf6 20.♗e3 ♗d7 21.♖bc1 ♖e8 22.b3 ♕e7 23.♕g6 ♖f6 24.♕c2 ♕f7 25.a3 ♔h8 26.b4 axb4 27.axb4

27...♖g8

At first sight 27...b5 looks good but is not enough! White more or less wins after 28.cxb5 ♗xb5 (28...♕xd5 29.♕xc7 ♕xb5 30.♘e4+–) 29.♕xc7 ♕xd5 30.♖ed1 ♕e6 (30...♕b3 31.♘e4) 31.♘e4.

28.♕d1 ♗f8 29.c5 bxc5 30.bxc5 dxc5 31.♘e4 ♖f4 32.♘xc5 ♗g4 33.f3

With 33.♕d2 White would not even have allowed Black the illusion of counterplay.

33...♗xf3 34.gxf3 ♖xf3 35.♘e4 g4 36.♗f2 h5 37.♖c2 ♗h6 38.d6 cxd6 39.♕xd6 ♗f4 40.♖c7 ♗xh2+ 41.♔h1 ♕f8 42.♕xf8 ♖gxf8 43.♔xh2 h4 44.♔g2 h3+ 45.♔g1 ♖8f7 46.♖xf7 ♖xf7 47.♗g3 ♔g7 48.♘f2 ♖f3 49.♗xe5+ ♔g6 50.♘xg4 ♖f5 51.♔h2

Black resigned.

Instructive mistakes were made, but on move 10 Black ought to have started preparing for ...f5.

Now what if White wants to use the loss of tempo (7...h6) to take on e5? Doesn't he just win a pawn?

□ **Davoud Pira**
■ **Sinisa Drazic**
Cannes 2005

1.d4 ♘f6 2.♘f3 g6 3.c4 ♗g7 4.♘c3 0-0 5.e4 d6 6.♗e2 h6 7.0-0 e5 8.dxe5 dxe5

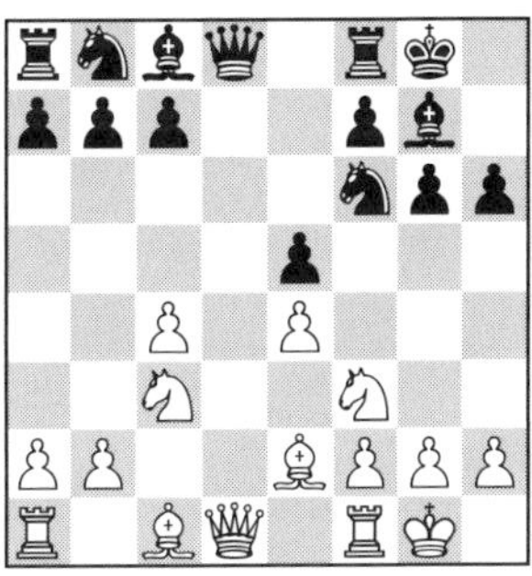

9.♘xe5

9.♕c2 ♘bd7 10.♖d1 ♘h5 11.♗e3 c6 12.b4 ♕e7 13.c5 ♘df6 14.h3. This plan is not so bad. White has a space advantage and more liberty to play, but he should be careful. 14...♘f4 15.♗f1 ♘6h5?! (a bad move, without a clear idea. 15...♘h7 is natural and good: 16.♖d6 ♘g5 17.♘xg5 hxg5 18.♗c4 ♗e6 19.♕b3 ♗xc4 20.♕xc4 ♖fd8 21.♖ad1 ♘e6 22.b5 ♘d4± and there is still a lot of poison in the position). Now correct is 16.♖d6 with the idea to double the rooks, and I can't see what Black's knight is doing on h5, White would have been much better. In Kuhne-Stolz, Potsdam 1995, 16.♔h2 was played and after several mistakes Black even won.

9...♘xe4!

The only move for equality, and the tactical justification for 7...h6.

9...♕e7? leaves White with a clear pawn up: 10.f4 (of course, even 10.♗f4± is possible) 10...c6 11.♗e3 ♘a6 12.♕c2 ♘c5 13.♖ad1 ♖e8 14.♗f3 a5 15.♕f2 ♗f8 Chytilek-Holemar, Brno 2001, and now 16.♖d2 should suffice – a pawn up and better development.

10.♘xe4 ♗xe5

11.♕xd8

11.♗xh6 ♕h4 (after this move Black doesn't have problems anymore!) 12.f4 ♕xh6 13.fxe5 ♕e3+! (an important move) 14.♘f2 ♘c6 15.♗g4 ♗xg4 16.♕xg4 ♘xe5 17.♕h4 ♖ae8∓ (instead, 17...♘d3 18.b3 ♖ae8 19.♖ad1 ♘xf2 20.♕xf2 is equal) 18.♖ae1 ♕b6 (after simple play, Black is slightly better) 19.♔h1 Gombac-Drazic, Nova Gorica 2010. And now instead of 19...f5 Black retains a slight edge with 19...♔g7.

11...♖xd8 12.♗xh6 ♗xb2 13.♖ad1

A good move. Ignoring the bishop on b2, which is not stronger here than on g7!

After 13.♖ab1 ♗g7 14.♗g5 (14.♖fd1 ♖xd1+ 15.♖xd1 ♘c6=) 14...♖e8 Black is equal.

13...♖e8

A good reply. Black keeps as many pieces as possible in the game, which can help to create winning chances.

After 13...♖xd1 14.♖xd1 ♘c6 15.♗e3 White is slightly better because Black has problems developing.

14.♖d2

14.♗f3 ♘c6 15.♖fe1 ♗f5 is unclear.

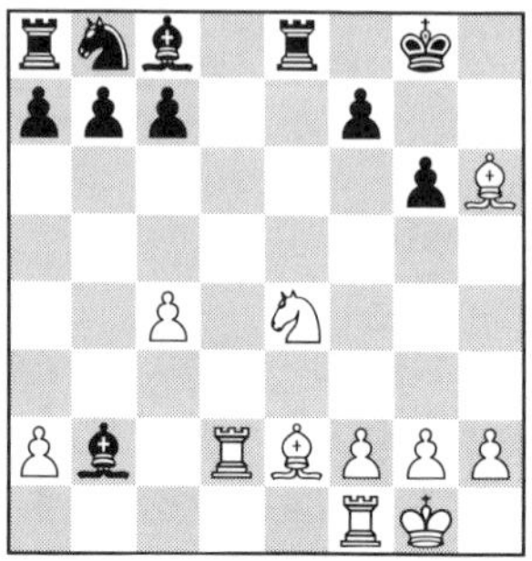

14...♗g7

This move isn't bad, but Black will have no more winning chances. Of course we can win any position in practical play, but this position is clearly drawish and any other result will be a surprise.

14...♗h8! was the best move. The idea is to support the knight, which will move to c6 and d4. Then Black will have an excellent position, with a strong knight in the centre! Still, with best play the game could end in a repetition after 15.♗f3 ♘c6 16.♘c5 (16.♗f4 ♗g4!∓) 16...♘e5 17.♗xb7 ♗xb7 18.♘xb7 ♖ab8 19.♘a5 ♘g4 20.♗f4 ♗c3 21.♖d5 ♘f6 22.♖c5 ♘e4 23.♖d5 ♘f6=.

15.♗xg7 ♔xg7 16.♘c5 ♘c6 17.f4 ♖b8

17...♘a5.

18.♗f3 ♘a5 19.♖c1 b6 20.♘b3 ♘xb3 21.axb3 a5 22.♔f2

And the game ended in a draw on move 59.

□ **Remus Cornea**
■ **Almos Szirti**
Marijampole 1994

1.d4 ♘f6 2.c4 g6 3.♘c3 d6 4.e4 ♗g7 5.♗e2 0-0 6.♘f3 e5 7.0-0 h6 8.d5 a5

As I mentioned above the alternative is 8... ♘h7 to prepare ...f5.

9.♖b1

I don't like this move, better is 9.♘d2 or 9.♘e1.

After for instance 9.♘e1 ♘a6 10.♘d3 ♘d7 we enter a typical standard King's Indian position. Play is dictated by the pawn chain. White will play on the queenside, and Black on the kingside.

9...♘a6 10.a3?!

A mistake, after which Black can have all the advantages which the King's Indian Defence can give!

10...♘c5

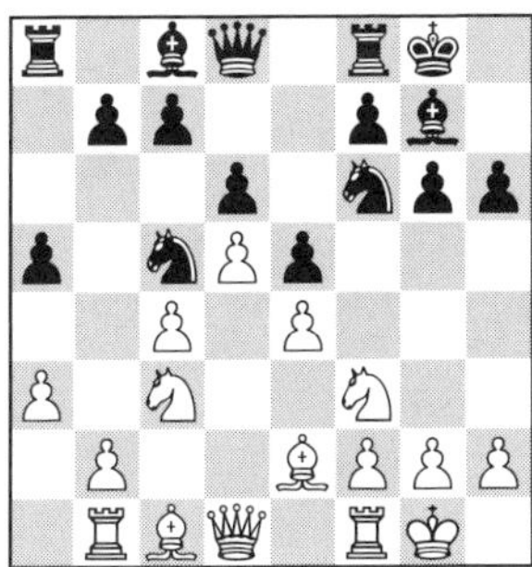

11.♕c2?

A direct mistake, connected with the badly-placed rook.

Black has a pleasant position after 11.♘d2 a4.

11...♘fxe4!

Possible because the rook is hanging.

12.♘xe4 ♘xe4 13.b4 ♘f6

And Black is a clear pawn up in an early stage of the game, with no compensation for White!

□ **Daniele Zarpellon**
■ **Sinisa Drazic**
Padova 2005

1.d4 ♘f6 2.c4 g6 3.♘c3 ♗g7 4.e4 d6 5.♘f3 0-0 6.♗e2 h6

If you are in a more provocative mood you can play 6...h6, like I did in this game.

7.0-0

7...a6

This is a novelty. 7...e5 would bring us back to our standard SOS position. The idea is of course to confuse the opponent, because without ...e5 or ...c5, White has nothing to do, except for developing his pieces, and Black might have the additional option to have a useful tempo if the position switches to the Benoni-Benko type later on. A note of warning: such half risky moves are especially good if you play against opponents weaker than yourself!

8.h3 e5

I opt for a set-up with ...e5. Which is more useful: the pawn on h3, the pawn on h6 – or the pawn on a6? Tactically there is something wrong with my play though.

9.dxe5

In case of 9.d5 Black's counterplay on the kingside would be faster than usual because of the target provided by h3.

9...dxe5 10.♕xd8

Correct was 10.♘xe5 ♘xe4 11.♘xe4 ♗xe5

12.♗xh6 ♕xd1 (12...♖e8 13.♕xd8 ♖xd8 14.♖fe1 ♗xb2 15.♖ab1 ♗g7 16.♗g5 ♖e8 17.♗g4+−) 13.♖axd1 ♖e8 14.♗f3 ♗xb2 15.♗f4 and with simple moves White has obtained a better position!

10...♖xd8 11.♗e3 ♘c6 12.♖fd1 ♗e6

13.b3

White is still somewhat better after 13.♘d5 ♖ac8 14.♘xf6+ ♗xf6 15.♗xh6 ♘d4 16.♘xd4 exd4 17.♗f4. He is a pawn up, but Black has some compensation.

13...♔h7 14.♖xd8 ♖xd8 15.♖d1 ♖xd1+ 16.♗xd1 The position is equal. With small positional mistakes later on, White lost the fight and the game. **16...♗f8 17.♗c2 ♔g7 18.♗b1** The game is even after 18.♘d5 ♘e8. **18...♘e8 19.♘e2** 19.♘d5 is still equal. **19...♗a3** 19...♗b4. **20.♘e1 f6 21.f3 h5 22.h4 ♔f7**

And after 97 moves Black scored the full point, from a totally equal position.

In another fairly recent game of mine White postponed castling, still the early ...h6 justifies its selection for this article.

□ **Corrado Astengo**
■ **Sinisa Drazic**

Milano 2010

1.d4 ♘f6 2.c4 d6 3.♘f3 g6 4.♘c3 ♗g7 5.e4 0-0 6.♗e2 h6 7.h3 e5 8.♗e3 exd4 9.♘xd4 ♖e8 10.♗f3 ♘bd7 11.♕c2

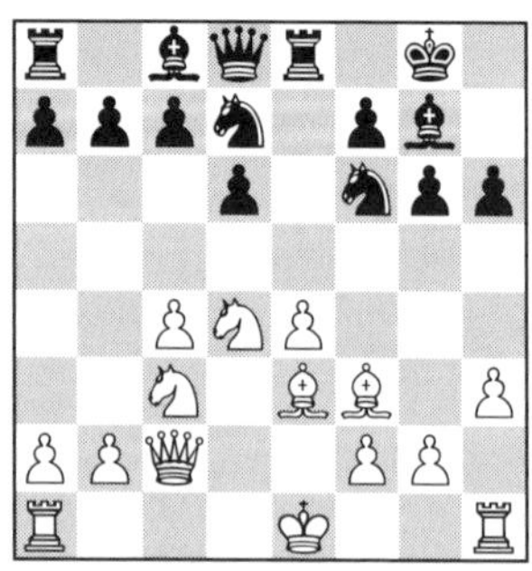

11...a6

11...♘b6 looks very attractive, but with a few strong moves White can punish this 'nice' move: 12.b3 d5 13.exd5 ♘fxd5 14.♘xd5 ♗xd4 15.0-0-0 ♗f5 16.♖xd4! ♗xc2 17.♘xb6 ♕e7 18.♘d5 ♕a3+ 19.♔xc2 ♕xa2+ 20.♔c3 and the pieces are superior to the queen.

A good alternative was 11...♘e5 12.♗e2 c5 13.♘f3 ♘c6 – Black has a weak point on d6, but on the other hand he controls square d4 and his pieces are better placed and he has the option to gain good counterplay with ...♗e6 and ...a6.

12.♖d1 ♕e7

Not 12...c5 13.♘b3 ♘e5 14.♗e2 ♕c7 15.♕d2±.

13.0-0

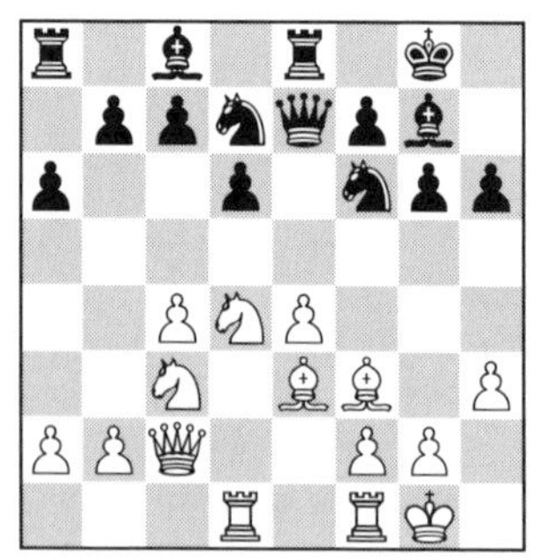

13...♘e5

Stronger was 13...c5. Black gains space, for the price of a small weak point, which is practically untouchable anyway! Tell me, after 14.♘b3 ♘e5 15.♗e2 ♗e6 16.♘d2 ♗d7 17.♘f3 ♘xf3+ 18.♗xf3 ♗c6, what's wrong with the black position? Of course, Black is OK (as Adorjan told us long ago!). In the game I lack space, and am soon inferiorly placed.

14.♗e2 ♗d7 15.f4 ♘c6 16.♗f3 ♘xd4 17.♗xd4

Black lacks space no doubt about it!

17...♗c6 18.♖fe1

Why didn't White play 18.e5, an obvious move, so natural and simple? It promises a clear advantage!

18...♖ac8

What should Black do? He can only wait for some mistakes, right?

19.♕f2 Or 19.b4 to gain even more space. **19...♘d7 20.♘d5 ♗xd5 21.cxd5 ♗xd4 22.♕xd4** 22.♖xd4 was better. **22...♕h4 23.♕d2 ♖e7**

This is the best position for Black since the start of the game.

Not 23...g5 24.♗g4.

24.♗g4 24.♖c1. **24...♖ce8 25.♗xd7 ♖xd7**

White plays for a draw, and just because of this Black gains time to consolide, and then to press the opponent for more! One more mistake is needed though.

26.e5?

Here it is! This often happens when you have only one result in mind. You should always play for the best moves and then press your opponent to defend, rather than exchanging pieces at any cost and slowly drift towards a weaker position. Once you wake up, you realize that you are in an already lost position!

26...♖de7

Black is slightly better, and with good technique and calculation he won the game.

27.e6 fxe6 28.dxe6 ♕f6 29.♕d5 b6 29...♕xb2∓. **30.♖d4 ♔g7 31.♖de4 ♕xb2 32.f5 ♖f8 33.♖f1** 33.♖g4 ♖f6 34.♖xg6+ ♖xg6 35.fxg6 ♕c3∓. **33...♖f6 34.♖g4 ♕e5 35.♕d3 b5 36.♔h1 c5∓ 37.♖f3 c4 38.♕b1 d5 39.♖fg3 ♕xf5 40.♖xg6+**

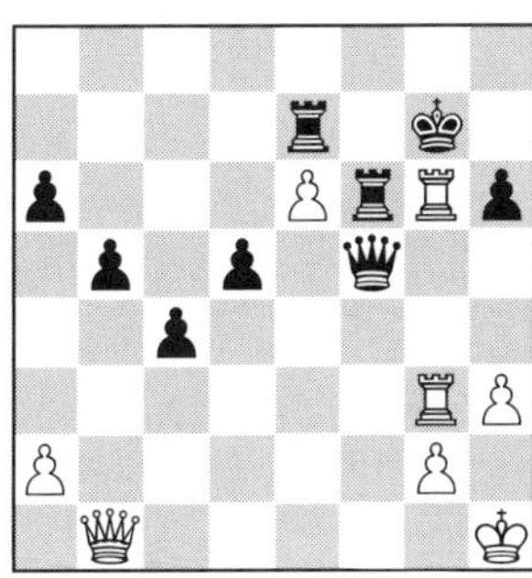

After **40...♔h7** Black won on move 64.

□ **Norbert Stull**
■ **Boris Gruzmann**
Davos 2008

1.d4 ♘f6 2.c4 d6 3.♘c3 g6 4.e4 ♗g7 5.♗e2 h6 6.♘f3 0-0 7.0-0 ♘a6

Here too Black postpones ...e5.

8.h3 ♕e8 9.♗e3 e5

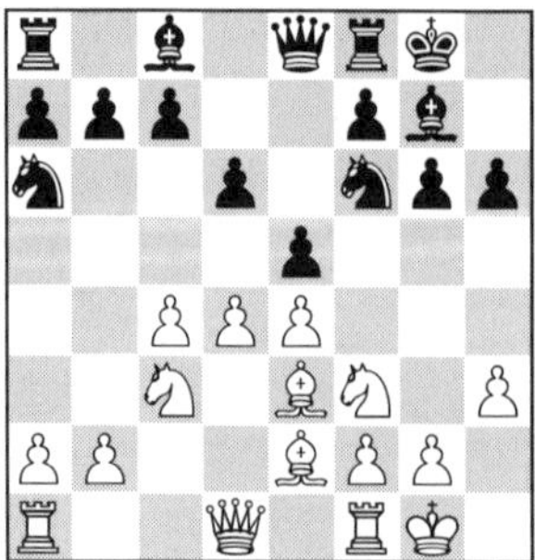

10.d5

10.dxe5 dxe5 11.a3 is an alternative. The move ...h6 is not necessary, but it's also not so bad. After a3, b4, ♕c2, White keeps the somewhat better prospects.

10...♔h7

I don't like this plan. Black will lose a lot of time to push ...f5. It was possible to play in a much simpler way.

Black has some compensation after 10...♘h5 11.♕d2 ♘f4 12.♗xf4 exf4 13.♕xf4 ♘c5 14.♖fe1 f5 15.exf5 ♗xf5 16.♕d2±.

Best is 10...♘h7 11.♕d2 h5 12.a3 f5 when things are not clear! It is the plan with ...♘h7 that you should remember when you decide to take up this King's Indian with ...h6.

11.♘d2 ♘g8 12.a3 f5 13.f3?!

13.exf5 gxf5 14.♕c2 ♘e7 15.f4 e4 16.♘b3 is a typical position in which White is clearly better. He must push g4 at the right moment, after some preparation. Black has an additional problem compared to similar positions, because he can't control the important square d4.

13...♘f6 14.b4 b6?

14...f4 was the only chance to attack the white king but objectively the first player is better after 15.♗f2 g5 16.c5.

15.♕a4??

15.exf5! gxf5 16.♗d3 was strong. What is the black king doing on h7?

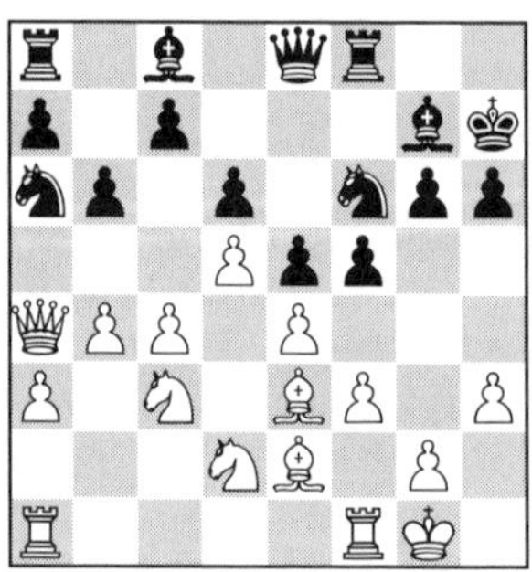

15...♕e7?

White is only slightly better after 15...♕xa4 16.♘xa4 ♘h5 17.♖fc1.

Now Black is forced to bury his pieces on the queenside. Still he will be successful, so should we really condemn his desire not to exchange queens?

16.c5 ♘b8 17.cxd6 cxd6 18.♖fc1 ♘h5 19.♕d1 ♗f6 20.♘b5 ♗g5 21.♗xg5 ♕xg5 22.♖c7+ ♔g8

23.♘f1?

After this mistake White will have no more chances to come back in the game!

23.♕e1 is much stronger: 23...♘f4 24.♗f1 ♘xh3+ 25.♔h1 ♘f4 26.♘xd6±.

23...♘f4 24.g3 fxe4 25.♘xd6 ♘xh3+ 26.♔h2 ♘f2 27.♕c1 ♕h5+ 28.♔g1 ♘h3+ 29.♔h2 ♘f4+

White resigned.

CHAPTER 7

Igor Lysyj

Queen's Indian: Chernyshov's Line

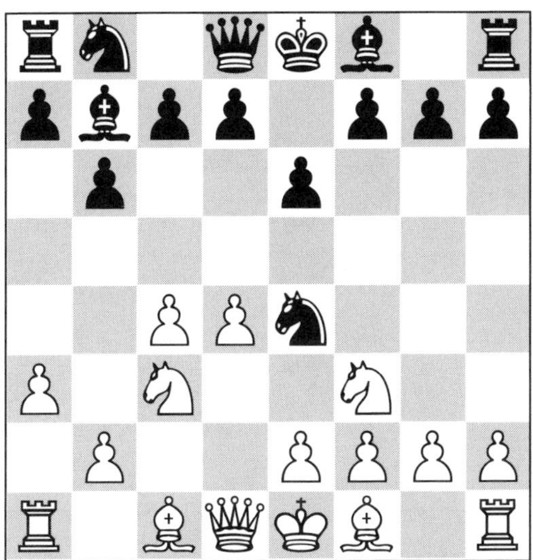

4.a3 ♗b7 5.♘c3 ♘e4!?

After five rounds of the Aeroflot Open I was completely disillusioned with my play and my tournament position. The pairings also did not inspire any optimism: in the sixth round I was black against grandmaster Vorobiov, who has a solid opening repertoire. In search of complicated play, I hit upon an unusual way of handling the Petrosian Variation of the Queen's Indian Defence, which I had observed being played by the inventive Russian grandmaster Alexander Chernyshov. After 1.d4 ♘f6 2.c4 e6 3.♘f3 b6 4.a3 ♗b7 5.♘c3 ♘e4!? my opponent responded in the most critical way with 6.♘xe4 ♗xe4 7.♘d2 ♗g6 8.g3. But first let us analyse less ambitious ways of playing for White...

□ **Tal Shaked**
■ **Nick De Firmian**
Denver 1998

1.d4 ♘f6 2.c4 e6 3.♘f3 b6 4.a3 ♗b7 5.♘c3 ♘e4!?

I should mention that the rare knight jump on the 5th move, with the idea of immediately beginning a piece battle for the key e4-point while retaining a flexible pawn structure, has quite an ancient history and was first employed in the game Simagin-Keres, Parnu 1947. I recommend this move to those who like unusual play. To those who are prepared to go in for a certain strategic risk in order to play for a win.

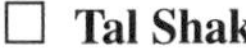

6.♗d2

White has also played 6.♕c2 ♘xc3, and now:

7.bxc3?! is illogical, as after 7...f5! Black successfully fights for the e4-point and creates counterplay against the opponent's doubled pawns:

– 8.g3 ♗e4! 9.♕b3 ♘c6! 10.♗g2 ♘a5 11.♕a4 ♗c6 12.♕d1 ♘xc4∓, Hanko-Chernyshov, Litomysl 1996.

– 8.e3 ♗e7 9.♗d3 0-0 10.e4 fxe4 11.♗xe4 ♗xe4 12.♕xe4 ♘c6 13.0-0 ½-½, Voloshin-Chernyshov, Frydek Mistek 1996. Black's position is more promising after 13...♘a5 14.♕d3 ♕e8 15.♖e1 ♕h5 I would prefer his position.

7.♕xc3 and now:

● 7...c5. The most logical continuation; Black clarifies the situation in the centre:

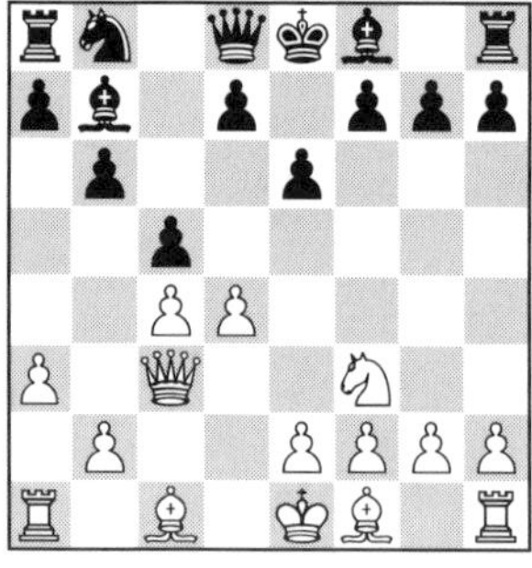

– 8.♗f4 cxd4 9.♘xd4 f6!? 10.♘f3 (10.♗g3 e5 11.♘c2 ♘a6 12.b4 ♖c8) 10...e5 11.♗e3 d5 12.cxd5 ♘a6 13.♖d1 ♖c8 14.♕d2 ♘c7 15.d6 ♘d5 is equal.

– 8.d5!? exd5 9.cxd5 ♗xd5 10.♗g5 f6 11.♖d1 ♗e6 12.♗h4 ♗e7 13.e4 0-0, White has compensation for the pawn, but no more, Munoz-Rios Parra, Medellin 2010.

– 8.dxc5 bxc5 9.♗f4 d6 10.♖d1 ♕b6 11.e3 ♘d7 12.♗e2 ♘f6 with an equal game.

● But 7...d6 is no worse, with the approximate variations:

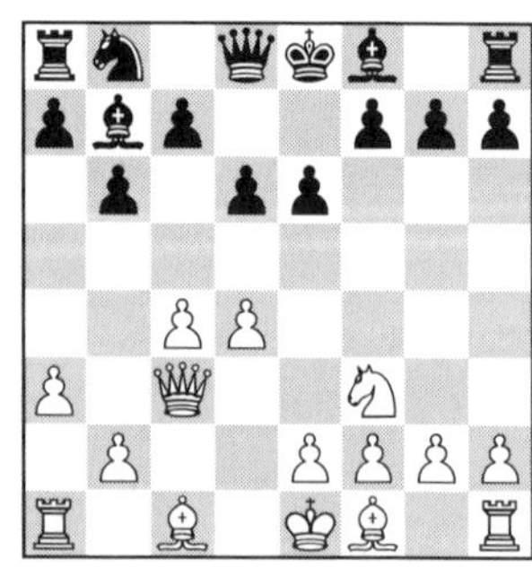

– 8.♕c2 c5 9.e3 (or 9.e4 cxd4 10.♘xd4 ♘d7, setting up a 'hedgehog') 9...♗e7 10.♗d3 cxd4 11.♘xd4 ♘d7 Black has counterplay.

– 8.g3 ♗e7 9.♗g2 ♘d7 10.♕c2 ♘f6 equal.

– 8.♕d3 ♘d7 9.e4 e5 10.d5 ♘c5 11.♕c2 a5 12.b3 c6, aiming to exploit the position of the white queen on the c-file, or 12...♕f6!? with the idea of 13...♕g6, putting pressure on the e4 pawn.

Black has good play in all lines since he has managed to exchange a pair of knights without making any concessions.

6...♗e7 7.d5

This principled continuation brings White nothing but problems. He should have preferred the modest 7.♕c2 ♘xd2 8.♕xd2.

7...f5!

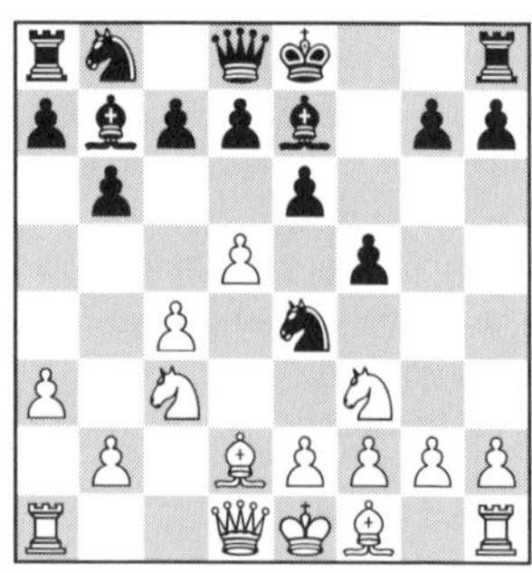

8.g3?!

I also prefer Black after 8.♘xe4?! fxe4 9.♘d4

exd5 10.cxd5 0-0 11.♕b3 ♗c5 12.d6+ ♔h8 13.dxc7 ♕xc7 14.e3 (14.♗c3? ♕f4–+) 14...♗xd4 (14...♘c6 15.♘xc6 ♗xc6∓) 15.exd4 ♘c6 16.♗e3 ♕d6 17.♖d1 ♘e7.

8...♗f6 9.♖c1 c6 10.dxe6

If White stubbornly avoids capturing on e6, then after 10.♗g2 0-0 11.0-0 cxd5 12.cxd5 ♘xc3 13.♗xc3 ♗xd5 14.♘d4 ♗xg2 15.♔xg2 ♘a6 he has no compensation for the material.

10...dxe6 11.♗g2 c5 12.0-0 ♘xd2 13.♘xd2 ♗xg2 14.♔xg2 0-0

The white knights have no prospects. Black, with his long-range bishop, has control over the central squares and a comfortable game.

15.b4

With this move White merely creates weaknesses for himself. He should have preferred 15.f4 ♘c6 16.♘f3 ♕xd1 17.♖fxd1 ♖ad8∓.

15...cxb4 16.axb4 ♘c6 17.b5 ♘a5 18.♘cb1 ♖c8 19.♕a4 ♕c7 20.♕a2 ♔h8 21.♔g1 f4?!

A sharp move. Black tries to create an attack on the opponent's king.

After 21...♕e7 22.♕a4 ♖fd8 23.♘b3 ♘xb3 24.♕xb3 ♕c5 he would have retained a solid advantage.

22.♘e4 ♗d4? Black still has counterplay after 22...♕e5 23.♘bd2 ♗e7 24.♔g2 h5.

23.♘bd2 ♕e5 24.♕b1

White has consolidated, and now his position is even slightly preferable.

24...♕h5 24...fxg3 25.hxg3 ♕f5 26.♔g2±. **25.♘f3 ♗c5?!** Now the white knights acquire comfortable posts, but the same cannot be said about the black steed on a5. 25...e5 was more resilient.

26.♖fd1 fxg3 27.hxg3 ♘xc4 28.♔g2!± ♗e7 29.♖d7 ♘a3 30.♕b2 ♕e8 31.♖cd1 31.♘e5!± was better. **31...♖c2 32.♕b3 ♖xe2 33.♕d3 ♖a2 34.♖xa7 h6 35.♘e5?** 35.♕b3! ♖e2 36.♕xe6 ♕h5 37.♖d3 would have won. **35...♕h5 36.♖xe7 ♕xe5**

37.♕e3?? A blunder. Of course, after 37.♖a7 ♕f5 38.♔g1 White's position is preferable, despite the pawn deficit.

37...♖axf2+

White resigned.

□ **Piotr Staniszewski**
■ **Igor Lysyj**
Warsaw 2010

1.d4 ♘f6 2.c4 e6 3.♘f3 b6 4.♘c3 ♗b7 5.a3 ♘e4 6.♘xe4 ♗xe4 7.e3

This modest continuation promises White a slight advantage in space. However, only two pairs of minor pieces are left on the board, and so White's spatial advantage is not so perceptible.

7...♗e7

I like this sound continuation. But if you

prefer sharp play, you can try 7...c5!? 8.♗d3 (the consequences of 8.d5!? are unclear; after 8...exd5 9.cxd5 ♗e7 Black has counterplay in the spirit of the Modern Benoni) 8...♗xf3! (weaker is 8...♗xd3 9.♕xd3, when after 9...cxd4?! 10.exd4 d5 11.0-0 ♗e7 12.♗f4 dxc4 13.♕xc4 ♘d7 14.♖fd1 White's lead in development is bound to tell; for example 14...0-0 15.d5! ♖c8 16.♕e2±) 9.♕xf3 ♘c6 and now:

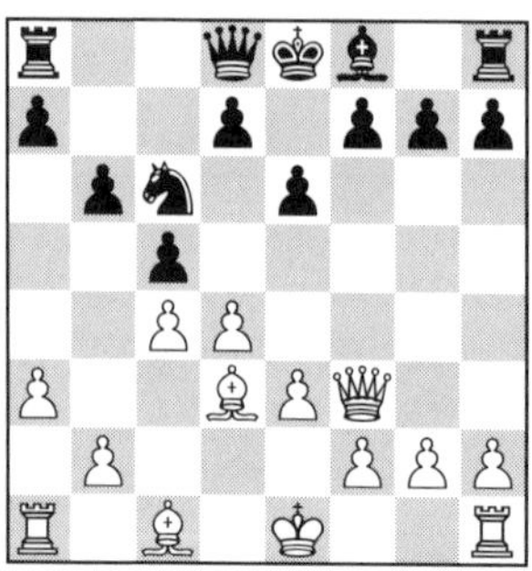

– 10.dxc5 ♘e5 11.♕e2 ♘xd3+ 12.♕xd3 ♗xc5 13.0-0 ♕c7 leads to equality.
– 10.♗e4 ♖c8 11.0-0 (11.dxc5 ♘e5!) 11...cxd4 12.exd4 ♕f6 13.♕xf6 gxf6 14.♗xc6 dxc6 is also equal.
– 10.♕g3 cxd4 11.exd4 ♕f6 (11...♘xd4 12.♗g5 ♕c8 13.0-0 is too risky) 12.♗e3 ♖c8 and Black has good play.

8.♗d3 ♗xd3 9.♕xd3 d6 10.0-0 0-0 11.e4 ♘d7

Black's position has no weaknesses, and although it is rather passive, it is very solid.

12.♗e3

If 12.b4 Black can respond in two ways:
– 12...c5 13.bxc5 bxc5 14.d5 ♖b8 (possible was 14...exd5!? 15.exd5 – 15.♕xd5 ♘b6 16.♕d3 ♕c8 17.♗b2 ♕e6 18.♖ac1 ♖ab8 19.♗a1 ♖fe8 20.♖fe1 ♗f6= – 15...♗f6 16.♖b1 ♘e5 17.♘xe5 ♗xe5 18.g3 ♖e8 with an equal game) 15.dxe6 fxe6 16.♗d2 and now, rather than spoil his pawn structure with 16...♘e5? as in the game Riazantsev-Asik, Dubai 2005, better is 16...♗f6 with the approximate continuation 17.♖ad1 ♘e5 18.♘xe5 ♗xe5 when the chances are even.
– 12...a5 13.♗b2 ♕c8! ♕d8-c8-b7 is a standard manoeuvre in this type of position. It is at b7 that the queen is most harmoniously placed. The following games demonstrate the soundness of Black's defences: 14.b5 ♕b7 15.♖fe1 ♖fe8 (15...♖ad8 16.h4 e5 17.♖ad1 exd4 18.♘xd4 ♗f6 19.g3 ♖fe8 20.♕c2 ♗xd4 21.♖xd4 ♖e7 22.♖d5 ♖de8 23.f3 ♕c8 24.♔g2 ♘e5 25.♗xe5 ½-½, Van Wely-Ivanchuk, Monaco 2002) 16.♖ad1 ♖ad8 17.♕c2 ♗f8 18.h3 g6 19.♖e2 ½-½, Vitiugov-Khairullin, St. Petersburg 2006.

12...♕c8 13.♖ad1 ♕b7 14.♖fe1 a5 15.d5 e5

Or 15...a4!? 16.e5 exd5 17.exd6 dxc4 18.♕xc4 cxd6 with even chances.

16.♕b3?!

16.b3 is stronger, not allowing the fixing of the pawn on b2: 16...♘c5 (16...a4 is unfavourable because of 17.b4±) 17.♕c2 h6 18.♘d2 ♕c8 with sufficient counterchances.

16...a4! 17.♕b5 ♘f6 18.♗g5 ♖a5 19.♕b4 h6 20.♗h4 ♖e8

Black has achieved an equal game. In the subsequent far from faultless play I managed to win.

□ **Tornike Sanikidze**
■ **Evgeny Romanov**
Aix-les-Bains 2011

1.d4 ♘f6 2.c4 e6 3.♘f3 b6 4.a3 ♗b7 5.♘c3 ♘e4 6.♘xe4 ♗xe4 7.♗f4

This 7th move also does not claim to be an attempt to refute Black's opening set-up. White simply develops his pieces and transfers the weight of the struggle to the middlegame.

7...♗e7 8.e3 a5!? 9.♗d3 ♗xd3 10.♕xd3 d6

This position, but via a different move order (8...d6 9.♗d3 ♗xd3 10.♕xd3 a5), was three times successfully reached by Portisch.

11.0-0

Portisch's opponents played more accurately – 11.b3, not allowing the fixing of the queenside by a5-a4, but after 11...♘d7 all the same they did not achieve any advantage:

– 12.0-0 0-0 13.h3 ♖e8 14.e4 e5! 15.♗e3 (15.dxe5?! dxe5 16.♗g3 – 16.♘xe5?? ♘xe5 17.♕xd8 ♗xd8–+ – 16...f6 17.♖fd1 ♘c5 18.♕e3 ♕c8 19.b4 axb4 20.axb4 ♘e6∓) 15...exd4 16.♗xd4 ♘e5 (16...♗f6=) 17.♕c3 ♗f6 18.♖ad1 ♘xf3+ 19.♕xf3 ♗xd4 20.♖xd4=, Nikolic-Portisch, Reykjavik 1991.

– 12.e4 0-0 13.0-0 ♖e8 14.♖fd1 ♕c8 15.e5 (this leads to an equal game; 15.♖e1 also does not give White any advantage after 15...♕b7 16.♖ad1 ♖ab8 17.d5 ♗f6 18.e5 with mass exchanges in P.Cramling-Portisch, London 1996) 15...dxe5 16.♘xe5 ♘xe5 17.♗xe5 ♗d6 18.♕g3 ♗xe5 19.dxe5 ♕b7=, Gelfand-Portisch, Moscow 1990.

11...a4!? 12.e4 0-0 13.♖ad1 ♘d7 14.♖fe1 ♖e8 15.h3 ♘f8

Play is even after 15...♕c8 16.e5 ♕b7.

16.♕c2 ♕d7 17.♖e3 ♘g6 18.♗h2 ♖ed8 19.♖c3 ♖ac8

Or 19...♖a5!? which changes nothing about the evaluation that the game is equal.

20.♖cd3 ♕e8 21.♗g3 h6 22.♖1d2 ♔h8 23.♖d1 ♔g8 24.♖1d2 ♔h8 25.♖d1

Draw.

□ **German Pankov**
■ **Nikolay Ogloblin**
Sochi 2007

1.d4 ♘f6 2.c4 e6 3.♘f3 b6 4.a3 ♗b7 5.♘c3 ♘e4 6.♘xe4 ♗xe4 7.♘d2 ♗g6

7...♗b7 is unthematic. A few years ago I witnessed the following crushing defeat: 8.e4 ♕f6 (in the event of 8...♘c6 9.♘f3 the drawback to the bishop's position on b7 becomes apparent – the e4 pawn is not under attack) 9.d5 ♗d6 10.♗d3 a5 11.♘f3 ♘a6?? (11...h6 12.0-0±) 12.e5! ♕e7 (12...♗xe5 13.♗g5+–) 13.exd6 ♕xd6 14.0-0 and White converted his extra piece, Zabotin-Chernyshov, Serpukhov 2007.

8.e4 ♘c6! 9.d5 ♘d4

10.♘f3

With this move White exchanges the active black knight, without any pretentions to gain an advantage.

But 10.♗d3 also does not promise White anything. The best that he can hope for in this variation is a complicated battle where three results are possible:

– 10...e5 11.0-0 (11.h4 h5 12.♘f3 ♘xf3+ 13.♕xf3 ♗e7 14.♕g3 0-0=) 11...♗d6 (11... c5=) 12.b3 c5 13.♘b1 0-0 14.♘c3 a6 Black has a perfectly good game. His position is at least equal. 15.g3 ♕e7 16.f3 f5 17.exf5 ♗xf5 18.♘e4 h6 19.g4 ♗g6∓, Krasenkow-Chernyshov, Warsaw 2002.

– 10...♗d6!? is no worse than Chernyshov's continuation, for example: 11.0-0 (11.h4 h5 12.♘f3 ♘xf3+ 13.♕xf3 ♗e5) 11...0-0 12.♘b3 ♘xb3 13.♕xb3 ♖e8 with counterplay.

– Best is 10...♕g5 11.0-0 ♗h5 12.♘f3 ♘xf3+ 13.♕xf3 ♕xc1 14.♖axc1 (14.♕xh5 ♕xb2 15.e5 ♗c5∓) 14...♗xf3 15.gxf3 ♗d6∓.

10...♘xf3+ 11.♕xf3 ♗c5

The less standard 11...♗d6!? is also possible, with good play for Black against the enemy centre. For example 12.♗d3 and now:

– 12...♗e5 13.0-0 ♕f6 14.♕xf6 ♗xf6=.

– 12...0-0 13.0-0 f5 (13...♕h4!? 14.g3 ♗h5 15.♕e3 ♕f6 16.♖e1 ♗e5 17.♖b1 exd5 18.cxd5 ♖ae8) 14.exf5 ♗xf5 15.dxe6 ♗xd3 16.♕xd3 dxe6 17.♕e2 ♕f6 18.♗e3 ♗e5=.

– 12...exd5 13.cxd5 0-0 14.0-0 c6 15.dxc6 dxc6∓.

12.♗d3 0-0 13.♗e3 exd5

Also good is 13...♗d6 14.0-0 (14.h4 f5) 14...f5 15.exf5 ♗xf5 16.♗xf5 ♖xf5 17.♕g4 ♕f6, and Black's position is not worse.

14.cxd5 ♗xe3 15.♕xe3 f5 16.0-0

16...f4?! An attempt to complicate the play.

After 16...fxe4 17.♗xe4 ♕f6 a draw can be agreed upon.

17.♕h3 17.♕d4! c5 18.dxc6 dxc6 19.♕c3±. **17...♕e7 18.♖ac1 ♕d6 19.e5**

This simplifies the position. Black was wrongly hoping for 19.♖fd1! ♖ae8 20.f3 ♖e5 with double-edged play, although after 21.♕h4! ♖h5 22.♕f2 ♗e8 23.♗f1 ♕h6 24.h3± things would not have been easy for him.

19...♕xe5 20.♗xg6 hxg6 21.♕xd7 ♖f7 Draw.

□ **Claude Landenbergue**
■ **Konstantin Chernyshov**
Cappelle la Grande 2006

1.d4 ♘f6 2.c4 e6 3.♘f3 b6 4.a3 ♗b7 5.♘c3 ♘e4 6.♘xe4 ♗xe4 7.♘d2 ♗g6 8.g3!

The only way of fighting for an appreciable advantage. The white bishop eyes the long diagonal, which has only just been abandoned by his opponent. It appears that in the opening battle the scales are beginning to tip in favour of White, but...

8...♘c6! 9.e3 e5! 10.d5 ♘a5

11.b4

If 11.♗g2, then 11...♗d6 12.0-0 0-0. Black should not prematurely play 12...♗d3?! 13.♖e1, when his bishop comes under attack, for example 13...f5 (13...♘xc4? 14.♕b3+–) 14.b4 ♘xc4 15.♕b3 ♘xd2 16.♕xd3 ♘e4 17.f3 ♘f6 18.♕xf5±.

● No advantage is given by 13.b4 ♘b7 14.♗b2 a5! 15.♘e4 (15.f4 exf4 16.exf4 f6 17.f5 ♗f7 18.♗c3 ♖e8 19.♖e1 ♖xe1+ 20.♕xe1 ♕f8 21.♘e4 ♖e8 with sufficient play) 15...axb4 16.axb4 ♖xa1 17.♕xa1 ♗xb4 18.♗xe5 ♖e8 19.♕b2 ♗f8 20.♘d2 ♘c5, when Black has a strong point at c5 and stands at least equal.

● 13.♕e2 ♘b7, and now:

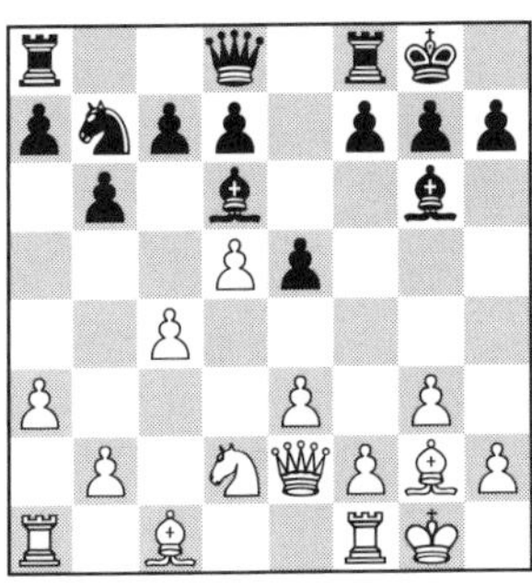

– 14.h4 h6 (14...a5 is also possible, since 15.h5 is not dangerous in view of 15...♗c2 16.♘b1!? ♗b3!? 17.e4 a4 18.♘d2 ♘a5 with play against the c4 pawn; White has nothing better than 19.♘xb3 ♘xb3 20.♖b1 ♗c5∓) 15.h5 ♗h7 with complicated play.

– The pawn sacrifice 14.b4 a5 15.c5 bxc5 16.b5 is interesting, but insufficient on account of 16...a4! 17.♘c4 ♘a5∓.

– 14.♘e4 ♗xe4! 15.♗xe4 f5 16.♗g2 e4 17.b4 a5 18.♗b2 ♕e7∓.

If 11.b3, avoiding creating any targets for attack on the queenside, Black employs the standard piece arrangement in this variation: 11...♗d6 12.♗b2 ♘b7 13.♗e2 0-0 14.0-0 ♕e7.

11...♘b7 12.♗b2 ♗d6! 13.♗g2 a5 14.♗c3 14.♕b3 ♕e7 15.0-0 0-0 16.♗c3 ♗d3 17.♖fc1 e4 strengthening the outpost.

14...♕e7

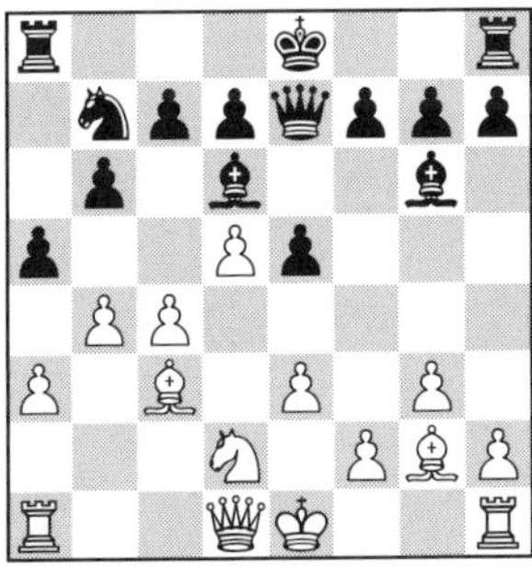

It was this position that I had aimed for in my preparation. The positioning of the black pieces seems unprepossessing, but, strangely enough, they are all making life uncomfortable for White's attractive classical set-up. The bishop on g6 is ready at any moment to establish itself at d3. The bishop on d6 is preventing the activation of the g2 bishop and supporting the e5 pawn, and together with the queen and the rook on a8 it creates pressure on the white a3 and b4 pawns, trying to win the c5-point for the black knight.

15.0-0 0-0 16.♕b3 ♗d3 17.♖fe1 e4
The unusual placing of the black pieces does not prevent them from successfully coordinating.

18.♕b2 f5 19.♗f1 ♗xf1 20.♖xf1 c6 21.dxc6 dxc6 22.♖fd1 c5 23.bxa5 ♘xa5 24.♗xa5 bxa5 25.♖ab1 a4
Black's game is easier. White has a temporarily inactive knight and a fixed pawn weakness on a3. In the subsequent far from faultless play the main expert on the variation went on to win.

□ **Evgeny Vorobiov**
■ **Igor Lysyj**
Moscow Aeroflot Open 2011

1.d4 ♘f6 2.c4 e6 3.♘f3 b6 4.a3 ♗b7 5.♘c3 ♘e4 6.♘xe4 ♗xe4 7.♘d2 ♗g6 8.g3 ♘c6 9.e3 e5 10.d5 ♘a5 11.h4

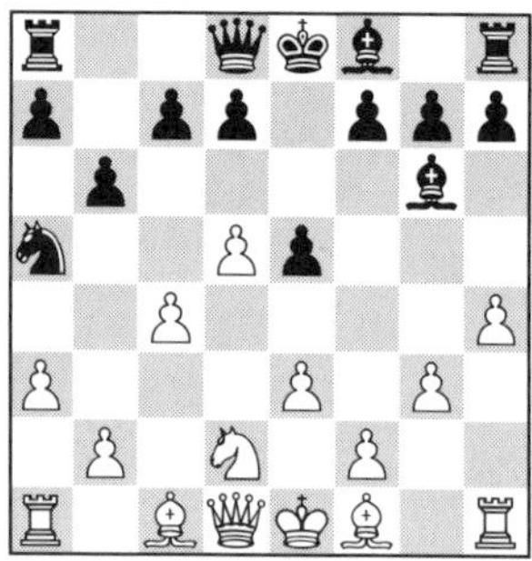

An attempt to exploit the position of the bishop on g6.

11...h6 12.e4
After the impetuous 12.h5 there follows 12...♗h7 13.b4 ♘b7 14.♗b2 ♗d6 15.♗h3 a5 with pressure on the b4 pawn, traditional for this set-up. The best chance for White would appear to be the sacrifice 16.c5 bxc5 17.b5.

After 12.♗h3 in the game Borovikov-Chernyshov, Pardubice 2004, there followed 12...♘b7! 13.0-0 a5 14.b3 ♘c5!? (the alternative is 14...♗d6 with the approximate continuation 15.♗b2 0-0 16.f4 exf4 17.exf4 f6=) 15.e4 ♗d6 16.♗f5 ♕f6∓.

12...♗d6
12...♗c5!? is stronger: 13.♗d3 ♘b7 14.b4 ♗d4 15.♖b1 0-0 (15...a5!? 16.0-0 axb4 17.axb4 0-0) 16.h5 ♗h7 17.♘f3 c5 18.dxc6 dxc6 19.0-0 c5 with good play.

13.♗d3
If 13.♗h3, then 13...h5!? 14.0-0 ♘b7 15.♗f5 ♕f6 16.♕c2 ♗xf5 17.exf5 0-0 18.♘b3 g6 is equal.

13...♘b7 14.♗c2 a5 15.b3
After 15.h5!? ♗h7 16.♕g4 Black can go into an equal endgame by 16...♕g5 17.♕xg5 hxg5.

15...♕e7 16.♗b2 h5!? 17.♕e2 ♘c5?!
In this non-standard position Black is the first to go wrong. After 17...c6!? 18.0-0 0-0 19.f4 f6∓ his position is certainly not worse.

18.f3?!
Returning the favour! After 18.0-0 0-0 19.b4! (if 19.f4 there can follow 19...f6 – it looks very risky to play 19...exf4 20.gxf4 ♕xh4 21.f5 ♗h7 22.e5 ♗e7 23.♖f2 – 20.f5 ♗f7 21.♔f2 ♘b7) 19...axb4 20.axb4 ♘b7 21.c5 bxc5 22.b5 ♖xa1 23.♖xa1 ♖b8 24.♘c4 the position is unclear. Although White is material down, he has excellently-developed 'working' pieces, whereas Black has problems in finding a sensible plan and

making progress in improving the placing of his pieces.

18...c6

Or 18...0-0!? 19.g4 ♔h8 20.♔f2 c6 21.♖ag1 f6.

19.♘f1

19.♔f2 0-0! 20.g4 f6 21.♖ag1 ♘b7∓.

19...♘b7 20.♘e3 ♔d8?!

Black tries to be excessively original. He should have played 20...♗c5 21.a4 (or 21.dxc6 dxc6 22.♘f5 ♗xf5 23.exf5 0-0-0 24.♔f1 ♗d4) 21...0-0-0 22.0-0-0 f6 with a solid position, but not 20...0-0?! 21.g4 ♗c5 22.0-0-0!? ♗xa3 23.gxh5 ♗xb2+ 24.♔xb2 ♗xh5 25.♖hg1, when the open g-file causes him problems.

21.♔f2 ♔c7 22.♔g2 ♗h7

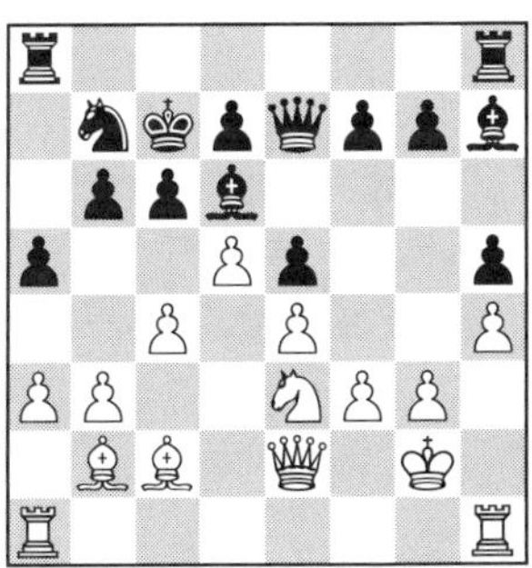

23.dxc6?

Prematurely releasing the tension. 23.♘f5 promised more benefits. After 23...♗xf5 24.exf5 f6 25.♖he1 ♖he8 26.♕d2 White dominates the entire board.

23...dxc6 24.♘f5 ♗xf5 25.exf5 f6 26.♖hd1 26.♖he1 ♖he8=.

26...♖ad8 27.f4?

A repetition was possible after 27.♔h3 ♗c5 28.♖e1 ♕d7 29.♖ed1 ♕e7.

27...♖he8

After 27...exf4 28.♕xe7+ ♗xe7 29.gxf4 ♗c5 30.♔f3 Black cannot exploit the opponent's pawn weaknesses, whereas White begins to fasten on to the g7 and h5 pawns. Chances are even.

28.fxe5 ♗xe5 29.♗xe5+

It was possibly better to keep the queens on. After the approximate 29.♖xd8!? ♕xd8 30.♖e1 ♘d6 31.♗xe5 ♖xe5 32.♕f2 ♘f7 33.♗d1 ♖xe1 34.♕xe1 ♘e5 35.♗xh5 ♕d4 Black dominates, but White retains drawing chances.

29...♕xe5 30.♕xe5+ ♖xe5 31.♖xd8 ♔xd8 32.♔f2 ♘d6 33.♖e1?

The only saving chance was 33.♖d1! ♔d7!? 34.♖d4 b5 35.♖f4 bxc4 36.bxc4 c5 37.♗a4+ ♔c7 38.♗c2 ♖e8 39.g4 ♘f7 40.gxh5 ♘e5∓.

33...♖xe1 34.♔xe1 a4! 35.bxa4 ♘xc4 36.♗d1 ♘e3 37.♗xh5 ♘xf5 38.♗g6 ♘d6

Black has a decisive advantage, which he easily converts into a win.

39.♔d2 ♔e7 40.♔c3 ♔e6 41.♔b3 ♔d5 42.g4 ♔d4 43.♗c2 ♘c4 44.g5 fxg5 45.hxg5 c5 46.g6 ♘d2+ 47.♔b2 c4 48.♗f5 ♘b3 49.♗d7 ♔d3 50.♗h3 ♔d2

White resigned.

Chapter 8

Jeroen Bosch

An Unusual Taimanov

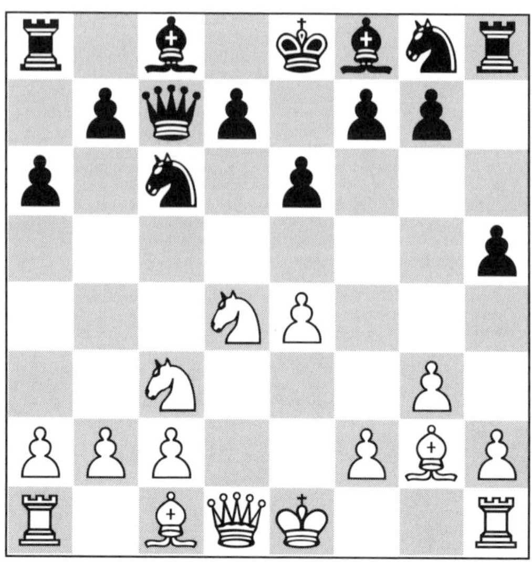

7...h5!?

□ **Alexander Berelowitsch**
■ **Francisco Vallejo**
Germany Bundesliga 2010/11

1.e4 c5 2.♘f3 ♘c6 3.d4 cxd4 4.♘xd4 e6 5.♘c3 ♕c7

The Taimanov Variation of the Sicilian, which these days is often met by 6.♗e3, followed by 7.♕d2 and queenside castling. One of White's main (and most solid) options has always been the kingside fianchetto, though.

6.g3

Many top players favour 6.g3, but Michael Adams deserves special mention as the main supporter of this line.

6...a6 7.♗g2 h5!?

Attaboy! It is unusual in such a theory-heavy opening as the Sicilian to see a top player like Vallejo leave the well-trodden paths at such an early stage in the game. The audacious 7...h5 was first played by Bent Larsen in a period when he experimented with many opening ideas. The launch of the h-pawn may remind you of coffee-house chess (or ICC blitz), but it really isn't just about attacking bluntly on the kingside. Positionally speaking, the move 7...h5 is quite sound: 1. To stop the h-pawn in its tracks White would have to play 8.h4 here, which weakens the g4-square (as f4 is a normal part of White's plan).

2. Playing 8.h3, to meet 8...h4 with 9.g4, on the other hand, weakens the dark squares.
3. Allowing Black to play ...h4 gives him the opportunity to open the h-file whenever he wants to, and also weakens the g4-square somewhat (in these fianchetto lines White often wants to play h3 to protect g4, but this isn't possible when Black and White have exchanged their h-pawns on g3).
The main line is 7...♘f6 (your database will easily list some 3500 games!), but we do well to remember that 7...d6 8.0-0 ♗d7 9.♖e1 ♗e7 10.♘xc6 ♗xc6 11.♕g4 h5!? 12.♕e2 h4 is another not unpopular line that scores very decently for Black: 13.a4 hxg3 14.hxg3 ♘f6 is then the normal continuation.

8.h3

A logical response to the threat of ...h5-h4.

● Ignoring the advance of the h-pawn is possible: 8.0-0, castling into the storm, or obtaining a useful edge in development?
8...h4 9.♖e1 hxg3 10.hxg3 ♗c5 (Black fights for the initiative; not 10...♘f6 11.♘d5! – 11.♘xc6 bxc6 12.e5 ♘d5 is OK for Black – 11...exd5 12.♘xc6 bxc6 13.exd5+ ♔d8 14.dxc6, and White has great compensation for the piece). Now:
– 11.♗e3 ♘e5 12.♗f4?! (12.♘f5! ♗xe3 – too dangerous is 12...exf5? 13.♘d5 ♕d6 14.♗xc5 ♕xc5 15.exf5 – 13.♘xe3 is slightly better for White, while 13.♘d6+ ♔f8 14.♖xe3 ♘f6 is less clear) 12...d6 13.♘b3 ♗a7 14.♕e2 ♘f6 15.♖ad1 b5 is an ideal Sicilian for Black. His positional advantages are obvious, while his king is relatively safe in the centre: 16.♘d4 ♗d7 17.♘f3 ♘fg4! 18.♖f1 b4 19.♘xe5 ♘xe5 20.♘b1 ♗b5, and Black won an exchange and soon afterwards the game in S.Collins-A. Kogan, Port Erin 2002.
– 11.♘xc6 is a very decent alternative: 11...bxc6 (11...dxc6? 12.e5±) 12.e5! ♘e7 (12...f5!?) 13.♗g5 (13.♘e4!) 13...♔f8 14.♘a4 ♗a7 15.♗e3 (15.c4!?) 15...♗xe3 16.♖xe3 ♘f5 17.♖b3 ♖b8 18.♘c5?! ♖b5! 19.♖xb5? cxb5 20.b4 ♕xe5, and although the win is still not that easy, Black clearly had the upper hand in Ocantos-R.Swinkels, Maastricht 2010.
– Black should meet 11.♘b3 with 11... ♗e7 (11...♗a7 12.♗f4), when he should be happy to have achieved the withdrawal of the knight from the centre, for example 12.a4 d6 13.a5 ♘f6, with about equal chances.
– 11.♗f4!? is a very concrete attempt. Black must reply with 11...e5, when it all depends on 12.♘d5 ♕b8 and now 13.♘xc6 (13.♘b3 exf4 14.♘xc5 fxg3 with sharp play. Black has achieved a lot on the kingside, but White has an advantage in development) 13...dxc6 (if 13...dxc6 is too mundane for you, then you may well wish to investigate the sharp 13...♗xf2+ 14.♔xf2 bxc6) 14.♗e3 ♗xe3 15.♘xe3 ♗e6 is equal.

● White can prevent ...h4 by withdrawing his knight to f3, but this is harmless: 8.♘f3 ♗e7 9.♗f4 d6 10.♕d2 ♘e5 11.♘e2 ♗d7 12.♕c3!? ♘c6!? 13.e5

13...d5! (13...dxe5 14.♗xe5 ♕b6 15.♗xg7 ♗b4 16.♗xh8 is unclear) 14.a3 ♖c8 15.h4 ♘h6 16.0-0 ♘g4, and Black was better in the stem game Terkelsen-Larsen, Aarhus 1959.

● Moving the knight to b3 has also occurred in practice. This immediately gives Black an easy game. 8.♘b3 h4 9.0-0 (9.♗f4 ♘e5) 9... hxg3 10.hxg3 ♘f6 11.♕e2 ♘e5 12.♗g5

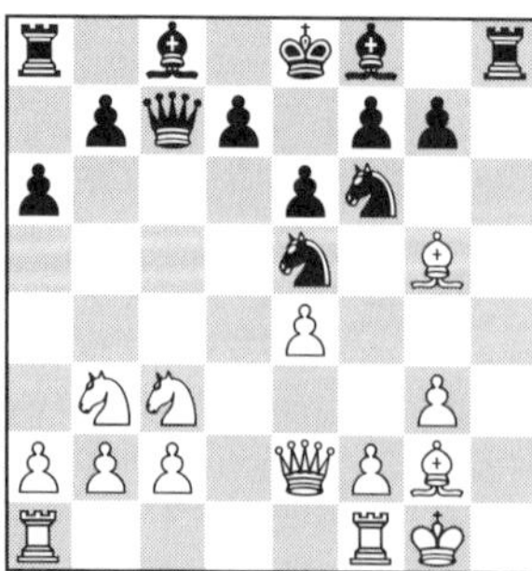

and now Black has many good options to obtain the better game 12...♗b4 (12...♘fg4; 12...d6; 12...b5) 13.♘d1 ♕c4 14.♕xc4 ♘xc4, and Black had a very comfortable queenless middlegame in Misailovic-Kontic, Cetinje 1992.

● 8.h4 – stopping the cheeky rascal in its tracks. Let's follow the example of Spanish GM Arthur Kogan: 8...♗c5 9.♘b3 ♗a7 10.♗f4. It's normal to develop the bishop to f4 (moving a pawn to f4 would accentuate the weakness of square g4). 10...♘e5 11.♕e2 d6 12.0-0-0 ♘e7 (12...♘f6!?) 13.♗e3 b5 14.♗xa7 ♖xa7 15.♕d2?! (15.f4) 15...♘c4 16.♕g5 (a shot in the dark; the black king doesn't mind moving to f8 anyway) 16...b4 17.♘e2 ♔f8 18.♔b1 e5! 19.♕c1 a5!

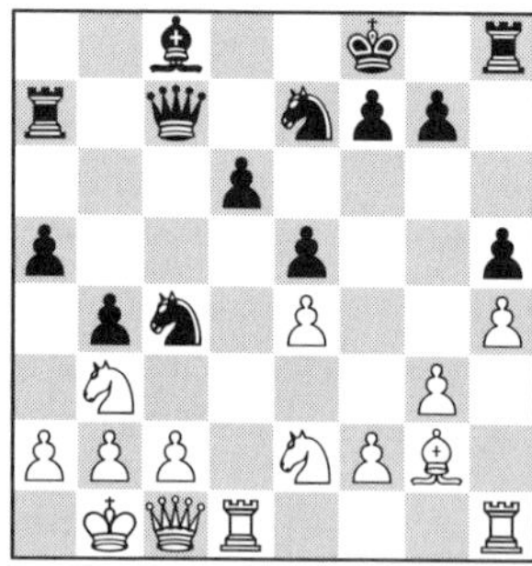

and Black's chances are to be preferred, Remiro Juste-Kogan, Spain 2004.

● 8.♗e3 ♘f6 (8...h4 is a bit rash when White hasn't castled kingside and has spent no time on preventing ...h4. White could, for instance, play 9.♘xc6 bxc6 10.♕d4, intending to castle queenside) 9.h3. White reacts belatedly to the threat of ...h4. With his next move Black exploits the early development of the bishop to e3: 9...♘e5! 10.♕e2 ♗b4 11.♗d2 ♘c4 12.0-0-0 ♘xd2 13.♕xd2 d6. White has no compensation for having lost the important dark-squared bishop. Black has a slight edge. 14.♘de2 ♗d7 15.♕g5 (just like in our previous example, this yields nothing) 15...♔f8! 16.♖d2 ♖c8 17.♖hd1 ♗c5 18.♔b1 ♖h6 19.♖d3 b5 20.a3 a5! favoured Black in Heidenfeld-Miladinovic, Leon Ech-tt 2001.

● A concession is 8.♘xc6, when after 8...dxc6 (8...bxc6) 9.♗e3 ♘f6 10.h3 e5 Black has obtained an equal game: 11.♘a4 ♘d7 12.♕d2 b5 13.♘c3 ♗e7 14.♖d1?! ♘b6 15.♕e2 (15.b3) 15...♗e6 (15...h4). This enables White to exchange some pieces: 16.♗xb6! ♕xb6 17.♘d5! ♕a7 18.♘xe7 ♕xe7 19.b3?! h4!

20.g4?! ♕b4+ 21.♕d2 ♕xd2+ 22.♖xd2 ♔e7, and due to the weak dark squares on the kingside White is worse, Draganova-Djingarova, Veliko Tarnovo ch-BUL 2005. Here we see illustrated one of the main positional ideas behind 7...h5.

● 8.f4, and now:

– I would recommend 8...b5!?, when 9.♘xc6 (9.e5 ♗b7) 9...♕xc6 10.♕e2 ♗b7 is fine for Black.

– 8...h4?! 9.♗e3 (9.g4) 9...hxg3 10.hxg3 ♖xh1+ 11.♗xh1, with a slight advantage for White.

– 8...d6?! 9.♗e3 ♗d7 10.♘xc6 ♗xc6 11.♕e2 ♗e7 12.♗d4 e5 13.♗e3 ♗f6? 14.0-0-0! and Black's plan has failed completely. Genzling-Vila Gazquez, Sibenik jr 2007.

8...h4

This is certainly consistent, but not the only move to consider.

– 8...♗c5?! 9.♘xc6 dxc6 10.♕e2 e5 11.♗e3, as played in Garcia Brion-Vila Gazquez, La Pineda de Vila 2009, is slightly better for White. Normally, in such positions taking on c6 promises little, but here the inclusion of ...h5 and h3 favours White. White will castle queenside and Black will find it difficult to equalize.

– 8...♘f6 9.0-0 ♗c5

is a position that has occurred in several games (sometimes via the move order 7...♘f6 8.0-0 h5!?). This is playable. One fairly recent example between two strong grandmasters is Sutovsky-Safarli, Baku 2010: 10.♗e3 (10.♘b3 ♗a7 11.♗f4 ♘e5 12.♕e2 d6 13.♖ad1 b5 14.♘c1? b4 was a clear edge in Makka-Lanchava, Varna Ech 2002; 10.♘xc6 dxc6 11.e5!? ♕xe5 12.♗f4 is a decent pawn sacrifice that has occurred in practice) 10...d6 11.♕d2 ♘e5 (after 11...♘xd4 12.♗xd4 ♗xd4 13.♕xd4 e5 14.♕d2 h4 the chances are equal) 12.b3 h4!

13.f4 (13.g4? ♘fxg4 14.hxg4 h3 15.♗h1 h2+ 16.♔g2 ♘xg4 with long-term positional compensation for the piece) 13...♘g6 14.g4 e5! 15.fxe5 dxe5 16.♘f5 (16.♘de2) 16...♗xf5 17.exf5 ♘f4 18.♖ae1 ♖d8 19.♕f2 ♘xg2 20.♗xc5 ♘xe1 21.♖xe1, and the players, somewhat surprisingly, agreed on a draw. Objectively, White seems to be struggling to prove that he has enough for the exchange.

9.g4

9...♘ge7

Taimanov's favourite knight manoeuvre in his very own Sicilian. Vallejo aims to control as many dark squares as possible, which is why the knight should be developed to e7 (and not to f6) and from there to g6 or c6. Black can also opt for the immediate knight swap, followed by ...♘e7: 9...♘xd4 10.♕xd4 ♘e7 11.♗e3 b5 12.0-0 (12.0-0-0!?) 12...♘c6 13.♕d1 (13.♕d2) 13...♗b7 14.♘e2 (14.f4 ♘a5∓) 14...♘e5 15.b3 ♖c8 16.c3 ♗c5, and Black was quite happy with the outcome of the opening, Radovanovic-Bakic, Kladovo ch-YUG 1992.

10.♘de2

Berelowitsch avoids the knight swap but Black doesn't really mind. In fact, Black's knight is fairly useful on g6, while there is no real future for the 'superfluous' knight on e2 (as square g3 is controlled by Black's h-pawn).

In case of 10.♗e3, Black should continue 10...♘e5 (rather than 10...♘xd4 11.♕xd4 ♘c6 12.♕b6, with a slight edge for White), when he is doing OK.

After 10.0-0 the exchange of knights is best though: 10...♘xd4 11.♕xd4 ♘c6 12.♕e3 (12.♕d1 ♗c5) 12...♘e5.

10...♘g6 11.0-0

Instead, 11.f4 weakens the diagonal g1-a7. After 11...♗c5 12.e5 d5 13.exd6 Black should not exchange queens (13...♕xd6?! 14.♕xd6! ♗xd6 15.♘e4, with a slight advantage for White, Marinkovic-Kontic, Podgorica 1993, or 15.♗e3 ♗c7 16.0-0-0, with a slight advantage for White), but play 13...♗xd6.

11...b5

12.a3

Black may reject the sacrificial 12.a4 b4 13.♘d5!? with 13...♕a5, but he can also accept the piece with 13...exd5 14.exd5 ♘d8 (14...♗d6 15.dxc6 dxc6 16.♘d4 0-0), and now:

– 15.♖e1 ♗d6;

– 15.♘f4!? ♘xf4 16.♖e1+ ♘de6 17.♗xf4 (17.dxe6 ♘xh3+!) 17...♕xf4 18.dxe6 fxe6 19.♗xa8 ♗d6, with sufficient compensation for the exchange;

– 15.d6 ♕b8 16.♗xa8 ♕xa8 17.♖e1 ♘e6 favours Black.

12...♗c5 13.♔h1 ♗b7

Black has a very agreeable Taimanov Sicilian. Note that the h4 pawn is more a strength than a weakness. Vallejo makes all his useful moves first, before finally castling kingside.

14.f4 ♖d8!? 15.♕e1 ♗a7

16.♗d2

White understandably wants to finish his development, but this passive move gives Black plenty of leeway.

Best is perhaps 16.f5 ♗b8 (16...♘ge5 17.♗f4) 17.♘f4 ♘ge5.

After 16.e5 Black can advantageously sacrifice a piece with 16...♘cxe5!? (16... ♘d4 17.♘xd4 ♗xg2+ 18.♔xg2 ♗xd4 is also fine) 17.fxe5 ♗xg2+ 18.♔xg2 ♕c6+ 19.♔h2 ♘xe5, when he will regain his material with interest: 20.♗f4 (20.♘g1 ♗xg1+

21.♔xg1 ♘f3+ 22.♖xf3 ♕xf3 23.♕e3 ♕xe3+ 24.♗xe3) 20...♘f3+ 21.♖xf3 ♕xf3.

16...♘ce7 17.♘c1?

Improving the position of the poorly placed knight, but it was necessary to anticipate ...d5.

– 17.♖d1 is also met by 17...d5.

– 17.f5!? ♗b8 18.♘f4 ♘e5, and now Black has good dark-square control after 19.♗e3 g5! 20.fxg6 ♘7xg6 21.♘xg6 ♘xg6 22.♗g1 but White is still fully in the game too.

17...d5! 18.♘d3

18.exd5 ♘xd5 19.♘d3 0-0 20.♘xd5 ♗xd5 21.♗xd5 ♖xd5 is very pleasant for Black, as is 18.e5 0-0.

18...dxe4 18...0-0!?. **19.♗xe4 ♖d4!?**

Enterprising play by Vallejo. 19...0-0 is the simple way. **20.♗f3?!** 20.♗xb7 ♕xb7+ 21.♔h2. **20...0-0 21.♕e2 ♘d5 22.♘xd5 ♗xd5 23.♗xd5?!**

23.♗e3 looks like the best way to keep Black's advantage within drawing limits.

23...exd5!

Well-played! The isolated pawn provides Black with a useful stronghold on e4.

24.♗c3 ♖e4 25.♕g2 ♖e3 26.♖ae1?

26.♖f3 was the only move, but White is in deep trouble after 26...♖xf3 27.♕xf3 ♖e8 when 28.♕xd5 ♖e3! is hard to meet, and most other moves will lose a pawn somewhere.

26...♖g3

Well, that h-pawn certainly came in useful!

27.♕xd5 White can resign after 27.♕h2 d4. **27...♖xh3+ 28.♔g2 ♖g3+ 29.♔h2 ♖xg4 30.♖e4 ♖g3**

Even stronger was 30...♕c8!, with the threat of 31...♖g2+.

31.♖fe1 ♗b8

The easiest win was 31...♕c8 32.f5 ♖g5!, but Vallejo finishes in style:

32.♖e8

32...♖xd3! 33.♖xf8+ ♘xf8 34.♕xd3

Or 34.cxd3 ♕xf4+ 35.♔g1 h3–+.

34...♕xf4+ 35.♔g2 ♕h2+ 36.♔f1

36.♔f3 h3–+.

36...♗g3! 37.♕d4 ♕h1+ 38.♔e2 ♕g2+ 39.♔d3 ♗xe1 40.♗xe1 h3

White resigned.

CHAPTER 9

Maurits Wind

The Mayet Defence

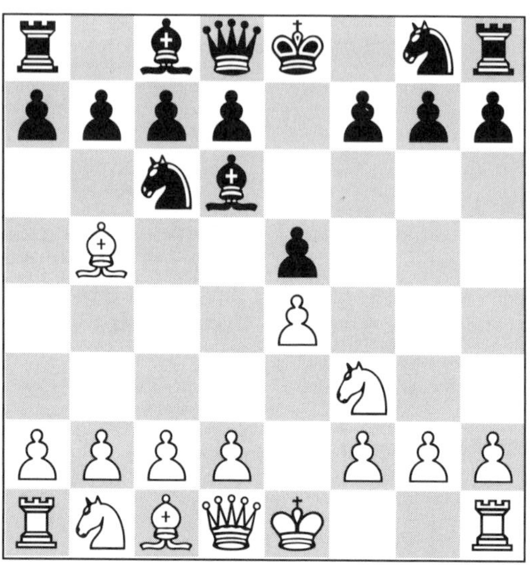

Spanish with 3...♗d6

Carl Mayet (1810-1868) was a German chess master who lived in Berlin. Mayet was a member (and in 1836 the president) of the prestigious Berliner Schachgesellschaft. He was one of the seven chess masters, who were collectively known as the *Berliner Siebengestirn* or the *Plejades*. The names of these seven players are Von Bilguer, Von der Lasa, Hanstein, Horwitz, Bledow, Mayet and Schorn. These seven players frequently came together to discuss opening theory, to play free games and to test their ideas in corr. chess with other German chess clubs.

One important chess opening that was being examined was the Spanish Opening. After 1.e4 e5 2.♘f3 ♘c6 the move 3.♗c4 had long been considered strongest. However, it became more and more apparent that Black can neutralize White's initial onslought and obtain equality. In particular the work by theoretician Paul Bilguer on 3...♘f6 (the Prussian game or Two Knights Defence) was a breakthrough. Attention then began to shift towards 3.♗b5, the move proposed by Lopez in 1561. The members of the Berliner played a leading role in this exploration. Without pre-existing theory, a wide range of defences was examined. For example set-ups with ♕f6 & h6, ♘ge7, ♗c5, ♗d6. In later years these early attempts were superseded by stronger ideas such as 3...♘f6, nowadays called the Berlin defence, and 3...a6, Morphy's continuation.

It was Carl Mayet who endorsed the defence 3...♗d6 in the Spanish. The idea did not gain much support but was occasionally tried in games. Then Paul Rudolf von Bilguer and Tassilo von der Lasa began their monumental work on the first encyclopedia of chess openings: the *Bilguer*. The first edition [reference 1] appeared in 1843. The section on the defence 3...♗d6 in the Spanish was written by Carl Mayet. Nine lines of analysis were presented, most resulting in a ± verdict. (Note: the modern ⩲ and ⩱ assessments were not in use then!) Nevertheless, the author comments: 'Gegen diesen Zug, so schlecht derselbe der Theorie nach zu sein scheint, ist es dennoch für Weiss sehr schwierig zu spielen.' Later editions of the Bilguer present essentially the same analysis, only in a condensed form. This is an indication that the analysis of 3...♗d6 was old, already a closed topic, when it was included in the Bilguer of 1843.

I believe this is sufficient ground to name the defence 3...♗d6 in the Spanish opening after Carl Mayet. J.Ganzo, in a booklet on the Spanish opening [2], mentions 3...♗d6 and names it the Bilguer Defence. In my opinion it is appropriate to name an opening system after its inventor, instead of to the first book in which it is treated.

Current theory rejects the defence 1.e4 e5 2.♘f3 ♘c6 3.♗b5 ♗d6 as poor. In fact many openings books ignore the move 3...♗d6 altogether! ECO [4] adorns the move with a question mark and cites a short variation from the Bilguer. Khalifman [5] is equally dismissive. But is this poor reputation justified?

Recently I performed the following experiment with the strong chess programme Rybka 3. I checked several of the offbeat third move alternatives that Black has in the Spanish Opening. And while Rybka dismissed most of them easily, it gave a thumbs to 3...♗d6. Quite a surprising outcome! This result triggered my interest in both the theoretical aspects and the history of 3...♗d6, with the present article as a result.

In tournament and match play the ...♗d6 defence was occasionally played. If 19th century masters chose it, they tended to prefer the version 3...♘f6 and 4...♗d6. In modern chess praxis the defence 3...♗d6 only occurs in lower level competition. However, a few examples can be found in correspondence chess. The Polish IM Leszek Ostrowski (Elo 2330) has played in at least two games, and so has S. Daenen in the French correspondence championship 2008/2009.

While grandmasters shy away from 3...♗d6, they are certainly willing to play the bishop move when they feel the conditions are right. Malaniuk has played 1.e4 e5 2.♘f3 ♘c6 3.♗b5 a6 4.♗a4 ♘f6 5.0-0 b5 6.♗b3 ♗b7 7.d3 ♗d6!?

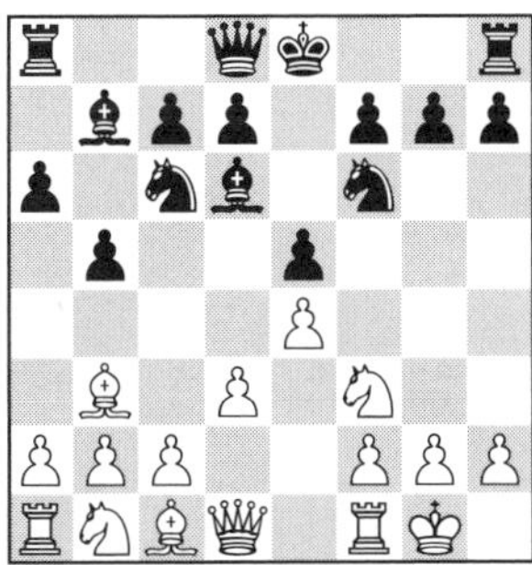

on three occasions, scoring 2½ out of 3. This is now considered a respectable line in the Arkhangelsk Variation.

Tiviakov-Carlsen, Wijk aan Zee 2010 saw 5...♗d6 in the Worrall Variation: 1.e4 e5 2.♘f3 ♘c6 3.♗b5 a6 4.♗a4 ♘f6 5.♕e2 ♗d6 and the game ended in a draw after 27 moves.

Finally there is the analogy with a currently fashionable line in the Spanish Four Knights Opening: 1.e4 e5 2.♘f3 ♘c6 3.♘c3 ♘f6 4.♗b5 ♗d6!?.

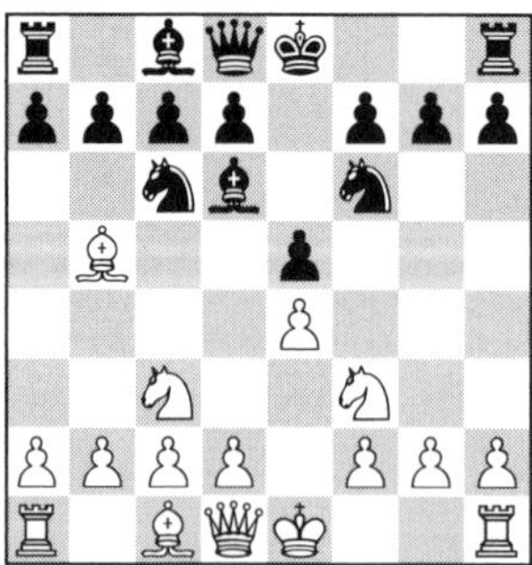

This was the subject of an interesting article by Jeroen Bosch in SOS-1 [3]. Black's plan in this system is to play ...0-0, ...♖e8, ...♗f8 and then ...d5.

It should be noted that in the last three systems White settles for a pawn centre with a pawn on d3. Yet, after 3...♗d6 White can go for a classical centre with c3 and d4. This is considerably more testing for the second player. We shall now examine how the 3...♗d6 defence holds up.

1.e4 e5 2.♘f3 ♘c6 3.♗b5 ♗d6

Back's plan is straightforward. He intends to play ...♘f6, ...0-0, ...♖e8, ...h6 on the kingside and centre, in combination with the standard moves ...a6, ...b5, ...♗b7 on the queenside. Once this set-up is complete, Black will make a crucial decision on how best to reposition the bishop on d6.

Variation A – 4.c3
Variation B – 4.0-0

Other continuations are less critical:

● 4.♘c3 ♘f6 transposes to the 4...♗d6 variation of the Spanish Four Knights. Play may continue: 5.d3 a6 6.♗a4 h6 7.h3 b5 8.♗b3 ♗b7 9.a3 ♗c5 10.0-0 0-0 11.♘d5 ♘d4 12.♘xd4 ♗xd4 13.c3 ♗a7 14.♘xf6+ ♕xf6=, Jonkman-Sokolov, Leeuwarden ch-NED 2002. This game is annotated in SOS-1.

● 4.d3 a6 5.♗a4 b5 6.♗b3 ♘f6 7.c3 ♗b7 8.0-0 0-0 9.♘bd2 h6 10.♖e1 ♖e8 11.♘f1 ♗f8 12.♘g3 ♘a5 13.♗c2 c5=, Dolmatov-Saveliev, Krasnoyarsk 2003.

● 4.d4 ♘xd4 (more accurate than 4...exd4 5.0-0) 5.♘xd4 exd4 and now:

– 6.♕xd4 ♕e7! 7.f4 (7.♕xg7?? ♗e5 8.♕g4 ♕b4+–+) 7...♘f6 8.♘c3 c6 and Black equalizes easily.

– 6.0-0!? ♕f6 7.f4 ♗c5 8.♘d2 ♘e7 9.♕h5 with compensation.

Variation A

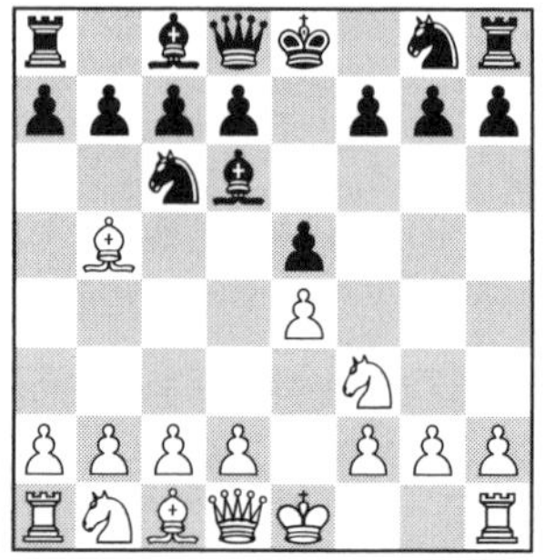

4.c3

The move preferred by the Bilguer [1]. White intends to build a classical centre with moves like d4, 0-0, ♖e1. The early 4.c3 (instead of 4.0-0) has the point that the bishop on b5 may return via a4 to c2 in one move instead of two (a4-b3-c2). However, the move is also a bit slow and allows Black the sharp response ...f5.

4...a6 5.♗a4

Others:

– 5.♗xc6 dxc6 is a harmless version of the Exchange Variation.

– 5.♗c4 is okay, but annuls the point outlined above. After 5...♘f6 6.0-0 (or 6.d3) 6...b5 the bishop is forced to b3, transposing to Variation B.

– Stefan Bücker points to the interesting

move 5.♗d3!?. White prevents 5...f5, while still intending to play 0-0, ♗c2, ♖e1 and d4. However, Black has an excellent reply in 5...♗e7! 6.♗c2 d5, equalizing comfortably.

5...f5!

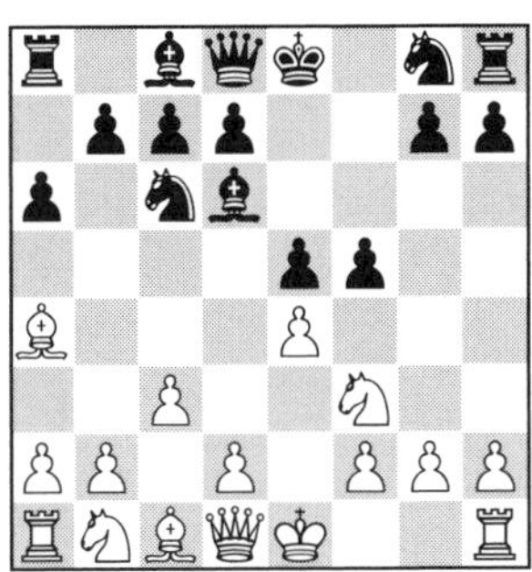

This fine move is a proposal by Stefan Bücker. It may seem odd that Black can afford such a sharp move in combination with the defensive 3...♗d6, but the idea holds up well in analysis.

The Bilguer [1] gives 5...b5, analysing 6.♗b3 ♘f6 7.0-0 to advantage for White after both 7...♘xe4 (given an !) and 7...0-0. See Variation B. The Bilguer also mentions 6.♗c2 as a recommendation by Von Bardeleben. This move is indeed stronger and it is the reason why I recommend 5...f5 rather than the natural 5...♘f6 to which this line may transpose.

Surprisingly, the natural development of Black's kingside knight with 5...♘f6?! is inaccurate. The point is that 4.c3 has enabled White to withdraw his bishop to c2 gaining an important tempo on Variation B below. After 6.0-0 0-0 (the 'Open Spanish' treatment with 6...♘xe4 turns out to be too risky. After 7.♖e1 the complications are clearly in White's favour. See 7...b5 8.♗b3! – Stefan Bücker – 8...♘c5 9.♗c2 ♘e6 10.d4 exd4 11.cxd4 ♗b4 12.d5±) 7.♖e1 ♖e8 8.d4 b5 (note that the attempt to win pawn e4 by means of 8...exd4, fails to 9.♗xc6 dxc6 10.e5 and White wins a piece)

9.♗c2! (here the weaker continuation 9.♗b3 transposes to B)

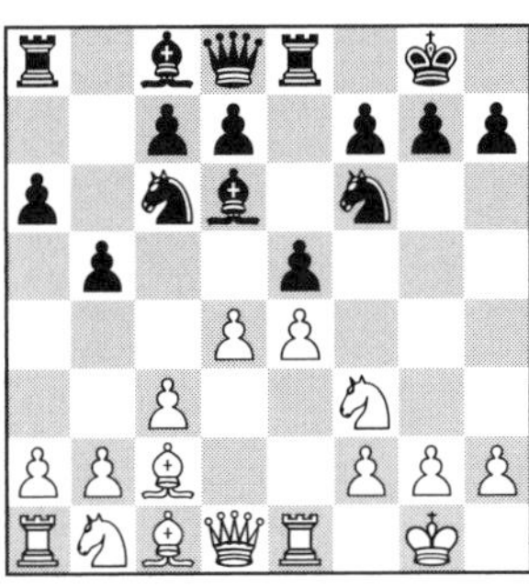

the thematic continuation is 9...♗b7, after which White plays 10.♘bd2, when both 10...h6 11.h3 and 10...♖b8 11.h3 ♗a8 (11...♕e7!?) 12.a3 h6 transpose to positions from Variation B or Variation B3, with the important difference that White has a useful tempo (h3) extra. Although Black's position might still be tenable, White must be significantly better.

Therefore Stefan Bücker and I have also investigated the interesting 9...a5!?, a move with which Black tries to gain counterplay and space on the queenside. Still, on the whole White will be able to gain an advantage, which is why I prefer 5...f5!.

6.d4

This appears to be the only way for White to fight for a small advantage. The alternatives give Black an easy game.

- 6.exf5 e4 and now:

– 7.♘d4 ♕h4 8.♗c2 ♘f6 9.d3 ♘xd4 10.cxd4 exd3 11.♕xd3 0-0 equal.

– 7.♕e2 ♕e7 8.♘d4 ♗c5 9.♕h5+ ♔f8 10.♗xc6 dxc6 11.0-0 ♘f6 12.♕h3 ♕e5 with even chances.

- 6.d3 fxe4 7.dxe4 ♘f6 8.0-0 0-0 9.♗e3 ♘g4

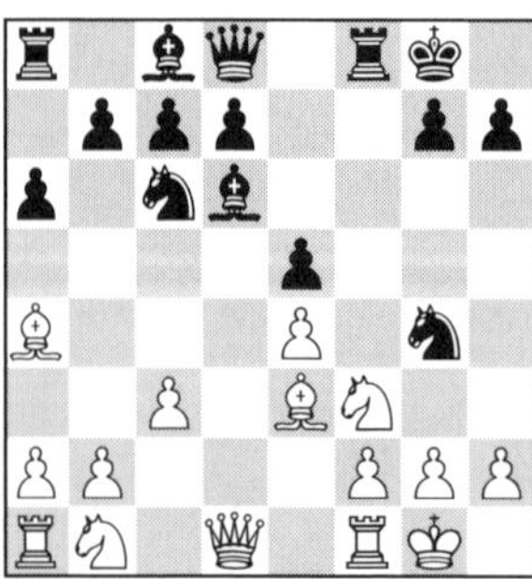

and now:

– 10.♗g5 ♗e7 11.♗xe7 ♕xe7 12.c4 d6 13.♘c3 ♘f6 14.h3 ♗e6 15.♘d5 ♕d8=.

– 10.c4!? ♘d4! 11.♗xd4 exd4 12.h3 ♘e5 13.♘xd4 ♗c5 14.♘c3 d6 15.♘ce2 ♔h8 16.♖c1 ♕h4 with full compensation for the pawn.

6...exd4

After 6...fxe4?! 7.♘xe5 ♘f6 White has the strong move 8.♘g4! which yields him the advantage. After 8...0-0 9.♗c2 pawn e4 becomes vulnerable.

7.0-0

An ambitious alternative is 7.exf5!? ♕e7+ 8.♔f1 ♘f6 9.cxd4 b6! (also interesting is 9...b5!? 10.♗b3 ♗b7 11.♘c3 0-0-0 and now 12.a4 or 12.♗g5) 10.♘c3 (or 10.g3 ♗b7 11.♔g2 0-0-0 12.♘c3 ♕e8 unclear) 10...♗b7 11.h4!? (11.♗xc6?! dxc6!) 11...0-0-0 12.♖h3. White has obtained the double-edged position he was looking for. Objectively Black can be satisfied since chances are roughly equal.

7...fxe4 8.♖e1 ♘f6

The safest continuation. After 8...♗e7?! White obtains a pleasant edge: 9.♖xe4 ♘f6 10.♖e1 0-0 11.cxd4 (harmless is 11.♘xd4 ♘xd4 12.♕xd4 d5 13.♗g5 c5=) 11...d5 12.♗xc6 bxc6 13.♘e5 ♗b7 14.♕c2±.

9.♘bd2 0-0 10.♘xe4 ♘xe4 11.♖xe4 ♗e7 12.♘xd4 ♘xd4!

This is better than 12...d5, after which White maintains the initiative and a small advantage with 13.♘e6 ♗xe6 (13...♕d6? 14.♗b3±) 14.♖xe6 ♕d7 15.♖e2 ♗c5 16.♗e3 ♗xe3 17.♖xe3±. White's bishop is stronger than Black's knight and pawn d5 is vulnerable.

13.♖xd4

The exchange of the central pawns and the knights has resulted in a simplified position. White still exerts some pressure, but with accurate play Black should be able to hold the balance. In my opinion there are two good methods with which Black can steer towards equality.

– 13...♗f6 14.♗b3+ ♔h8 15.♖f4 d6 16.♗e3 ♗e5 17.♖xf8+ ♕xf8 18.♕h5 g6 19.♕h4 ♗d7 20.♖e1 ♖e8.

– 13...♗c5 14.♗b3+ ♔h8 15.♖f4 ♕e8! (prevents 16.♕h5) 16.♖xf8+ ♕xf8 17.♗e3 ♗xe3 18.fxe3 d6 19.♕h5 ♕e7 20.♗c2 g5.

Variation B

4.0-0

The strongest and most flexible move. White can follow-up with a classical set-up (♖e1, c3, d4), but sharper lines with a direct d4 are also an option.

4...a6

Clearly best. Khalifman [5] only mentions the weak move 4...♘f6?, which he refutes by 5.d4! ♘xe4 6.♕e2 f5 7.dxe5 ♗c5 (7...

♘xe5? 8.♘xe5 ♗xe5 9.f3 c6 10.♗d3+−) 8.♘bd2! ♘xd2 9.♗xd2 with a clear advantage for White.

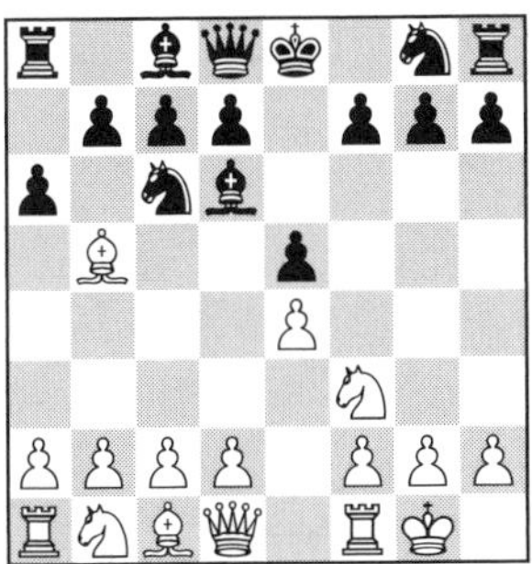

5.♗a4

Here White has two important alternatives.

- With 5.♗xc6 White can go for the Exchange Variation, in which Black has committed himself to the ...♗d6 system. However this is not a big concern, since this particular line is currently considered safe for Black. It is frequently being tested in high level competition. After 5...dxc6 6.d4 exd4 7.♕xd4 f6 play usually goes 8.♗e3 ♘e7 9.♘bd2 ♗e6 and now:
  - 10.♕c3 ♘g6 11.♘d4 ♕e7 12.♘xe6 ♕xe6 13.♕b3 ♕xb3 14.axb3 0-0-0 15.♖fd1 with a small edge for White.
  - 10.♖ad1 ♘g6 11.♘c4 ♗xc4 12.♕xc4 ♕e7 13.♖fe1 0-0-0 with balanced chances.
- 5.♗c4!? is well worth considering. After 5...b5?! 6.♗d5 ♘ge7 7.d4 exd4 8.♘g5 White obtains good chances. Better is 5...♘f6. Now 6.♖e1 b5 7.♗b3 transposes to the main line, while after 6.d3 Black can play 6...♗c5 with an Italian Game. More interesting is 6.d4 0-0 7.♖e1 b5 8.♗d3(!) ♖e8 9.c3 ♗b7. The Spanish bishop has arrived at square d3 instead of b3. This possibility presents an argument in favour of the move order 3...a6 4.♗a4 and only now 4...♗d6.

5...b5

This move is essential in Black's plans, so it is best to play it right now. Otherwise White can play c3, preparing the retreat of ♗a4 to square c2. Indeed 5...♘f6?! is already inaccurate since 6.c3! transposes to 4.c3 a6 5.♗a4 ♘f6 a line that I consider inferior.

6.♗b3 ♘f6

It is also perfectly sound to play 6...♗b7 first. Both 7.c3 ♘f6 and 7.d3 ♘f6 transpose to positions examined below.

7.c3

By transposition we have reached a position examined by the Bilguer [1] and ECO [4]. White's plan is to apply the Spanish Torture by establishing the classical pawn centre supported by ♖e1 and ♘bd2. Other continuations:

- 7.d3 is too timid to challenge the validity of the Mayet Defence. Nevertheless the continuation is of theoretical relevance. After 7...♗b7 (Black can also delay this by playing 7...0-0) we have reached a position from the Arkhangelsk Variation: 1.e4 e5 2.♘f3 ♘c6 3.♗b5 a6 4.♗a4 ♘f6 5.0-0 b5 6.♗b3 ♗b7 7.d3 ♗d6. The last move 7...♗d6!? gained recognition when the Ukrainian GM Vladimir Malaniuk played it successfully around 1990. Nowadays this is main line theory, frequently tested in tournament practice. Play may go: 8.a3 0-0 9.♘c3 h6 10.♗e3 (White has also tried 10.♖e1, 10.h3, 10.♘e2 and 10.♗a2) 10...

♘g4 11.♗d2 ♗c5 12.♗d5 (12.♘d5!?) 12... d6 13.b4 ♗b6 14.♗b3 ♘e7 with equal chances in Inarkiev-Vasquez, Linares 2003.

● 7.♖e1 0-0 8.d4 ♗b7. Now 9.c3 transposes to the main line. Kononenko-Tarlev, Kharkov 2007, took an original course: 9.c4!? ♗b4 (9...♘xd4 is also playable) 10.dxe5 ♘g4 11.♗g5 ♗xe1?! (courageous; 11...♕e8 equalizes) 12.♗xd8 ♗xf2+ 13.♔h1 ♖axd8 14.h3 ♘gxe5 15.cxb5 axb5. White won in 56 moves.

● 7.d4 ♗b7 8.dxe5!? (8.c3 0-0 see main line) 8...♘xe5 9.♘xe5 ♗xe5 10.f4 ♗d6 11.e5 ♗c5+ 12.♔h1 ♘e4 13.♕e1 ♕e7 14.♘d2 ♘xd2 15.♗xd2 0-0-0 16.a4 f6 with sharp play and balanced chances.

7...0-0

The Bilguer [1] and ECO [4] consider 7... ♘xe4 as good (or as bad!) as the text-move. The Bilguer even assigns an exclamation mark to 7...♘xe4. However, the tactics are clearly in White's favour: 8.♖e1 (also very strong is 8.d4±) 8...♘c5 (equally insufficient are 8...f5 9.d4 and 8...♘f6 9.d4 e4 10.♘bd2) 9.♗c2 ♘e6 10.d4 exd4 11.cxd4 ♗b4 12.d5±. A valid alternative to the text move is 7... ♗b7. It should transpose to the main line after 8.d4 0-0.

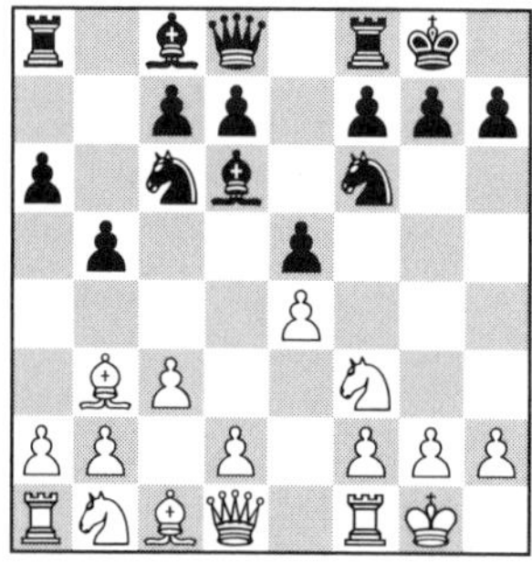

8.d4

Or 8.♖e1. ECO [4] stops here and assesses the position as ±, referring to the Bilguer [1]. There we find the following line: 8...♖e8 9.♘g5 ♖e7 10.f4 with a dangerous attack both after 10...exf4 and 10...h6. However, Black should play instead 8...♗b7!. After 9.d4 h6 10.♘bd2 ♖e8 we reach the main line. Moves like 8.d3, 8.a4 and 8.♕e2 are playable but pose no particular threat to Black.

8...♗b7

Black should avoid the trap 8...♘xe4?? 9.♗d5! ♘f6 10.♗xc6 dxc6 11.dxe5 and White wins a piece.

9.♘bd2 h6

A useful precaution. Before playing ...♖e8 Black takes away square g5 from White's knight and bishop. The odd alternative 9...♕b8?! most likely transposes to a dubious line from B3 after 10.♗c2 ♖e8 11.♖e1 h6 12.h3.

10.♖e1

Sharp complications can arise from 10.dxe5!? ♗xe5 11.♘xe5 ♘xe5 12.f4 ♘eg4 13.♕e2 c5!. It appears that Black is okay: 14.h3 c4 15.hxg4 cxb3 16.e5 ♖e8 equal; or 14.♗c2 c4 15.♘f3 ♖e8 16.h3 ♘xe4! 17.hxg4 ♘xc3 18.♕f2 ♖e2 unclear.

10...♖e8

Black has completed his development and is now ready to retreat his bishop from d6 to f8.

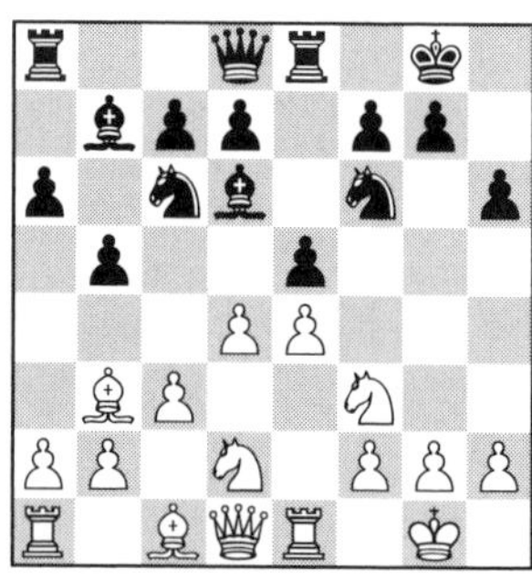

11.♗c2!

With this move White strengthens pawn e4 and indirectly discourages Black's intended bishop retreat. The importance can be seen in the next variation:

● 11.h3 ♗f8 12.♘xe5 ♘xe5 13.dxe5 ♖xe5. Now the intended move 14.♘f3 is not feasible since pawn e4 is insufficiently protected. Hence White plays 14.♗c2, but after 14...d6 Black is okay.

● 11.d5 ♘e7 12.♘f1 is comfortably met by 12...c6 (also good is 12...♘g6) 13.dxc6 dxc6 14.♘h4 c5 15.♕f3 c4 16.♗c2=.

● 11.a4 ♗f8 12.h3 d6 13.♗c2 exd4 14.cxd4 ♘b4 15.♗b1 c5 16.d5 g6 17.♘f1 ♗g7 =. A classical Spanish position in which Black has good counterplay. Chances are equal. Drawn in 29 moves, Gueci-Ostrowski, correspondence game 2008.

After the text-move (11.♗c2) we have reached a key position for the 3...♗d6 Spanish. The position can be reached by numerous move orders. It has been tested in a small number of correspondence games. Now that both sides have completed their development, the main issue to be resolved is the repositioning of the bishop on d6. Black has the choice between three strategies:

1. to retreat the bishop to f8;
2. to exchange pawns in the centre;
3. to postpone a decision, waiting to see how White resolves the central tension, either by advancing the d-pawn to d5 or by exchanging it on e5. We examine:

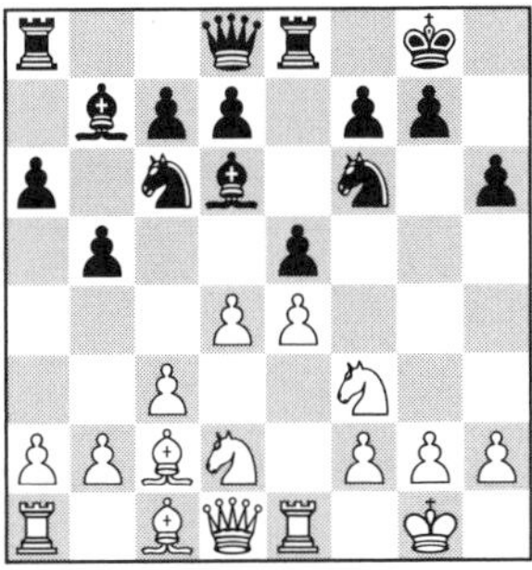

Variation B1 – 11...♗f8
Variation B2 – 11...exd4
Variation B3 – 11...♖b8

Variation B1

11...♗f8

With this bishop retreat Black signals his wilingness to transform the position to a classical variation by following up with ...d6. However, as we shall see the move comes down to an exchange sacrifice, the value of which can be disputed.

12.♘xe5

The right way for White to take advantage. After 12.h3 d6 13.a3 we would reach a position from the Smyslov/Zaitsev/Flohr Variation (ECO code C93) with balanced chances. Note that instead of the text-move (12.♘xe5), the capture 12.dxe5(?) is inaccurate since it allows the good reply 12...♘g4! e.g. 13.♘b3 ♘gxe5 14.♘xe5 ♘xe5=.

12...♘xe5 13.dxe5 ♖xe5 14.♘f3

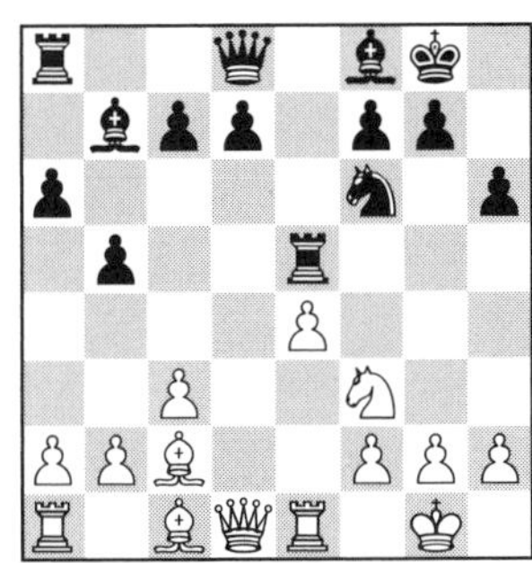

14...♖xe4

This exchange sacrifice is the point of Black's play. It is also forced, because if the rook would retreat then White has 15.e5± with a dominating position.

15.♗xe4 ♘xe4

Weaker is 15...♗xe4 because of 16.♘e5.

After the textmove we have reached an important position. Black has sacrificed the exchange, for which he has obtained fair compensation in the form of a pawn, the bishop pair and activity. Whether this is really sufficient is difficult to say. In the databases I found four correspondence games reaching this position. White scored +1 =3 –0.

16.♗f4

The 2008 correspondence game Germann-Sueess went: 16.♗e3 ♗d6 (16...c5!?) 17.a4 (17.♘d4 ♕h4 18.h3) 17...b4 18.♕c2 ♖c8 19.♗d4 ♘g5 20.♘d2 ♘e6 21.♘e4 ♗f8 22.♖ad1 d5±, draw in 34. Other reasonable moves are 16.♘d4 and 16.a4.

16...♖c8

An alternative is 16...d5 17.♘d2 ♘c5 18.♘b3 ♘e6.

17.♘d4 ♕f6 18.♕g4 c5 19.♘f3 c4 20.♗e3 ♕e6 21.♕xe6 dxe6 22.♖ed1 ♗d5 23.♘e5 ♖c7

White is still better, but Black's position is resilient. Tombette-Daemen, correspondence game 2008 was drawn in 48 moves.

Variation B2

11...exd4

In my opinion this is a sound move, worth testing in practice.

12.cxd4 ♗f8

The pawn exchange has left White in control of the centre. However, if he plays slow then Black will obtain counterplay by attacking the centre with ...c5. For example: 13.a3 d6 14.h3 ♘e7 15.♘f1 ♘g6 16.♘g3 c5 17.d5 ♘d7 18.♘f5 ♘de5 19.♗d2 ♗c8 and White has only a small edge.

13.e5!?

A sharp advance. White obtains square e4 plus chances along b1-h7, but Black gets square d5 for his knight and the chance to attack the centre with ...d6. The other central advance is also of interest. 13.d5!? ♘a5 14.h3 ♖c8 15.a3 c5 16.b3 g6 17.♗b2 ♗g7 18.♖c1 d6 19.♗b1 ♔h7 with a tense position. White is slightly better.

13...♘d5 14.♗e4 ♘b6 15.a3

White intends to play ♕c2 and first takes control over square b4. Another possibility is 15.b3 ♖b8! 16.♗b2 ♘e7 17.♗xb7 (or 17.♖c1 ♗xe4 18.♘xe4 ♘ed5 19.g3 d6±) 17...♖xb7 18.♘e4 ♘ed5 19.g3 (idea: ♘h4) 19...♗e7 followed by ...d6. White is slightly better.

15...♕c8

There are other defensive set-ups that are worth considering:

– 15...d6 16.♕c2 ♕d7 17.♗h7+ ♔h8 18.♗f5 ♕d8 19.b3 ♘e7±.

– 15...♖b8 16.♕c2 ♕c8 17.♗h7+ ♔h8 18.♗f5 ♘e7 19.♗g4 ♗d5±.

16.♗b1

With the idea of bringing the bishop to a2. After 16.♕c2 ♘d8 White has little.

16...d6 17.♕c2 g6 18.♘e4 ♗g7 19.♗a2 ♘e7±

We have reached a tense and interesting middle game position, in which White holds the slighty better chances.

Variation B3

11...♖b8!?

A semi-useful waiting move. Black maintains the central tension and wants to see what White will do. Obviously there are similar waiting moves Black may consider. The main problem is to give them meaning if White follows suit by playing another preparatory move. For example:

– 11...♕c8?!. Hoping for 12.h3, when 12...exd4 13.cxd4 ♗f8 14.e5 ♘d5 15.♗e4 ♘ce7 is interesting. However after 12.a3(!) I fail to see a good follow-up for Black.

– 11...♕b8?!. The 2008 correspondence game Khachaturov-Ostrowski went 12.a3 ♗f8 13.♘xe5 ♘xe5 14.dxe5 ♖xe5 15.♘f3 ♖xe4 16.♗xe4 ♗xe4 with play similar to that in B1. Better might be 12.h3(!), e.g. 12...♕a7?! (12...a5?! 13.a4!) 13.♘b3. Black has achieved nothing with his odd manoeuvres, since the intended line 13...exd4 14.cxd4 ♘b4 15.d5 ♘xc2 16.♕xc2 – while achieving the desired exchange of knight versus light-squared bishop – clearly favours White.

12.h3

The main alternative is 12.a3. One option for Black is to play 12...♗f8. More interesting is the continuation 12...♗a8!?, and now:

– 13.b4 a5 (a good move to prepare this pawn advance is 13...♕c8) 14.bxa5 ♘xa5 15.♘xe5 ♗xe5 16.dxe5 ♖xe5 17.f4 ♖e8 18.a4 ♕e7 19.axb5 ♕c5+ 20.♔h1± Zielinski-Frenzel, correspondence game 2006.

– 13.h3 ♗f8 (other continuations like 13...♕c8?! are too slow) 14.dxe5 ♘xe5 15.♘xe5 ♖xe5 16.♘f3 ♖xe4 17.♗xe4 ♘xe4 18.♗e3 c5. The position is similar to those discussed in B1. Black's chances may have improved, due to the fact that his rook has access to square b6 and from there to the kingside (f6 or g6).

12...exd4 13.cxd4 ♗f8 14.e5 ♘d5

15.♘f1!?

After the logical move 15.♗e4 we see a key-point of 11...♖b8, the bishop on b7 is protected by the rook. Play goes 15...♘b6 16.a3 ♘e7 17.♗xb7 ♖xb7 18.♘e4 ♘ed5±. Black has firm control over square d5 and he will soon follow up with ...d6.

15...d6 16.♕d3 g6 17.e6 f5 18.♗d2 ♕e7

We have reached a rich and complicated position, with chances for both sides.

Final Thoughts

It seems to me that Rybka's first impression was right: the Mayet Defence 3...♗d6 in the Spanish Game is indeed much stronger than its poor reputation suggests. After 4.c3 a6 5.♗a4 Black has an excellent response: 5...f5!. The main line positions arising from 4.0-0 are interesting and playable, in particular the line 11...exd4 12.cxd4 ♗f8 examined in B2.

White has a lot of options to consider in this opening, e.g. whether to play d3 and a4, or go for a classical centre with c3 and d4. In the latter case there are issues whether to exchange pawns on e5; or to close the centre with d5; or to go for the standard knight manoeuvre ♘d2-f1-g3. On the other hand Black's play is fairly straightforward, making this an easy to learn system that can be employed as a surprise weapon in tournament play.
In this article I have focused on ...♗d6 at move three. Since Black's plan involves standard moves like a6, b5 and ♘f6, other move orders can be considered. The variation 3...a6 4.♗a4 ♗d6 comes to mind. This is at least equivalent to 3...♗d6, and perhaps slightly more accurate; this way one sidesteps possibilities like 5.♗xc6 and 5.♗c4 in B. Furthermore one may take the Archangelsk Variation 3...a6 4.♗a4 ♘f6 5.0-0 b5 6.♗b3 ♗b7 as a starting point. This move order allows one to defer ...♗d6 to move 5, 6 or 7. Of course this would spoil the surprise factor a bit.

References

1. Bilguer und Van der Lasa: Handbuch des Schachspiels (1843)
2. J. Ganzo: *La apertura Spanola*, Madrid 1957
3. Bosch: *Sokolov's Surprise*, SOS-1 (2003)
4. *Enzyklopädie der Schacheröffnungen*, Volume C (1974)
5. Khalifman: *Opening repertoire according to Anand*, Book 1 (2003)

Acknowledgement. The author wants to thank FM Stefan Bücker for his valuable contributions and his friendly advice.

CHAPTER 10

Arthur Kogan

English Opening: Early Inspiration

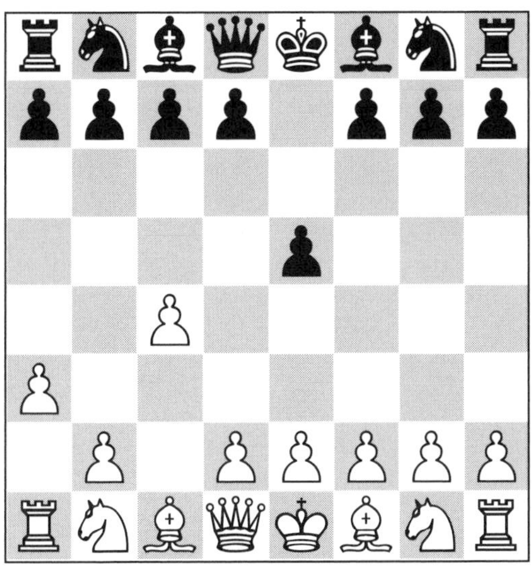

1.c4 e5 2.a3!?

When you surprise your opponent with a semi-useful move like 2.a3 it means offering him a world of choice. It is pointless, then to try and cover every possible reply. Indeed, our choice was to avoid theory, not to remember it! However, I do want to inspire you and like to present you with three annotated games.

□ **Manuel Bosboom**
■ **Loek van Wely**
Wijk aan Zee Blitz 1999

1.c4 e5 2.a3!?

Getting away from the main lines as soon as possible. This little pawn move has obvious merits though. Indeed, it is possible that you end up in a Sicilian a tempo up! In the Sicilian ...a6 is almost always a useful move, and in the English Opening this holds true as well. White prepares b4 and prevents ...♘b4 and ...♗b4. At the same time, White is employing the cyclist's strategy of 'sur place': he is waiting for Black to make the first 'move', to then respond in the proper way. Interestingly, the move 2.a3 was used from time to time that past genius Adolph Anderssen (even versus Morphy!). Later Leko played it (hoping for his Taimanov or Paulsen Sicilian with an extra tempo!), and even more aggressive players like Velimirovich, Galkin and Carlsen!

Please note that 2.♘c3 ♘f6 3.♘f3 ♘c6 4.a3 was covered by Mikhail Gurevich in SOS-3 (Chapter 17, p.131).

2...♘f6

This is the most common answer, and it makes it easier for White to imagine that he is playing a Sicilian a tempo up! I will mainly give examples without a knight on f3, but you could also use this chapter in combination with the article of Gurevich in SOS-3.

2...♘c6 3.b4 (after 3.♘c3 play could transpose to an open (or closed) Sicilian with a3 added – so no more Rossolimo Variation for example!) 3...f5 4.♗b2 d6 5.g3 (5.e3) 5...♘f6 6.♗g2 g5?! 7.d4?! (not the best, after 7.♘f3 g4 8.♘h4 the position looks dubious for Black) 7...♘xd4 8.♗xd4 exd4 9.♘f3 ♗g7 10.♘xg5 c5 (10...d5!) 11.♘d2 0-0 12.0-0 and White was slightly better in Galkin-Winants, playchess. com 2007.

3.e3

Played in Paulsen style.

3.d3!? was later played by 2.a3 expert Bosboom: 3...d5 4.cxd5 ♘xd5 5.♘f3 ♗d6 6.g3 0-0 7.♗g2 a5 8.0-0 c6 9.b3 f6 10.♗b2 ♗e6 11.♘bd2 c5 12.e3 ♘c6 13.♖c1 ♖c8 14.♘e4 b6 15.d4 cxd4 16.exd4 ♘xd4 17.♗xd4 ♖xc1 18.♕xc1 exd4 19.♕c6 ♘c3 20.♘xd4 and Black resigned in Bosboom-Pilgaard, Kemer 2007.

A few examples after **3.♘c3**:

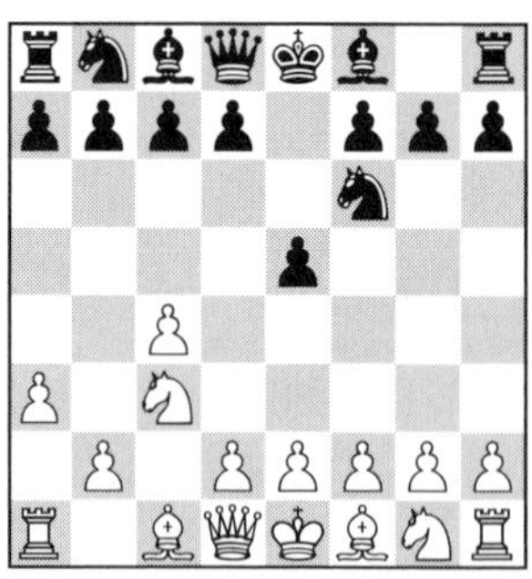

● 3...♘c6 4.e3 d5 5.cxd5 ♘xd5 6.♘f3 ♗g4 7.♗e2 (7.♕a4) 7...♘xc3 8.bxc3 f5 9.d4 e4 10.♘d2 ♗xe2 11.♕xe2 a6 12.0-0 ♗d6 13.♕h5+ g6 14.♕h6 and White held the initiative in the old game Tarrasch-Mendelsohn, Breslau 1879.

● 3...g6 4.d4!?. Just like in the Sicilian this move grabs the initiative! (4.g3 d5 5.cxd5 ♘xd5 6.♗g2 ♘e7 7.d3 ♗g7 8.h4 h6 9.♘f3 ♘bc6 10.♗d2 b6 11.0-0 ♗b7 12.b4±, Velimirovic-Todorovic, Obrenovac 2008; 4.♘f3 ♘c6 5.g3 ♗g7 6.♗g2 0-0 7.0-0 d6 8.b4 ♘d4 9.♗b2 c6 10.d3 ♖e8 11.♘d2 ♗e6 12.e3±, Carlsen-Eljanov, Moscow WCh Blitz 2010) 4...exd4 5.♕xd4 ♗g7 (5... ♘c6 6.♕e3+ ♕e7 7.♘d5±) 6.♕e3+! ♔f8 (6...♕e7 7.♕xe7+ ♔xe7 8.♗g5 favours White) 7.♕d3 (7.g3±) 7...♘c6 8.♘f3 d6 9.e4 h6 10.♗e2 ♗g4 11.♗e3± Velimirovic-Todorovic, Ulcinj 1997.

● 3...c6 4.♘f3 (4.d4! is also good) 4...e4 5.♘d4 d5 6.cxd5 ♕b6 7.e3 cxd5 8.d3 ♘c6 9.♘xc6 bxc6 10.dxe4 dxe4 11.♕c2 ♗f5 12.♗e2 ♗d6 13.g4! ♗g6 and now 14.♗d2! (an improvement over 14.g5 ♘d7 15.♘xe4 0-0 16.♕a4 ♗e5 and Black had compensation in Eljanov-Kalugin, Alushta 2000) 14...0-0 (14...♖b8 15.♘a4 ♕c7 16.♖c1±) 15.h4 with an attack.

● 3...c5 4.g3 (for 4.e3 or 4.e4 see my comments to the game Kacheishvili-Macieja) 4...♗e7 5.♗g2 0-0 6.♘f3 ♘c6 7.0-0 d6 8.d3 h6 9.♘d2 ♗e6 10.♘d5 ♕d7 11.b4 cxb4 12.♖b1 bxa3 13.♘xe7+ ♕xe7 14.♗xa3 with nice Volga-like compensation. Velimirovic-Vajda, Herceg Novi 2007.

● 3...d5 4.cxd5 ♘xd5. This is exactly what White wants by playing 2.a3: an open Sicilian with tempo up! Now just choose your favourite open Sicilian line.

– For example: the most principled way to fight for a quick edge is perhaps 5.e4, which makes sense as ...♘b4 is impossible! 5... ♘b6 (5...♘f4 6.d4!) 6.♘f3 ♗g4 7.h3 ♗xf3

8.♕xf3 ♗e7 9.♗b5+! c6 10.♗e2 0-0 11.0-0 c5 12.a4 ♘c6 13.a5 ♘d4 14.♕g3 ♘d7 15.♗c4, Schmidt-Schulz, Hamburg 2002.
– 5.♘f3 ♘c6 6.d3 (6.e4 and 6.♕c2!? are covered by Gurevich in SOS-3). The super popular Najdorf or Dragon Variations reversed with a tempo up can't be bad, right? 6...♗e7 7.g3 0-0 8.♗g2 ♗e6 9.0-0 ♔h8 10.♗d2 f5 11.♖c1 ♗f6 12.♘a4 ♕e7 13.♘c5 (White holds the initiative) 13...e4 14.dxe4 fxe4 15.♘g5 ♗g8 16.♘gxe4 ♗xb2 17.♖b1 ♗xa3 18.♗g5 ♕f7 19.♘xb7 ♗e7 20.♗xe7 ♘dxe7 21.♕d7±, Leko-Fontaine, Spain 1995.
– 5.e3 ♗e6 6.♘f3 ♗d6 7.♗e2 (7.d4!) 7...0-0 8.0-0 (8.d4 ♘xc3 9.bxc3 e4 10.♘d2 f5 11.f4!? g5?! – 11...♕h4+ 12.g3 ♕h3 13.♗f1 ♕h6 14.c4 c6 unclear, Anderssen-Morphy, Paris 1858 – 12.♗c4 ♗xc4 13.♘xc4 gxf4 14.exf4 ♕e8 15.0-0± ♕c6 16.♕b3 ♕d5 17.♖b1±, Anderssen-Morphy, Paris 1858) 8...♘xc3 9.bxc3 f5 10.d4 e4 11.♘d2 ♖f6 12.f4 ♖h6 13.g3 ♘d7 14.♘c4 ♗xc4 15.♗xc4+ ♔h8 16.♖a2 ♕e7 17.a4 ♘f6 18.♕b3 b6 19.♗e6 was played in one of the first games of all time with 2.a3 between two legendary players. White later won in Anderssen-Morphy, Paris 1858.
– 5.g3 is a 'Dragon'.

3...c6 4.♘f3

4.d4 is also logical. This is an Alapin Reversed, of course. 4...exd4 5.♕xd4 (5.exd4 d5 6.♘f3 is also playable. White aims for an isolated pawn position where a3 is useful) 5...d5 6.♘f3 ♗e7 (6...♗d6 7.♘c3 dxc4 8.♗xc4 0-0 9.e4?! – 9.0-0 is more promising – 9...♗c7 10.♕xd8 ♖xd8 11.♘g5?! – 11.0-0 ♗g4 12.♗e3 was equal – 11...♖f8 12.f4 h6 13.♘xf7 ♖xf7 14.e5 ♘fd7 15.♗e3 ♘f8 16.♗xf7+ ♔xf7 and by now Black was slightly better in Bosboom-Tiviakov, Hilversum 2007) 7.♘c3 0-0 8.cxd5 cxd5 9.♗e2 ♘c6 10.♕d3 ♗g4 11.0-0 ♕d7 12.b3 ♖fd8 13.♗b2 ♗f5 14.♕d1 d4 (Black has completely equalized) 15.exd4 draw, Galkin-Alsina, Lugo 2009.

4...e4 5.♘d4 d5 6.cxd5 cxd5 7.d3

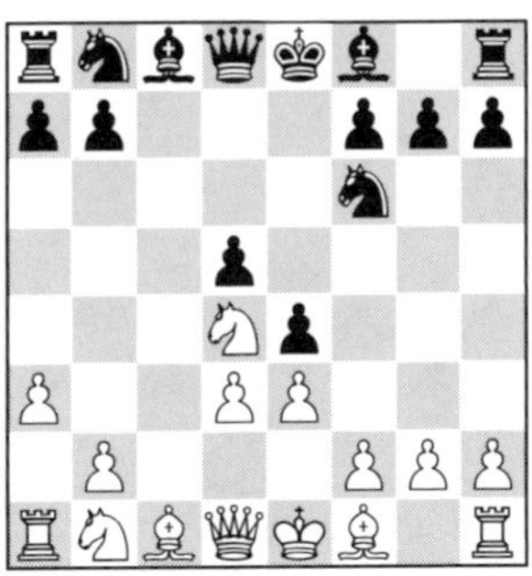

And here we are in a Sicilian Alapin reversed, where a3 is very useful.

7...a6!?

It seems that Van Wely is now making a small joke by returning the tempo. He prepares ...♗d6 and does not want to be disturbed by ♘b5.
– 7...♗c5 is a better option, but White can still look forward to typically complex play after 8.♘c3 (8.dxe4 dxe4 9.♗e2; 8.♘b3 ♗d6 9.♘c3, pressing the centre) 8...0-0 9.♗e2 ♕e7 10.0-0 ♖d8 11.b4 ♗xd4 12.exd4 ♘c6 13.♗e3 ♗f5 14.dxe4 (14.♖e1) 14...dxe4 15.♕d2 ♕e6 (15...♗e6 16.f3) 16.♖fd1 ♘e7, Milov-Godena, Cannes 2006. Now instead of 17.♗g5 White could improve with 17.d5! ♘fxd5 (17...♕d7 18.d6) 18.♗c4 ♗g4 19.♘xd5 ♗xd1 20.♖xd1 ♘xd5 21.♗xd5 ♕f5 22.♕a2 ♖d7 23.h3! ♖ad8 (23...h5 24.♖d4) 24.g4 ♕f3 25.♖d4 ♕xh3 26.♖xe4±.
– 7...♘c6 8.♘xc6 bxc6 9.♕c2 ♗d7 10.♘d2 exd3 11.♗xd3 Camacho Calle-Franco Ocampos, Dos Hermanas 2004.
– 7...♗e7 8.♘c3 0-0 9.♗e2 ♘bd7 10.♘f5!? (10.dxe4 dxe4 11.0-0±) 10...exd3 11.♗xd3 ♗c5 12.♘a4 g6 13.b4! ♗b6 14.♘xb6 ♘xb6 15.♘d4 ♗g4 16.♕b3 (16.♘e2) 16...♖c8

17.0-0 ♘c4 18.h3 with unclear play in Shlegin-Shukh, Saratov 2009.

8.♘c3 ♗d6 9.dxe4 dxe4 10.♗e2

10.♕c2 0-0! 11.♘xe4 ♘xe4 12.♕xe4 ♖e8 13.♕c2 will leave Black with attacking chances for the pawn, and Bosboom clearly prefers to attack!

10...0-0

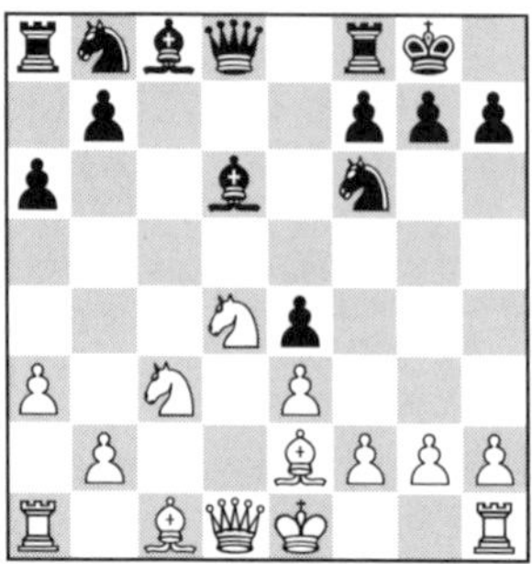

11.g4!

A very ambitious and risky way to fight for the centre! A perfect Bosboom plan, certainly in a blitz game like this!

11...♖e8 12.g5 ♘fd7 13.h4!

Now Black should sacrifice the e-pawn for some compensation, otherwise, having his king safe in the centre, White might even play ♗f1, ♗g2 and ♕c2 and win it for nothing...

13...♘c5 14.b4 ♘d3+!

14...♘e6 15.♘f5 (not 15.♘xe4?! ♗e5 16.♗b2 ♘xd4 17.exd4 ♗f4) 15...♗e5 16.♗b2 with the better chances.

15.♗xd3 exd3 16.♕xd3 ♗e5!

Black surely has some compensation for the pawn, but he should be very concrete, since if White manages to finish his development and/or get his king safe, then he is simply a pawn up!

17.♘ce2 ♕d5 18.e4

Bosboom is never afraid of complications – he simply enjoys them, winning or losing. 18.f3, hiding the white king on f2, was also an idea.

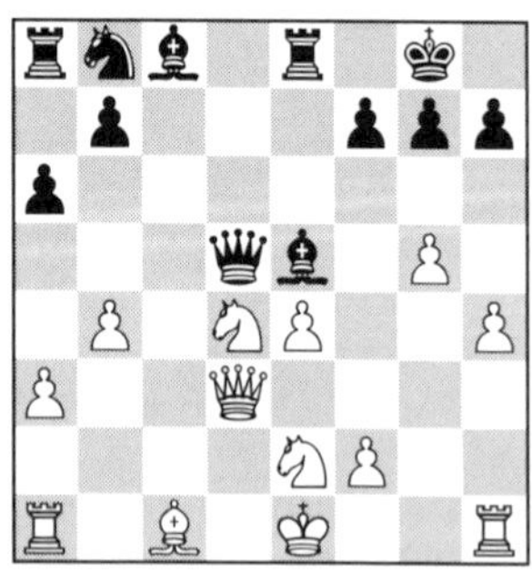

18...♕d6

18...♗f5!! could make it even hotter, with nice pins and hanging pieces from all sides!! 19.f3 is the only move (19.exd5 ♗xd3–+). 19...♘c6! 20.♗b2 ♗xd4! 21.♗xd4 (21.♘xd4 ♗xe4!–+) 21...♗xe4! 22.fxe4 ♖xe4 23.0-0-0!! (the only move, otherwise Black is winning!) 23...♖d8 and Black will regain his piece: 24.♖he1! g6 25.♘c3 ♕xd4 26.♘xe4! ♕xd3 (26...♕a1+ 27.♕b1 ♕xa3+ 28.♕b2) 27.♖xd3 ♖xd3 28.♘f6+ ♔g7 29.♘e8+ ♔h8 30.♘f6 ♖d8 31.♔b2 with even chances.

19.♗e3 a5!? 19...♘c6 20.♖d1. **20.b5 ♘d7 21.♖d1 ♘c5 22.♕c2**

And suddenly Black's compensation for the pawn seems dubious. White managed to finish his development, and even his king is quite safe! I will give the remaining moves of this blitz game with only a few notes.

22...♕e7 23.♘f5 23.♘c6! was better.

23...♗xf5 24.exf5 ♖ac8 25.0-0

25.f6!? ♕e6! (25...gxf6 26.♖g1 ♔h8 27.♕f5 with an attack).

25...♗b8 25...♘e4! 26.♕d3 ♖ed8 27.♕b1 h6! is unclear.

26.♘f4?! 26.♖c1 b6 (26...♕d6 27.♗f4) 27.♖fd1. **26...♘e6** 26...♘e4!. **27.♕d2 ♘xf4 28.♗xf4 ♗xf4 29.♕xf4 ♕xa3**

After a few not so accurate moves, White seems to be fighting for a draw, but he still manages to make some Bosboom magic...

30.f6!? 30.♖d7 ♖e7=. **30...♕c5 31.♖b1 ♕d5** 31...♕c4!. **32.♖fd1 ♕e6** 32...♖e4; 32...♖c4. **33.♖d6 ♕a2 34.♖bd1 a4 35.♖d7 a3** Loek is an optimist as usual and plays for the win! 35...♕e6 with ♖c4 coming was more to the point.

36.h5

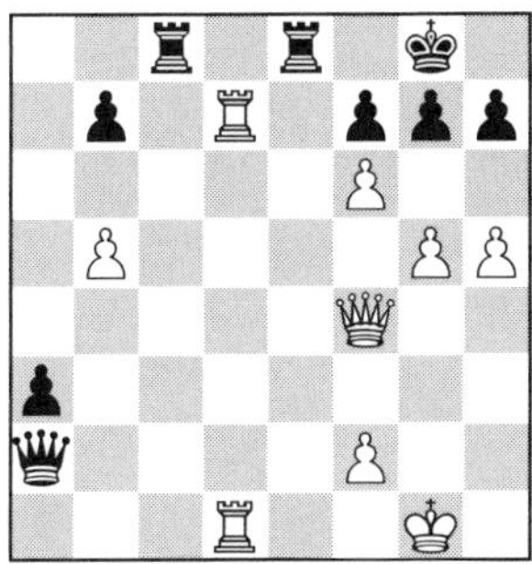

36...♖f8?? 36...g6 was the only move, and even though it looks already dangerous for Black, I don't see more than a draw after 37.hxg6 hxg6 38.♕h4 ♕e2! 39.♕h6 ♕g4+ 40.♔f1 ♕e2+ 41.♔g1 ♕g4+=.

37.fxg7 ♖fe8 37...♔xg7 38.♕f6+ ♔g8 39.h6 ♕b2 40.♖7d4+–. **38.g6!**

Loek probably missed this small pawn push, and as you already know Bosboom is a big fan of small pawn moves!

38...fxg6 39.hxg6

Black resigned.

□ **Andrey Deviatkin**
■ **Konstantin Landa**
Serpukhov 2008

1.c4 e5 2.a3! c6

Planning ...d5 is also logical of course. Still, a3 comes in useful, and you can choose your favourite line against the Alapin!

3.d4!

Time to get rid of Black's central pawn. Without a knight on c6, the queen feels quite good on d4!

– 3.♘f3 e4 4.♘d4! is also good: 4...d5 5.cxd5 cxd5 6.d3 exd3 7.♕xd3 ♘c6 8.♘c3 (8.g3! would be the Rubinstein response in this Tarrasch structure) 8...♘f6 9.♗g5 (9.g3) 9...♗e7 10.e3 ♗e6 11.♗e2 0-0 12.0-0 ♘e5 13.♕b5 was better for White in Brener-Schaffer, playchess.com 2007.

– 3.e3 is also possible, offering to play a French Defence, but it is a bit too passive to my taste: 3...d5 4.d4 e4 5.♗d2 ♘f6 6.cxd5 cxd5 7.♗b4 ♗d6 8.♗xd6 ♕xd6 9.♘e2 0-0 10.♘bc3 ♘c6 11.♘f4 with approximate equality Bunzmann-Yakovich, Saint Vincent 2000.

3...exd4 4.♕xd4

4...d5

And here White can also choose according to his taste (and the line he likes to play with Black a tempo down!). The bishop may be developed to f4 or g5. Or White can play e3 and first finish his development before placing it on b2.

5.♘f3 ♘f6 6.♗g5

Also good looks 6.♘c3 ♗e7 7.cxd5 cxd5 8.g3!? (or 8.♗f4).

6...♗e7 7.cxd5

7.♘c3 c5?!, and now 8.♕f4! is strong (not 8.♕d2? d4 9.♗xf6 ♗xf6 10.♘d5 ♗e6 11.e4 dxe3 12.fxe3 0-0 13.♗e2 ♗xd5 14.cxd5 ♕d6=, Galkin-Ovetchkin, playchess.com 2007), since 8...d4? fails to 9.♗xf6! ♗xf6 10.♘d5 with excellent play for White.

7...Qxd5 7...cxd5 8.e3. **8.Nc3 Qxd4 9.Nxd4 g6 10.e4**

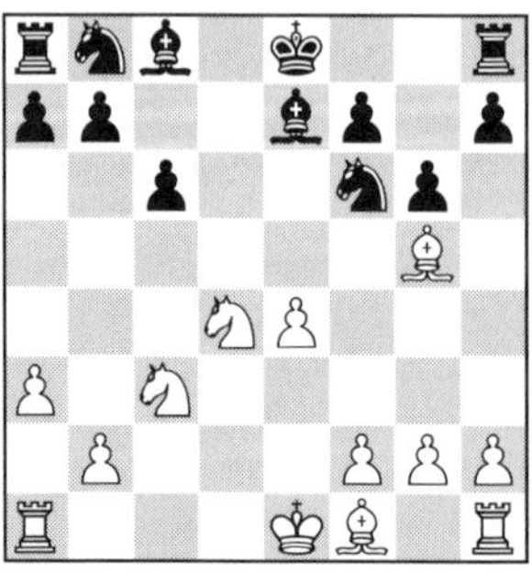

The middlegame without queens is more pleasant for White, who has more space and presence in the centre.

10...Nfd7 11.Be3 a5 12.Be2 Na6 13.f4 Nac5 14.0-0-0 a4 15.Rhe1 Nb6 16.e5 h5 17.Bf3 Bd7 18.Ne4 Nxe4 19.Bxe4 Nc4 20.Bf2 20.e6 is strong too. **20...0-0 21.Bd3 Na5 22.e6!** A very strong move, breaking Black's structure.

22...Bxe6 23.Nxe6 fxe6 24.Rxe6 Rxf4 25.Be3 Rf7 26.Bxg6 Rg7 27.Bh6 Nb3+ 28.Kb1 Nc5 29.Bxg7 Nxe6 30.Be5 The pair of bishops rules the board! **30...Nc5 31.Bxh5 Rf8 32.Bf3** White is a pawn up and has the bishop pair. He won on move 61.

□ **Giorgi Kacheishvili**
■ **Bartlomiej Macieja**
Istanbul 2003

1.c4 e5 2.a3 c5

This is not illogical. Black gains more control over square d4, but still it does weaken square d5. You could compare it to 1.e4 c5 2.c4. All the same we have our extra tempo.

■ White can also try to use his extra tempo after 2...f5?! 3.d4! To obtain a good French structure without the bad bishop! 3...e4 and now:

– 4.h4!? would be a typical way to gain control over the f4-square and to block the advance of black's pawns on the kingside: 4...Be7 5.g3 Nf6 6.Nc3 0-0 7.Nh3 d6 8.Bg5 (8.Nf4) 8...Ng4 9.Nd5 Bxg5 10.hxg5 Nc6 11.Qd2 (instead, 11.f3! would have crowned Bosboom's SOS strategy with a more or less winning position versus a strong GM: 11...exf3 12.exf3 Re8+ 13.Kd2) 11...Ne7 12.Ne3 Ng6 and now the chances were unclear in the blitz game Bosboom-Sokolov, Wijk aan Zee 1999.

– 4.Nh3!? is fine too.

– 4.Bf4 Nf6 5.h4 g6 6.Nc3 d6 7.e3 Bg7 8.Be2 Nc6 9.b4 Ne7 10.Qb3 c6 11.b5 h6 12.Nh3 Be6 13.Rd1 (White has an edge)

13...0-0 14.0-0 Bf7 15.Qb4! Nc8 16.c5 d5 17.bxc6 bxc6 18.Ba6 and White was already winning in Galkin-Winants, playchess.com 2007.

■ 2...a5?! 3.Nc3 Nf6 4.Nf3 Nc6 5.e3! d5 6.cxd5 Nxd5 7.Bb5 (7.Qc2 is strong too) 7...Nxc3 8.bxc3 e4 9.Nd4 Bd7 10.Qc2 again led to a good Sicilian for White. Clearly, ...a5 is much less effective than a3! 10...Nxd4 11.Bxd7+ Qxd7 12.cxd4 f5 13.d3 exd3 14.Qxd3±, Genov-Ozturk, Ankara 2010.

3.e3!

White is planning d2-d4 to gain more control over square d5. So Black will logically have to react with a quick ...d5, for otherwise he would end up with a backward pawn.

3.g3, to place a 'knife' on g2, always make sense in such structures: 3...♘c6 4.♗g2 f5 5.d3 g6 6.♘c3 ♗g7 7.b4 (7.♖b1±; 7.h4 h6 8.e4 d6 9.exf5 ♗xf5 10.♘d5 ♕d7 11.♘e2 ♘f6 was unclear in Kahn-Peredy, Budapest 1995) 7...d6 (7...cxb4 8.axb4 ♘xb4 9.♘b5±) 8.♖b1 with a pleasant edge for White.

Another logical option is 3.♘c3 ♘f6 4.e4! and then to organize the f4 pawn break.

3...♘f6 4.♘c3 ♘c6 5.♘f3 d5

Otherwise White will play d4, or ♕c2 and ♗d3, when Black is weak on the light squares.

6.cxd5 ♘xd5

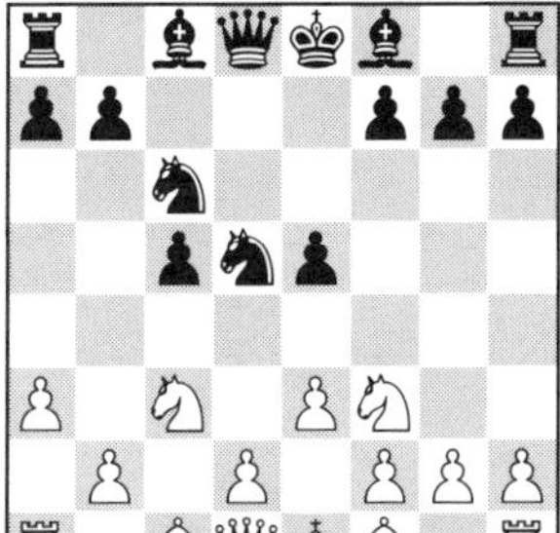

7.♕c2

Just like in the regular Sicilian where ...♕c7 is nearly always a good move. White is intending moves like ♘e4, ♗b5 or ♗d3, with excellent play.

7.♗b5 leads to a good Sicilian as well. Ideas as ...♘b4 are not possible here, and Black's centre is under pressure. (7...♘xc3 8.bxc3 ♗d6 9.0-0.)

7...♘xc3 8.bxc3

Also good is 8.dxc3 ♗d6 9.e4 0-0 10.♗c4 ♘a5 11.♗d5 c4 12.♗e3 ♕c7 13.♕e2 ♗d7 14.0-0 ♖ae8 15.♖ad1 ♗a4 16.♖de1 ♗c5 17.♘h4 and White held the initiative in Eljanov-Avrukh, Andorra 2003.

8...♗d6 9.♗c4 9.♗d3!? is playable too. **9...♕e7 10.♗d5** Placing the bishop on a dominating square. **10...♗e6 11.c4 f5 12.d3 0-0 13.♗b2**

13...♗xd5 Possibly Black should have preferred to keep the tension (and the structure). **14.cxd5 ♘d8 15.a4 ♖f6 16.e4 f4 17.♕c4 ♘f7 18.h4!? ♖g6 19.♔f1 h5 20.♗c3 ♖g4 21.♖b1** White has a pleasant edge. **21...♔f8 22.♖b5 ♖d8 23.a5 ♖d7 24.♕b3 ♔g8**

Black has everything defended for the moment, and it is not easy for White to break through. Kacheishvili now walks his king over to the queenside before engineering the g3-break on the kingside. It all takes a while, and I will only give a few light comments.

25.♕b2 ♖c7 26.♖g1 ♕d7 27.♕b3 ♕c8 28.♕c4 ♔h7 29.♔e2! ♖g6 30.♔d2 ♔h8 31.♔c2

The king is now out of the way. White is ready for the break.

31...♖g4 32.g3

32.♖bb1 was another useful move to make.

32...fxg3 33.fxg3 ♖g6 34.♖bb1 ♕h3 35.♕b5 ♖xg3?

Too greedy. White has a tactical refutation.

36.♕e8+ ♔h7 37.♖xg3 ♕xg3 38.♖f1?

White could win with 38.♘g5+! ♘xg5 39.♕xh5+ ♔g8 40.hxg5.

38...♕g2+?! 39.♘d2 ♘h6? 39...♖e7?. **40.♕xh5**

Material is equal, but White's structure is better and so are his pieces. White won on move 70.

CHAPTER 11

Alexander Finkel

Caro-Kann Advanced: an SOS Trend

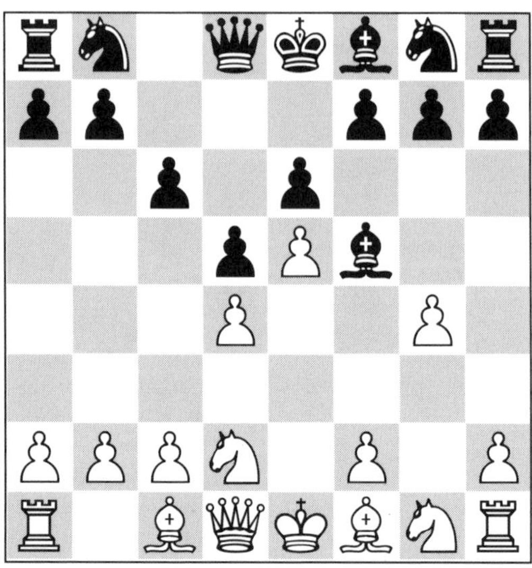

1.e4 c6 2.d4 d5 3.e5 ♗f5 4.♘d2 e6 5.g4!?

This chapter is dedicated to one of the latest trends in the Advance Variation of the Caro-Kann Defence.

I guess 'trend' isn't the right term to describe the state of affairs in the above-mentioned line, as we are definitely not talking about the mainstream variation. Although 4.♘d2 has been a legitimate and popular move against the Caro-Kann for quite some time, it has never been associated with aggressive kingside play by means of g4, followed by ♘ge2 and h4.

It's needless to mention that 4.♘c3 e6 5.g4 ♗g6 6.♘ge2 once enjoyed a tremendous popularity, but as the time passed Black succeeded to adjust to White's ultra-aggressive play in this line, so it slowly disappeared from tournament practice and was almost exclusively replaced by the less committal 4.♘f3.

The ideas behind 4.♘d2 e6 5.g4!? are obviously quite similar to those in the 4.♘c3 e6 5.g4 line, however the position of the knight on d2 affects the plans of both sides. Although White seems to waste an important tempo compared to the 4.♘c3 line (since he would need to move his knight once again to b3 in order to complete development), he clearly benefits from the possibility to cement his centre by c3 as well as a chance to hold on to the c5 pawn after a standard ...c5 break by Black. In other words, White gets a more solid and strategically more balanced version of the 4.♘c3 e6 5.g4 variation!

Since 5.g4!? has been re-introduced into practice by the Spanish grandmaster Francisco Vallejo back in 2009 (until that game it was never employed by a serious tournament player) we saw some strong players occasionally (and quite successfully) employ it, producing some sort of theoretical background for our article. Nevertheless, 4.♘d2 e6 5.g4 remains almost completely unexplored, so our readers get an excellent chance to shape the theory of this exciting variation!

□ **Francisco Vallejo**
■ **Anatoly Karpov**
San Sebastian (Donostia) 2009

1.e4 c6 2.d4 d5 3.e5 ♗f5 4.♘d2 e6 5.g4!?

Although 5.g4 has been tried before in a dozen games, Vallejo was the first one to employ it on the top level.

5...♗g6 6.♘e2

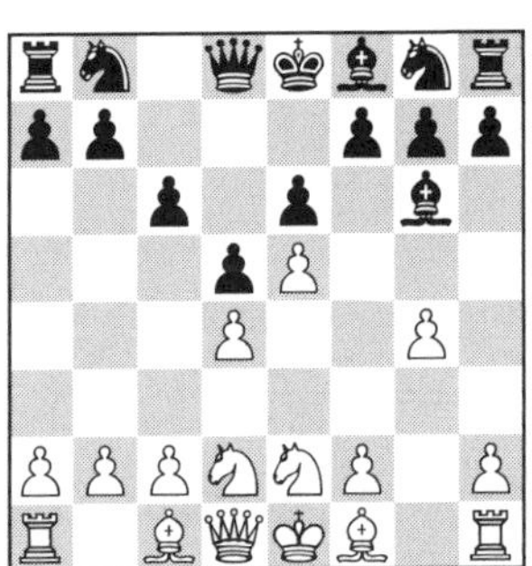

6...c5

The most natural and logical response, which is beyond any doubt the most crucial one to test the feasibility of White's set-up involving 4.♘d2 and 5.g4.

Worse is the other pawn break 6...f6?! 7.♘f4 ♗f7 8.♘f3 ♘d7 9.♕e2 fxe5 10.dxe5 ♗c5 11.♗d2 ♘e7 12.h4 h6 13.h5±, Vysochin-Csiszar, Ohrid 2009.

7.h4 h5

Karpov again opts for the most principled continuation. Another reasonable move is 7...h6, which is explored in-depth in the next game Vysochin-Bruchmann.

8.♘f4 ♗h7!

In a recent game between two strong Italian youngsters Black successfully tried 8...♘e7!?, which obviously caught White off-guard, as he reacted rather poorly with 9.gxh5?! (the right way to meet 8...♘e7 appears to be 9.♘xg6 ♘xg6 10.gxh5 ♘xh4 11.♕g4 ♘f5 12.dxc5 ♘c6 13.♘f3 ♗xc5 14.♗d3 with a minimal advantage) 9...♗f5 10.dxc5 ♕c7 11.♗b5+ ♘ec6 12.♘b3 ♗xc5 13.♕e2 ♗b6 and Black got an excellent position in Dvirnyy-Rombaldoni, Siena 2010, even though it was White who celebrated a victory at the end of the day.

9.♘xh5 cxd4 10.♘b3

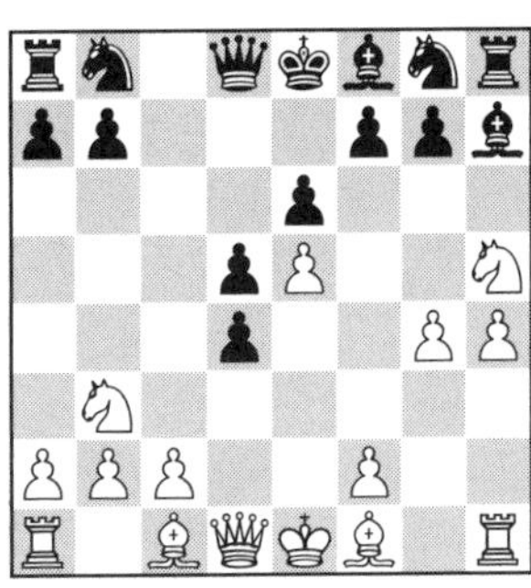

10...♘c6

Another reasonable option was 10...♕c7 11.♘xd4 ♕xe5+ (the greedy 11...♗b4+? fails to 12.c3 ♗xc3+ 13.bxc3 ♕xc3+ 14.♕d2 ♕xa1 15.♗b5+ ♘d7 16.0-0+–) 12.♗e3 (12.♗e2 ♘c6 13.♘b5? ♘b4!) 12...♘c6 13.♗b5 ♕c7 14.c3 ♘e7 15.f4 0-0-0, with a highly complicated struggle.

11.♘xd4 ♘ge7

The pawn on e5 is not going anywhere. The immediate 11...♘xe5 12.♗g5 ♕c7 13.♗b5+ ♘c6 14.c3 ♘e7 is quite similar to the game.

12.c3

Black has more than sufficient compensation for the pawn after 12.f4?! ♘xd4 13.♕xd4 ♘c6 14.♕f2 ♕a5+ 15.♗d2 ♕a4.

12...♘xe5 13.♗g5 ♘5c6 14.♗b5 ♖c8

14...♕c7 15.♕a4.

15.♕e2

All White's pieces have taken up very active positions, but Black has everything covered, while the strong pawn chain in the centre may become a formidable force. This is exactly the kind of position we treat as 'dynamic equality'!

15...♕d6 16.♖h3

Bringing another piece into play. The following line is very illustrative (even though not necessarily forced) to emphasize the hidden potential of Black's position: 16.0-0-0 a6 17.♗f4 ♕d7 18.♗xc6 ♘xc6 19.♘f5 f6 20.♘fxg7+ ♗xg7 21.♘xg7+ ♔f7 22.♘h5 ♘b4, and things get really messy.

16...a6

It's too early for the liberating 16...e5?!, as White seizes the initiative with 17.♘xc6 bxc6 18.♗a6 ♖b8 19.f4.

But the cunning 16...♗g6!? 17.♘f4 ♗e4 was worth the try: 18.♘d3 f6 19.♗e3 a6.

17.♗xc6+

Grabbing a pawn hardly promised White anything at all: 17.♗xe7 ♕xe7 18.♗xc6+ bxc6 19.♕xa6 ♕c7, with terrific compensation.

17...♘xc6 18.♖d1 ♘xd4 19.♖xd4

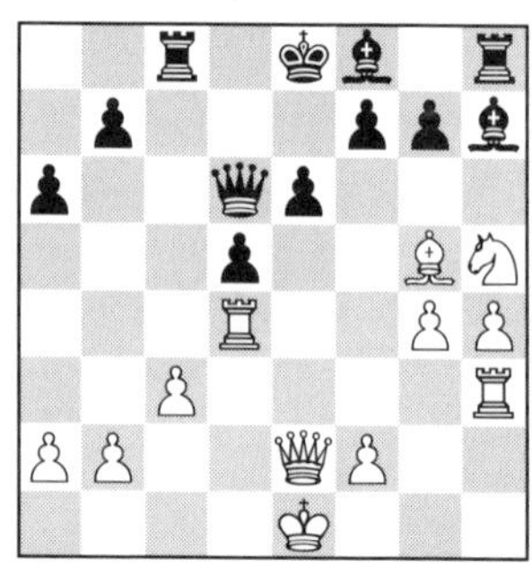

19...♗b1?

Black had two reasonable options at his disposal, but it's perfectly understandable why he wasn't too eager on entering the massive complications after 19...f6 20.♖e3 e5 (20...♔f7 21.♖f4 ♗e4 22.♘xf6 gxf6 23.♖xf6+ ♔g8 24.f3) 21.♗xf6 gxf6 22.♖xd5 ♕c6 23.g5 ♗e7 24.♘xf6+ ♗xf6 25.gxf6 ♔f7 26.♕h5+ ♗g6 27.♕xe5 ♖he8 and White has four pawns for the piece in an unclear position.

However, the solid 19...♗e4 20.♖e3 ♕h2 would've secured him at least equal chances in the forthcoming struggle.

20.♕d1!

A nasty move, which was probably overlooked by the former world champion.

20...♖xh5?!

It was better to admit his mistake and return to h7: 20...♗h7 21.♖e3 ♔d7 22.♗f4 ♕c5 23.♗e5, although White's pieces are dominating the field.

Instead, 20...♗e4 fails tactically to 21.♘xg7+! ♗xg7 22.♖xe4±.

21.gxh5 ♗f5 22.♖e3

Black does not have enough compensation for the exchange.

22...♕h2

22...♔d7 23.♗f4 ♕c6 24.♖g3±.

23.♕f3 ♗e4 24.♖exe4

Returning the exchange for a 'simple' position a pawn up.

24...dxe4 25.♕xe4 ♕c7 26.♔d1!?

White is just a pawn up, so in terms of top-level chess the rest is a matter of technique. But Karpov puts up tenacious resistance.

26...♗c5 27.♖d2 ♕c6 28.♕d3

It is not perfectly clear if White is winning after 28.♕xc6+ bxc6 29.h6 gxh6 30.♗xh6 ♔e7 31.b4 ♗b6 32.♗f4.

But after 28.♕g4! ♗f8 29.♕d4 it would be tougher for Black to organize his defence.

28...♗e7 29.♔c1

29.♗xe7!? ♔xe7 30.♕d4.

29...b5 30.a3 a5 31.♔b1 b4 32.cxb4 axb4 33.axb4 f5

White remains with a clear edge after 33...♕c1+ 34.♔a2 ♖a8+ 35.♔b3 ♕c6 36.b5 ♖b8 37.♗xe7 ♔xe7 38.♔b4.

34.♗xe7 ♔xe7 35.♖d1 ♕b7 36.b5 ♕c7 37.♕d2 ♖b8 38.♕g5+ ♔f8 39.h6 ♔g8

40.hxg7?!

40.♖d6! would have won on the spot.

40...♕c4 41.♖d8+ ♖xd8 42.♕xd8+ ♔xg7 43.♕d7+ ♔f6 44.♕c6

The queen ending is winning. I give the remainder without comments.

44...♕a4 45.♕c3+ ♔g6 46.♕d3 ♔h5 47.b6 ♕c6 48.♕d4 ♕b5 49.b4 e5 50.♕c5 ♕f1+ 51.♕c1 ♕d3+ 52.♔a2 f4 53.♕c5 ♔xh4 54.♕xe5 ♕c2+ 55.♔a3 ♕xf2 56.♕e7+ ♔g3 57.b7 ♕a7+ 58.♔b3 ♔f3 59.♕c7

1-0.

□ **Spartak Vysochin**
■ **Stephan Bruchmann**
Ohrid 2009

1.e4 c6 2.d4 d5 3.e5 ♗f5 4.♘d2 e6 5.g4 ♗g6 6.♘e2 c5 7.h4 h6!?

The main idea behind this move is not to keep the h-pawn, but to take under control the very important g5-square, which could be comfortably occupied by the white bishop in case of 7...h5!?.

8.♘f4 ♗h7 9.dxc5 ♗xc5

Although Black suffered a crushing defeat after 9...♘c6 things are not perfectly clear in that case too: 10.♘b3 ♕c7 11.♗b5 ♕xe5+ 12.♗e3 ♘f6 (12...♕xb2!?) 13.♕e2 ♗e7 (13...♕xb2) 14.0-0-0 ♘d7 15.♘h5 g5?! 16.hxg5 hxg5 17.♕d2±, Satyapragyan-Ismagambetov, Kolkata 2009.

10.♘b3

Less accurate is 10.♗b5+?! ♘c6 11.♘b3, allowing Black to flick in 11...♕b6!, after which White should be happy to keep the balance: 12.♗xc6+ ♕xc6 13.♘xc5 ♕xc5 14.c3 ♘e7 15.♘h5 ♗e4 (15...0-0!) 16.♖h3 0-0-0 17.♗e3 ♕c7 18.♗d4 (18.♘xg7 ♕xe5 19.♗d4 ♕d6 20.f3 ♗h7 is unclear) 18...♘c6 19.♕e2, ½-½ Boros-Böhnisch, Rijeka 2010.

10...♗b6 11.♗b5+ ♘c6 12.♘h5 ♔f8 13.♗xc6 bxc6 14.♗e3!

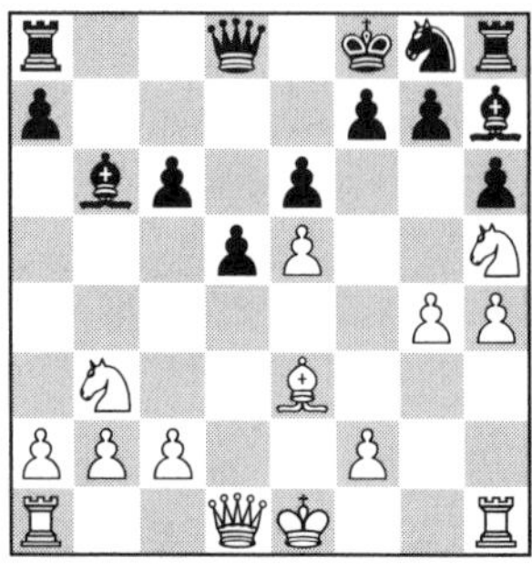

14...♗g6

Less convincing is 14...♗xe3?!, opening up the f-file for the white pieces: 15.fxe3 ♕b6 16.♕d2 a5 17.0-0 (17.♖f1!?) 17... ♘e7 18.♕f2 ♗g6 19.♘f4 ♔g8 20.♘d4 ♔h7 (20...♖a7 21.h5 ♗e4 22.♘fe2 ♘c8 23.♘c3±) 21.♘xg6 ♘xg6 22.♕xf7 ♘xe5 23.♕xe6 ♖he8 24.♕f5+ ♔h8 25.b3±, Bentivegna-Dziuba, Bratto 2010.

Black could consider 14...♕e7!?.

15.♘f4 ♗e4!

Black comes up with an excellent defensive idea, sufficient for equality.

15...♘e7 16.♘c5 ♔g8 17.h5 ♗h7 18.♕d2 ♘c8 19.0-0-0 ♗xc5 20.♗xc5 ♘b6 21.♘e2±.

16.♖h2 h5! 17.♘c5

White doesn't have a choice but to allow ...hxg4, as after 17.g5 or 17.gxh5 the black knight would get a fantastic outpost on f5.

17...♕e7 18.♘xe4 dxe4 19.♗xb6 axb6

19...♕b4+ 20.♕d2 ♕xb6 21.0-0-0 hxg4 22.h5 favours White, who is intending 22...g5? 23.hxg6! ♖xh2 24.♘xe6+ fxe6 25.♕f4+.

20.♕d4 ♖d8 21.♕xe4 hxg4 22.♘d3 ♕a7!?

The pawn on c6 is worth a couple of tempi, essential to consolidate Black's position.

Unclear is 22...c5 23.0-0-0 ♖d4.

23.♕xc6 ♘e7 24.♕c4 ♕a5+ 25.c3

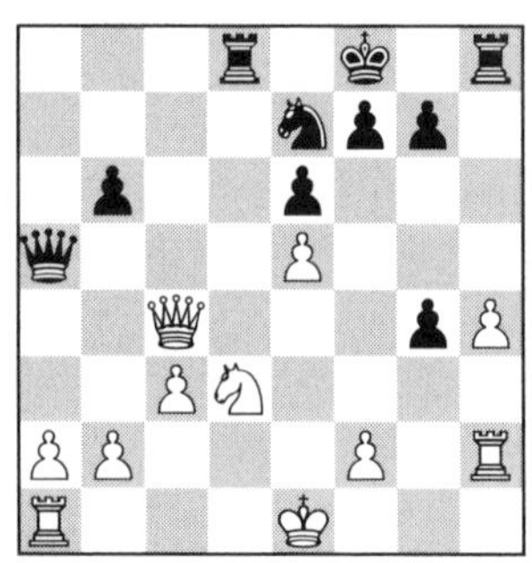

25...g6?!

Thus far Black's play was just about perfect, but he goes astray just one step from liquidating into the comfortable endgame arising after 25...♕d5! 26.♕xd5 ♖xd5 27.0-0-0 ♖h5 28.♔c2 ♘g6 and it is White who has to be careful to keep the balance.

26.0-0-0 ♔g7 27.♔b1 ♖d5?! 27...♖a8 28.a3 ♕a4±. **28.♕xg4**

White is just two pawns up, while Black's play on the queenside can be easily neutralized.

28...♖hd8 29.♖h3 ♘c6 30.f4 ♕a4

31.♕f3?

A rather silly mistake, which could've turned things around had Black found a nice attacking resource on the 35th move: 31.♕e2 ♖a8 32.b3 ♕a5 33.h5+–.

31...♖a8! 32.a3 ♕b3 33.♖hh1 ♖ad8?

Refusing to take the gift generously offered by White a couple of moves ago: 33...♖xa3! 34.h5 ♕a2+ 35.♔c2 (35.♔c1 ♖xc3+ 36.bxc3 ♖b5–+)

35...♖xc3+!! (this nice move was missed by both sides in their calculations) 36.♔xc3 ♕a5+ 37.♘b4 (37.b4 ♘xb4!–+) 37...♖c5+ 38.♔d2 ♕xb4+∓.

34.h5

Now it's all over.

34...♘a5 35.hxg6 ♘c4 36.♕g2 fxg6 37.♖dg1 ♘xa3+ 38.♔c1 ♕c2+ 39.♕xc2 ♘xc2 40.f5! ♖xd3 41.f6+ ♔f8 42.♖h8+ ♔f7 43.♖h7+ ♔f8 44.♖xg6

1-0.

□ **Daniele Vocaturo**
■ **Nazi Paikidze**
Moscow Aeroflot 2011

1.e4 c6 2.d4 d5 3.e5 ♗f5 4.♘d2 e6 5.g4 ♗g6 6.♘e2 ♘e7!?

Another possible way to meet 5.g4: Black prefers to carefully prepare the advance of the c-pawn rather than to enter the complications inevitably arising after 6...c5. I believe White should be able to get the upper hand after the text-move, but it is by no means trivial.

7.♘f4

Not 7.♘g3 c5 8.♗b5+ ♘ec6 9.f4 h6 10.f5 ♗h7 11.0-0 ♕b6 12.♕e2 cxd4 13.♗d3 ♘d7∓, Agrinsky-A.Lundin, Moscow 1998.

7...h5

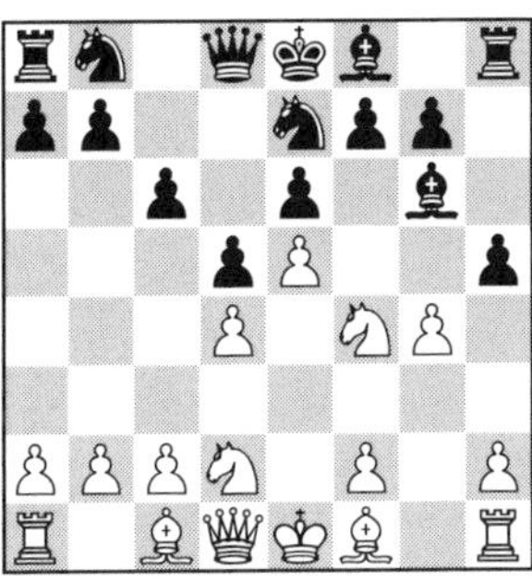

8.gxh5?!

I don't particularly like this capture, letting Black comfortably develop his pieces prior to performing the typical ...c5 break.

The right way to meet 6...♘e7 followed by 7...h5 is once again 8.♘xg6!? ♘xg6 9.gxh5 ♘f4 and now:

– Unclear is 10.h6!? g6 11.♘b3 ♗xh6 12.♕f3 ♘h5 13.♗xh6 ♖xh6 14.♕e3 ♖h7 15.0-0-0 ♘d7, but

– 10.c3 ♘xh5 (10...♕h4 11.♘f3 ♕g4 12.♖g1 ♕f5 13.♘g5) 11.♘f3 (intending to put pressure on f7) 11...c5 (11...♕b6 12.♘g5 c5 13.♕f3 ♕c7 14.♗e3 cxd4 15.cxd4 ♗b4+ 16.♔d1 with a dangerous initiative) 12.♕a4+ ♘c6 13.♗e3 ♕b6 14.0-0-0 leads to a somewhat better position for White.

8...♗f5 9.♘b3 ♘d7 10.♗e3 ♕c7 11.♕d2

An attempt to prevent ...c5 by 11.♘d3 would run into 11...♗e4 12.f3 ♗xd3

13.♕xd3 ♘f5, with a comfortable position for Black.

11...a6

Perhaps Black could gain a tempo by pushing ...c5 right away, but I don't think it's any better than the move in the game: 11...c5!? 12.♘xc5 ♘xc5 13.dxc5 ♕xe5 14.♗b5+ ♘c6 15.0-0-0 (15.♗xc6+ bxc6 16.0-0-0 ♗e4 17.♖hg1 ♕c7∓) 15...♕c7 with counterplay.

12.0-0-0

The knight on b3 is misplaced if White decides to push 12.c4?!, so Black gets a very comfortable position: 12...dxc4 13.♗xc4 0-0-0 14.♕e2 (14.0-0-0? ♘xe5) 14...♘b6 15.♗d3 ♗xd3 16.♘xd3 ♘f5.

12...c5 13.♘xc5

It makes perfect sense to trade the knights. 13.dxc5 ♘xe5 14.♘d4 ♘g4∓.

13...♘xc5 14.dxc5 ♘c6 15.♗d3

An interesting possibility was 15.h6!? g6 (15...♖xh6 16.♘d3 ♖h8 17.f4±) 16.♘d3 ♗xd3 17.♗xd3 ♘xe5 18.h4 ♗xc5 19.h5.

15...♕xe5

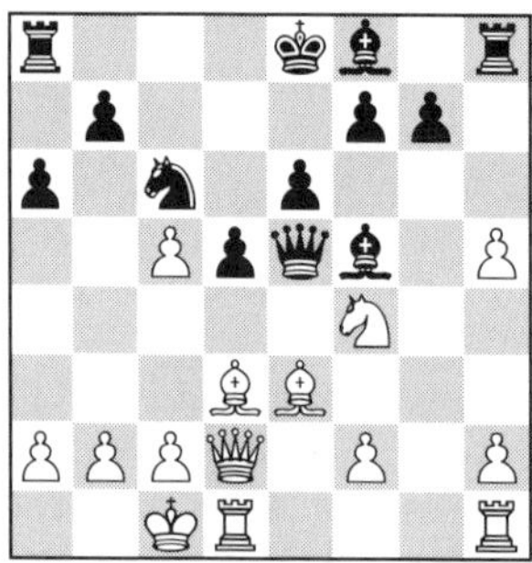

It is clear that Black has successfully solved the opening problems.

16.♖he1 0-0-0 17.♗xf5?!

Play is unclear after 17.c3!? ♗g4 18.♗e2 ♗xe2 19.♖xe2 (19.♕xe2 ♗xc5 20.♕g4 ♗xe3+ 21.♖xe3 ♕c7∓) 19...♕f6 20.♕c2.

17...♕xf5 18.♘e2 e5

Or simply 18...♕xh5!? 19.♘d4 ♘xd4 20.♗xd4 ♕xh2∓.

19.♘g3 ♕e6?!

Better is 19...♕f3∓.

20.c3 d4!?

Objectively White should be better after this move, but it requires very precise play to prove this. Normal was 20...♗e7.

21.cxd4 exd4 22.♗g5 ♕xa2 23.♗xd8 ♗xc5 24.♕c2 ♗b4

Up to this point none of the sides could've deviated from the forced line which was initiated by 20...d4!?.

25.♗b6?!

Giving away the chance to fight for a win after 25.♗e7!.

White would find himself under a very dangerous attack after 25.♗g5?! ♔b8 26.♖d2 ♖c8 27.♗f4+ ♔a7 28.♔d1 ♕a1+ 29.♔e2 ♖e8+ 30.♘e4 ♕a5.

But after the correct 25.♗e7! ♔b8 (25...♕a1+ 26.♕b1 ♕xb1+ 27.♔xb1 ♗xe7 28.♖e4±) 26.♗xb4 ♘xb4 27.♕b1 ♕a5! 28.♔d2 d3 29.♖e3 ♖c8 30.♔e1 Black's defensive task would be quite difficult.

25...♔b8 26.♕b1 ♕c4+ 27.♕c2 ♕a2 28.♘e4

Trying to squeeze something out of the position by avoiding the repetition with 28.♕b1.

28...♖c8 29.♘c5

Here 29.Nc3 leads to a draw after 29...dxc3 30.bxc3 Ba3+ (30...Qa3+ 31.Qb2 Qxc3+ 32.Qxc3 Bxc3 33.Re4±) 31.Kd2 Qd5+ 32.Qd3 Qa2+.

29...Bxc5

30.Qxc5??

Throwing away a well-played game.

It was necessary to take the draw after 30.Bxc5 Nb4 31.Bd6+ Ka7 32.Bc5+ (32.Qxc8 Qa1+ 33.Kd2 Qxb2+–+) 32...Kb8 (32...Ka8 33.Re8 Rxe8 34.Bxb4) 33.Bd6+=.

30...Qa1+ 31.Kd2 Qxb2+ 32.Qc2

32.Kd3 Nb4+ 33.Ke4 Rxc5 34.Bxc5 Qc2+–+.

32...Qxb6 33.Qf5?!

Better was 33.Rb1.

33...Qb2+ 34.Qc2 Qb4+ 35.Ke2 Ne5 36.Qe4 Qb5+

0-1

□ **Milos Perunovic**

■ **Bojan Vuckovic**

Vrnjacka Banja 2010

1.e4 c6 2.d4 d5 3.e5 Bf5 4.Nd2 e6 5.g4 Bg6 6.Ne2 Qb6?!

Although this move has a full right to exist it's clearly inferior to 6...c5 or 6...Ne7.

7.Nb3

This move is clearly better than the passive 7.c3?! c5 8.Nb3 Nc6 9.dxc5 Bxc5 10.Nxc5 Qxc5 11.Be3 Qa5 12.Bd4 Nge7=, Dmitriev-Sapis, Polanica Zdroj 1994.

But White could try to take advantage of the early 6...Qb6 by 7.c4!? Nd7 8.c5 Qc7 (8...Nxc5 9.dxc5 Bxc5 10.Qb3 Bxf2+ 11.Kd1∞) 9.Nf4 Ne7 (9...b6?! 10.h4 bxc5 11.h5 Be4 12.f3 cxd4 13.fxe4 Qxe5 14.Nd3 Qg3+ 15.Nf2±) 10.h4 h6 11.Nxg6 Nxg6 12.h5 Ne7 13.Rb1, with a very comfortable advantage.

7...Nd7 8.Be3 h5?! 8...c5!?. **9.Nf4 Be4 10.f3 Bh7 11.Qe2** 11.Nxh5 Nxe5. **11...hxg4 12.fxg4 a5! 13.a4** 13.c3 a4 14.Nc1 c5 15.Bg2 a3∓. **13...Be4** 13...Bb4+!?. **14.Bg2 Bxg2 15.Nxg2 c5**

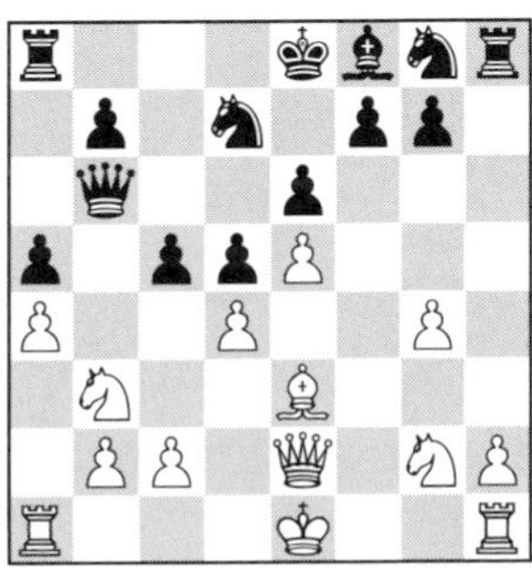

16.0-0

White's forces are much better mobilized, so once the position opens up Black's king would be in serious danger. Therefore serious consideration deserves 16.dxc5!? Qc7 (16...Nxc5?! 17.0-0↑) 17.Rf1 (17.0-0-0 Bxc5 18.Nxc5 Nxc5 19.Bxc5 Qxc5 20.Nf4 Ne7) 17...Qxe5 18.Qf2 Ngf6 19.0-0-0.

16...c4 17.Nd2 f6

Perhaps 17...Nh6!?, but dangerous is 17...Qxb2 18.Qf3 f6 19.Nf4 Qb6 20.Rae1.

18.b3!? 18.exf6 gxf6 19.Nf4 Bd6 20.b3 cxb3 21.Rab1±. **18...cxb3 19.c4 fxe5**

20.cxd5

20.dxe5 ♗c5 21.cxd5 exd5 would just transpose to the game.

20...exd5 21.dxe5 ♗c5 22.♖ab1 b2 23.♘f3 ♘e7 24.♖xb2 ♕a6

25.e6?!

It was just about time to seal the advantage by 25.♕xa6 ♖xa6 26.♖xb7 ♗xe3+ 27.♘xe3, enjoying an extra pawn in the endgame.

25...♕xe6 26.♘g5 ♕e5 27.♘f3 ♕e6 28.♗xc5 ♕xe2 29.♖xe2 ♘xc5 30.♘g5 b6

30...♔d7 31.♖f7 ♖he8 32.♘f4 ♔d6 33.♖xg7 ♖ac8 34.h4±.

31.♖f7

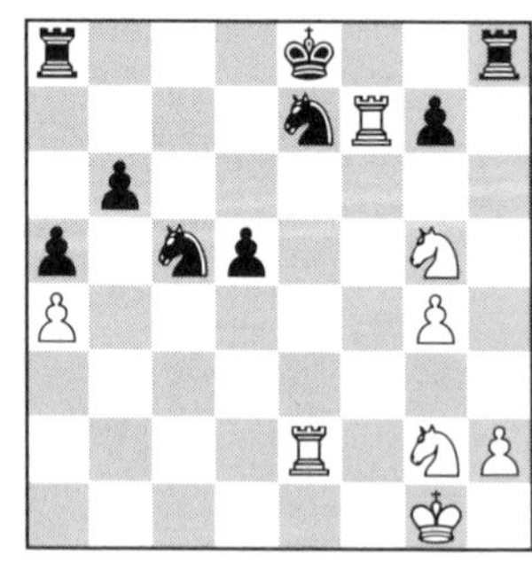

31...♘e4?

It was necessary to take care of the seventh rank by 31...♖a7, with excellent chances to hold the position: 32.♘e3 (32.♖xg7 d4 33.♘f4 d3 34.♖d2 ♖d7 unclear) 32...♘e6 33.♘xd5 ♘xg5 34.♖fxe7+ ♖xe7 35.♖xe7+ ♔f8 36.♖b7 ♖h4±.

32.♖xg7 ♘xg5

32...♔f8 33.♘e6+ ♔e8 34.♘gf4+–.

33.♖exe7+ ♔f8 34.h4 ♘f3+

A bit more stubborn was 34...♘e6, but White wins quite easily with 35.♖gf7+ ♔g8 36.g5.

35.♔f2 ♘xh4 36.♘f4 ♖h6 37.♖ef7+ ♔e8 38.♘xd5 ♖c8 39.♘f6+ ♖xf6+ 40.♖xf6

1-0.

CHAPTER 12

Matthieu Cornette

Grünfeld Fianchetto: a New Idea

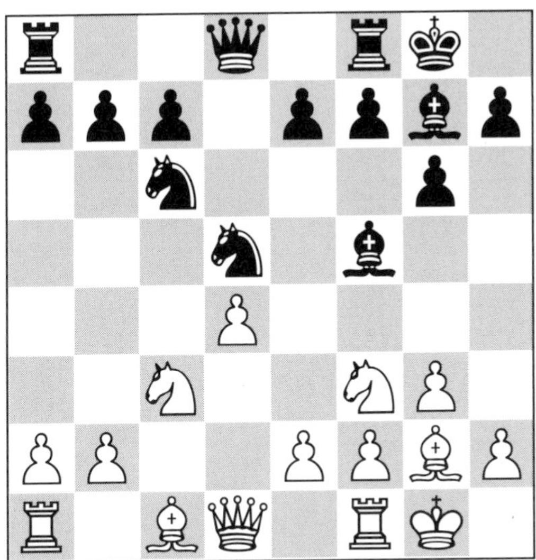

Avoiding the main line with 8...♗f5!?

1.d4 ♘f6 2.c4 g6 3.♘f3 ♗g7 4.g3

Many players like to play a fianchetto against the King's Indian or the Grünfeld Defence.

4...0-0 5.♗g2 d5 6.cxd5 ♘xd5 7.0-0 ♘c6

A 'tricky move' according to Boris Avrukh in his *1.d4 – Volume Two* (Quality Chess, 2010). However after 8.♘c3, apart from mentioning that 8... ♘b6 9.e3 leads to the absolute main line, he only considers 8... ♘xc3 and 8...♗e6. We have a surprise up our sleeve!

8.♘c3 ♗f5!?

Here we are! In my database, there are only 17 games with this 'malicious' bishop move, with a very decent score (=6 –6 +5). I began to play this variation in 2010, with good results. The first time I saw this move was in the game Meier-Vachier-Lagrave (see Game 1). I was very impressed with how easily Black equalized, and I decided to study it.

The main idea is to prevent White's e4. By waiting before he moves his knight from d5 Black keeps the options open between ...♘b4, aiming for the c2 square, and ...♘xc3 followed by ...♘a5 and ...c5 or of course ...♘b6.

The main line is 8...♘b6 and after 9.e3 ♖e8 theory is very complicated, and in constant progress. Everyone remembers Grischuk's dramatic loss in the final game of his World Candidates' match against Gelfand.

I'll analyse three games for you: the first one with the main line 9.♖e1, in the second one we'll see the lines in which White moves ♘f3, and the last one will cover the other moves.

In conclusion: I really think this variation is a perfectly valid alternative to the main line. The resulting positions are in pure Grünfeld style: unclear and very interesting.

□ **Georg Meier**
■ **Maxime Vachier-Lagrave**
France tt 2010

1.♘f3 ♘f6 2.c4 g6 3.♘c3 d5 4.cxd5 ♘xd5 5.g3 ♗g7 6.♗g2 0-0 7.0-0 ♘c6 8.d4 ♗f5!?

I perfectly remember this game, I was playing next to them and when I saw this move I was very curious to see what would happen next.

9.♖e1

The most common move. White wants to play e4.

9...♘xc3

The normal move, as 9...♘db4?! is no good after 10.e4 ♗g4 11.a3 ♘a6 12.e5!N (12.h3? Musaeva-Breslavskaya, Nikolaev 2000) 12...♗xf3 13.♗xf3 ♕xd4 14.♕xd4 ♘xd4 15.♗xb7 ♖ab8 16.♗xa6 ♘f3+ 17.♔f1 ♘xe1 18.♔xe1 ♗xe5 19.♔d2 ♖fd8+ 20.♔c2±.

I propose the novelty 9...♕d7! The main idea is to avoid the 11.♘g5 line below:

● 10.♘a4!? – the critical move for the evaluation of this novelty: 10...♘db4! 11.♘c5 ♕c8 12.e4 (12.d5 b6! – a very important reaction – 13.♘b3 – after 13.e4 ♗g4 14.♘d3 ♗xf3 15.♗xf3 ♘xd3 16.♕xd3 ♘e5 Black has equalized – 13... ♗c2 14.♕d2 ♖d8 15.e4 ♗xb3 16.axb3 e6! with a very sharp position) 12...♗g4 13.a3! ♘xd4! 14.axb4 ♖d8 15.♘d3! ♕d7 – the critical position:

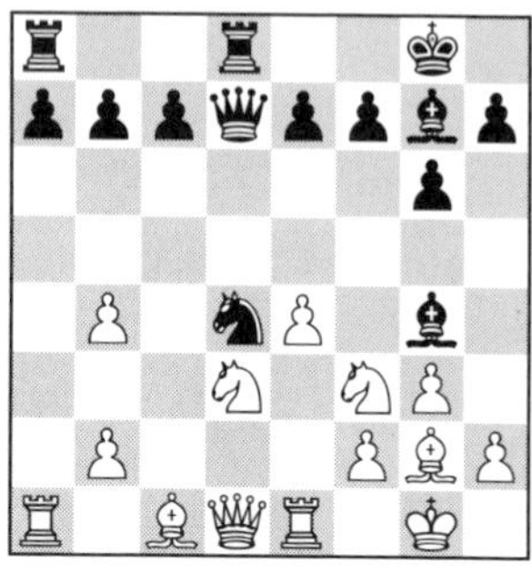

– 16.e5 ♘xf3+ 17.♗xf3 ♗xf3 18.♕xf3 ♕xd3 19.♕xb7 ♕d4! and I think the position is approximatively equal.

– 16.♖a3 ♘b5! 17.h3! (17.♖a5 b6! 18.♖xb5 ♕xb5 19.♗f1 a5; 17.♖b3 ♘d4 and the rook must come back to a3) 17...♘xa3 18.hxg4. Here Black has a choice. The computer likes both: 18...♕xd3 19.♕xd3 ♖xd3 20.bxa3 a5 and 18...♘b5 19.♗f1 ♕xg4 20.♕a4 c6.

– After 16.♖e3 ♗h6! White has nothing better than to return the rook to e1.

● 10.♘xd5 ♕xd5 brings White nothing.

● 10.♘g5 ♘db4!. A very strong move because now e4 isn't possible. The d4-pawn is under attack and the c2-square is very weak: 11.d5 (11.e4?! ♗g4!) 11...♘e5 (11...

♘d4!?) 12.♖f1 h6 13.♘ge4 c6 and the position is very unclear.

● 10.e4 is the most logical move, transposing to the game after 10...♘xc3 11.bxc3 ♗g4.

● 10.♘h4 ♗e6 11.e4 ♘xc3 12.bxc3 ♘a5 with a very decent position.

10.bxc3

10...♕d7

10...♗e4 was played twice. It's logical to prevent e4 but I don't think this is enough to equalize: 11.♗f1! (White is now threatening ♘g5 followed by e4. 11.e3 ♘a5 12.♘d2 ♗xg2 13.♔xg2 c5=, Poulsson-Zwaig, Oslo 1973) 11...♘a5 (11...e5 12.♘d2 ♗f5 13.d5! ♘a5 14.e4 ♗d7 15.♗a3 ♖e8 16.♗b4±) 12.♘g5N (12.♘d2!? ♗c6 13.e4 b6±, Burne-Andreassen, ICCF email 2007) 12...♗c6 13.e4 and I prefer White in this position.

11.e4

● 11.♗f4 and now: 11...♗e4 12.♗f1 (12.♘e5 gives nothing: 12...♗xe5 13.dxe5 ♕xd1 14.♖exd1 ♗xg2 15.♔xg2 ♖fd8 16.♖ab1 b6 17.♔f3 ♔g7=) 12...♘a5 (12...e5!? is also possible: 13.dxe5 ♕xd1 14.♖axd1 h6 15.h4 ♖fe8 16.♗g2 ♖e7 17.e3 ♖b8 18.♖e2 ♗xf3 19.♗xf3 ♘xe5=) 13.♘d2!? (13.♘g5 ♗d5 14.e4 ♗c4 15.♗h3 e6 with a very complicated position) 13...♗f5 14.e4 ♗g4 15.♕c2 b6 and I think Black is OK even if the most difficult is coming.

● 11.♘g5! is a very strong novelty. It's because of this move that I searched and found 9...♕d7! as mentioned above.

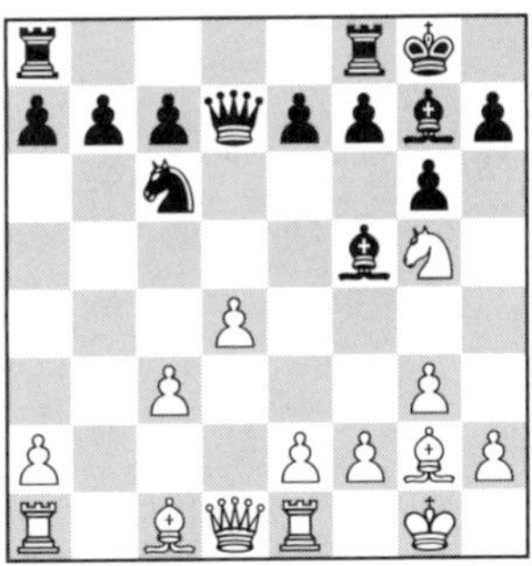

Now the computer recommends 11...♘xd4 but I don't really believe in it: 12.cxd4 ♕xd4 13.♗a3 ♕xa1 14.♕xa1 ♗xa1 15.♖xa1 c6 16.e4 ♗c8 17.e5 ♖e8 18.♖b1 a5 19.f4 a4 20.♔f2 I think this endgame is very unpleasant for Black.

11...♕c8 looks too ugly: 12.♕b3 h6 13.♘f3±.

So, after 11...h6 12.e4! the critical position is reached. I failed to find an easy way to equalize:

– 12...hxg5 13.exf5 ♕xf5 14.♗a3 (14.♕b3 ♖ab8 15.♗e4 ♕f6 16.♗a3 ♖fc8 17.♖ad1 e6 18.♕a4 ♗f8) 14...♖ab8 15.♖b1 ♗f6 16.♕e2 (threatening 17.♖b5) 16...a6 17.♖b2. A critical position. I think the position is unclear but even with a pawn up, Black's position is dangerous because of the activity of White's bishop pair.

– after 12...♗g4 13.f3 ♗h5 14.♘h3 g5 15.g4 ♗g6 16.f4 I really don't like Black's position.

● Black has counterplay after 11.♕b3 b6 12.♘g5 h6 13.e4 ♘a5 14.♕d1 (14.♕b4 ♗g4 15.h3 hxg5 16.hxg4 e5) 14...♗g4 15.f3 ♗h5 16.g4 ♗xg4 17.fxg4 hxg5 18.e5 ♖ad8 19.♗xg5 c5.

11...♗g4 12.♕b3

12.♖b1 doesn't seem very clever, because Black wants to play ...♘a5 anyway.

12.♗e3 ♘a5 13.♕d3 c5! (thematic) 14.d5 b6 15.♘d2 ♖ad8 is unclear. Black can play ...f5 sometimes or simply ...♕a4.

12...b6

13.♕d5

This move is a confession of failure, but other moves also fail to impress:

– 13.♗f4 ♗xf3 (13...♘a5 followed by ...c5 is even simpler) 14.♗xf3 e5! 15.dxe5 ♘xe5 16.♗e2 ♕h3 17.♖ad1 ♘g4 18.♗xg4 ♕xg4 is equal.

– 13.♘g5 ♘a5 14.♕c2 h6 15.h3 (15.♘f3 ♖fd8 followed by ...c5) 15...hxg5 16.hxg4 e5! (16...♕xg4 17.e5 ♖ad8 18.♖e4±) 17.♕d1! (17.d5 ♕xg4; 17.♗xg5 ♕xg4 18.♗e3 ♘c4=) 17...♖ac8! (17...exd4 18.e5 ♖ad8 19.♗xg5±) 18.d5 c6 19.♗xg5 (19. d6?! ♗f6 and the pawn on d6 is too weak; 19.dxc6 ♕e7!=) 19...cxd5 20.exd5 ♖xc3 with a balanced position.

– After 13.♗e3 ♘a5 (13...e5!?) 14.♕b4 ♖ac8 (after the sacrifice 14...c5 15.dxc5 ♘c6 16.♕a3 ♖fd8 even the computer likes Black's position) 15.♖ad1 (15.♘e5 ♗xe5 16.dxe5 c5∓) 15...♖fd8 16.♖d2 ♕e8 I really like Black's position. He can opt for ...c5 or ...e5.

13...♖fd8 14.♕xd7 ♗xd7 15.e5 ♘a5

Black has nothing to worry about. **16.♗a3** 16.♘g5 ♖ac8 17.e6 fxe6 18.♘xe6 ♗xe6 19.♖xe6 c5! is also equal. **16...c5**

Draw.

□ **Levan Pantsulaia**
■ **Matthieu Cornette**
Cappelle-la-Grande 2011

1.♘f3 ♘f6 2.g3 g6 3.♗g2 ♗g7 4.0-0 0-0 5.c4 d5 6.cxd5 ♘xd5 7.d4 ♘c6 8.♘c3 ♗f5 9.♘g5

A very aggressive approach. Even if at the time this move was a novelty, I was prepared. Other knight moves are:

● 9.♘d2 is an interesting idea from the young grandmaster Rodshtein.

9...♘db4 is the sharpest move, and now:

– 10.e4 ♗c8 11.d5 ♘d4

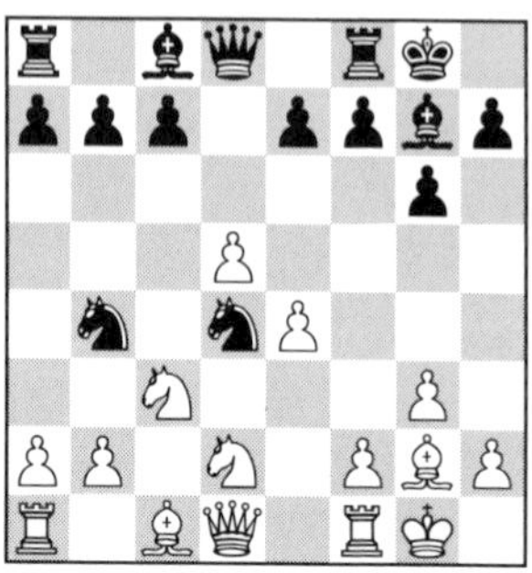

(a very strange position) 12.♘b3 ♘bc2 13.♘xd4 (13.♖b1 ♘xb3 14.axb3 ♘b4 15.♗g5 a5= followed by ...b6 and ...♗a6) 13...♘xd4 14.♗e3 e5 (14...c5!?) 15.dxe6 (15.f4 c5=) 15...♗xe6 followed by ...c6 or ...c5 with even chances.

– 10.e3 ♗c2 11.♕f3 e5! 12.d5 e4! 13.♘dxe4 ♘e5 and Black has the d3-square.

– 10.d5 ♗c2 11.♕e1 ♘d4 12.a3 ♘a6 13.b4 (13.e3 ♘b3 14.♘xb3 ♗xb3 15.♕e2 ♕d7 16.e4 ♘c5=) 13...♗f5 14.♖a2 ♘c2 15.♕d1 ♗xc3 16.♖xc2 ♗xc2 17.♕xc2 ♗g7 White has some compensation for the exchange.

Instead 9...♘b6 10.e4 ♗d7 11.♘b3 ♕c8 12.♗g5 h6 13.♗e3 ♗h3 14.♕e2 ♗xg2 15.♔xg2 ♖d8 16.♖ad1 was somewhat better for White, Rodshtein-Zhou Jianchao, Moscow 2011. Likewise, 9...♘f6 doesn't seem logical to me: 10.♘b3±.

However, 9...♘xc3!? is another possibility 10.bxc3 ♕d7!? and now crucial is 11.e4 ♗g4 12.f3 (12.♕c2 ♘a5 followed by ...c5 as usual) 12...♗xd4+! (the point) 13.cxd4 ♕xd4+ 14.♖f2 ♕xa1 15.♘b3 ♕b1 16.fxg4 ♖ad8 with a very unclear position. While after 11.♘e4 ♕e8! and 11.♖e1 ♗h3 12.♗h1 e5! I don't think Black's position is inferior.

● 9.♘e1 was played by Gelfand against Mamedyarov and then by Mamedyarov with white! 9...♗e6 and now:

– 10.e3 ♘xc3 11.bxc3 ♗d5 12.♗xd5 (12.♕c2 ♗xg2 13.♘xg2 ♘a5= followed by ...c5) 12...♕xd5 13.♕b3 ♖fd8 14.♘d3 (14.♕xd5 ♖xd5 is nothing) 14...b6 15.♕xd5 ♖xd5 16.c4?! ♖a5 17.a4 e5∓, Gelfand-Mamedyarov, Astrakhan 2010.

– 10.♘c2 ♘xc3 11.bxc3 ♘a5 12.e4 ♕d7 13.♗f4 and now 13…c6!? is the simplest way to equalize. The next move is 14...♘c4. Mamedyarov-Vachier-Lagrave, Moscow 2010, instead continued 13...♖ac8 14.h4 (14.♘e3 ♘c4 15.d5 ♘xe3 16.♗xe3 ♗g4 17.f3 ♗h3=) 14...♗g4 15.♗f3 ♗h3 16.♖e1 c5 with unclear play.

– 10.e4 ♘xc3 11.bxc3 ♗c4 12.♘d3 ♘xd4! 13.cxd4 ♕xd4 14.♘b2 ♗xf1 15.♕xf1 ♖ad8 followed by ...b6 and ...c5.

● 9.♘h4 is not so impressive but looks more logical to me than 9.♘e1: 9...♗e6 (logical) 10.e4 ♘xc3 11.bxc3 ♘a5 (as always) and now:

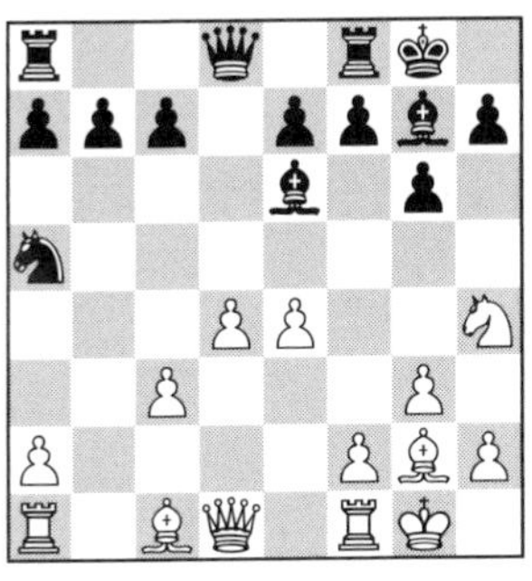

– 12.♘f3 c5 13.d5 ♗d7!? (13...♗g4) 14.♕d3 (after 14.e5 ♗b5 15.♖e1 ♗c4 Black's position is good because the d5 pawn is weak. 14.♕c2 ♘c4 15.♗f4 ♕a5) 14...b5 15.♗f4 ♘c4 leads to a very unclear position.

– 12.e5 ♗d5 13.♗xd5 ♕xd5 14.♗a3 (14.♕f3 c6=) 14...♖fe8 15.♘g2 ♘c4 16.♘e3 (16.♘f4 ♕c6 followed by ...e6) 16...♘xe3 17.fxe3 f6! (Black has no problem at all) 18.♕d3 fxe5 19.e4 ♕d7 20.d5 e6 draw, Zhou Jianchao-Vachier Lagrave, Moscow 2010.

– After 12.d5 ♗d7 13.♕d3 c6! (the thematic break) 14.♗g5 cxd5 15.exd5 h6 16.♗e3 (16.♗d2 ♖c8∓) 16...♕c7 17.♖ac1 ♖ac8 18.♗d4 e5! 19.dxe6 ♗xe6 the position is still about equal but White has to be accurate to keep the balance.

9...♘xc3 10.bxc3 ♘a5

10...h6?! 11.♘e4 followed by ...♘c5

11.e4

11.♗f4 h6 12.♘e4 b6 13.♘d2 ♖c8 14.e4 ♗e6 with an unclear position. There will follow ...♕d7 and Black will have the choice between ...c6 and ...c5.

11.♕a4 c5! followed by ...♗d7 and ...♖c8.

11...♗d7

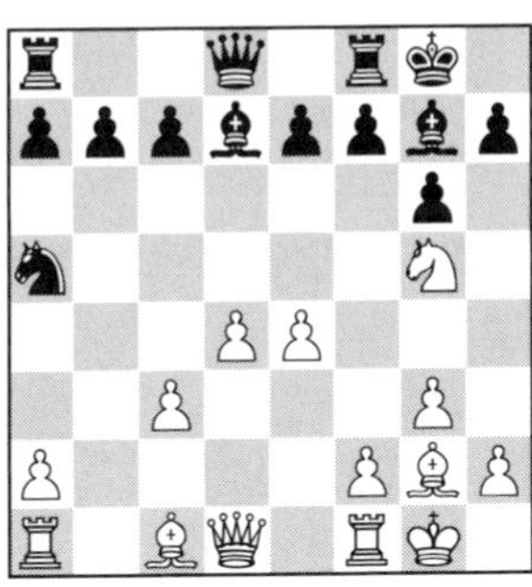

12.e5

– 12.♖b1 c5 13.e5 (13.dxc5 ♕c8 14.♗e3 h6 15.♘f3 ♘c4 16.♕d3 ♘xe3 17.♕xe3 b6! is thematic, Black seizes the initiative; 13.♖e1 ♖c8; 13.d5 b5!) 13...cxd4 14.cxd4 h6 15.♘e4 (15.♘f3 ♗e6=) 15...b6 16.♗e3 ♖c8 (16...♗e6? would now be a mistake because of 17.d5!) followed by ...♗c6 or ...♗e6 is equal.

– 12.♗f4 c5 13.e5 h6 14.♘e4 cxd4 15.cxd4 ♖c8 16.♖c1 (after 16.d5 g5 the e5 pawn is very weak) 16...b6 17.♕e2 ♗e6 18.♖xc8 ♕xc8 19.♖c1 ♕d7 20.d5!? ♗xd5 21.♖d1 ♗c4 22.♖xd7 ♗xe2=.

– 12.♕e2 c5 13.♗e3 a6 14.♖fc1 h6 15.♘f3 ♗b5 followed by ...♘c4.

12...c5 13.♖e1 cxd4

Not 13...h6?! 14.e6! hxg5 15.exd7 ♕xd7 16.♗xg5±.

14.cxd4 ♖c8 I think the position is balanced. **15.h4**

15.e6 gives White nothing: 15...♗xe6 16.♘xe6 fxe6.

15...♖c4!?

With the idea to sac an exchange! Instead, 15...♗f5 was the most logical move, when Black has no problems.

16.♗d5

Play is unclear after 16.♗e3 ♗a4 17.♕d2 ♖c2 18.♕d3 ♘c4 19.♖ec1 ♘xe3 20.♕xe3 b6. Instead 16…♗c6?! (the move I intended to play) is not so strong after 17.e6!.

16...♗c6! 17.♗xc4 ♘xc4 18.d5

After 18.♘e4 ♕d5 Black has definitely enough compensation for the exchange.

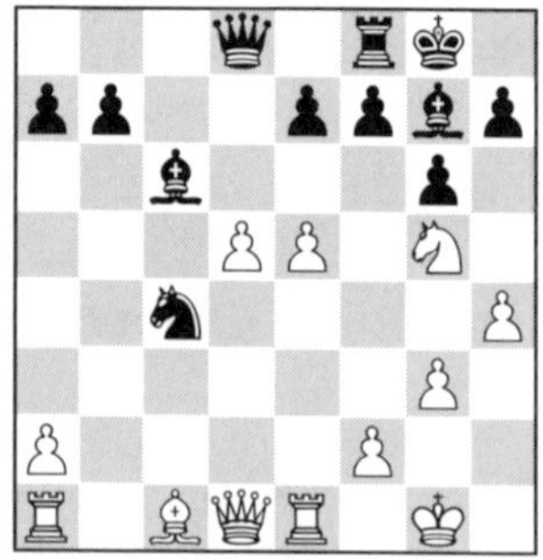

18...♗xe5??

It's very difficult for me to explain why I played such a bad move, especially as I saw the right varation.

18...♕xd5! is of course the best move!: 19.♕xd5 ♗xd5 20.f4 (20.♗f4 h6) 20...f6! 21.♖d1 e6 22.exf6 ♗xf6 23.♖b1 ♖c8 with an unclear position, but only Black can be better.

Also unbalanced is 18...♗xd5 19.♗f4 ♕a5 20.♕d4!.

19.dxc6 ♕xd1 20.♖xd1 ♗xa1 21.♗f4?

After this move Black is back in the game.

– 21.c7! ♗e5 (21...♘d6 22.♗f4) 22.♘xh7!. Ouch! This move wins on the spot.

– 21.cxb7!? ♗e5 22.♖d7! ♗d6 23.♗f4! ♗xf4 24.gxf4 ♘d6 25.♖xe7 ♖b8 26.♖d7 h6 was my main line, but even this is losing after 27.♖xd6 hxg5 28.♖d7.

21...♗e5 22.♗xe5 22.♖c1 b5!. **22...♘xe5 23.cxb7 ♖b8 24.♖b1 ♘d7 25.♘e4 ♔f8 26.a4 ♔e8 27.a5 a6 28.♖c1 ♔d8 29.♘g5 ♘e5! 30.f4 h6 31.♘e6+ fxe6 32.fxe5 ♖xb7 33.♖c6 ♔d7 34.♖xa6 ♖b5 35.♖a7+ ♔e8 36.a6 ♖xe5** Draw.

□ **Radoslaw Wojtaszek**

■ **Maxime Vachier-Lagrave**

Warsaw European Blitz 2010

1.d4 ♘f6 2.c4 g6 3.g3 ♗g7 4.♗g2 0-0 5.♘c3 ♘c6 6.♘f3 d5 7.cxd5 ♘xd5 8.0-0 ♗f5 9.♕b3!?

If the strong Polish grandmaster plays this move it must deserve some attention.

● 9.e3 is quite solid: 9...♘xc3 (the most logical move) 10.bxc3. Black has a choice:

– 10...♗e4!? (the simplest) 11.a4 (11.♘d2 ♗xg2 12.♔xg2 ♘a5 followed by ...b6 and ...c5.; 11.♖e1 ♘a5 12.♗f1 c5 13.♘d2 ♗c6=) 11...♘a5 12.♗a3 ♘c4 (after 12...b6 I think Black has no problems) 13.♘d2 ♗xg2 14.♔xg2 ♘xa3 15.♖xa3 c5= Ni Hua-Yang Kaiqi, Olongapo City 2010.

– 10...♘a5 (the move I played is also logical) 11.♘d2 c5 12.♘b3 cxd4 13.cxd4 ♖b8 14.♘xa5 ♕xa5 15.♗d2 ♕a6 16.♕b3 ♗d3 17.♖fc1 e5! when after 18.♗b4 Black was OK in Manea-Cornette, Aix-les-Bains ch-EUR 2011. The best chance for White was 18.♗d5! exd4 19.e4!.

● 9.♘xd5 ♕xd5 was what I played in a rapid tournament and many times on internet: after 10.♘e5?! (10.♘h4 ♕xd4 11.♘xf5 gxf5 – even if it's clear that White has some compensation, it's not enough to pretend having an advantage) 10...♕xd4 11.♘xc6 bxc6 and only Black can be slightly better.

9...♘b6

9...♘xc3!? (this novelty looks perfectly playable) 10.bxc3 (10.♕xc3?! ♘xd4∓) 10...b6 (10...♗e4?! 11.♕xb7!±). The rest is quite simple:

– 11.♘h4 ♗d7 12.♖d1 (12.♗g5 ♖c8 followed by ...♘a5 and ...c5) 12...♘a5 13.♕b4 ♖c8 14.♗e3 (White is trying to prevent ...c5) 14...♗e6 (with the idea ...♗d5) 15.d5 c5!. A very strong move. Black has no problems.

– 11.♗f4 ♘a5 12.♕a4 (12.♕b5 ♗e4 13.♖ad1 ♖c8 14.♘e5 ♗xg2 15.♔xg2 ♕e8=) 12...♗e4 13.♖ac1 ♖c8 14.♖fd1 ♕e8=.

– After 11.♕b5 ♗e4 12.♖d1 ♘a5 I don't see any reason why White should be better.

10.♖d1

10.d5 gives an interesting position after 10...♘a5 11.♕b4 ♘ac4 12.e4 a5 13.♕b3 ♗g4 14.♗f4 ♕d7.

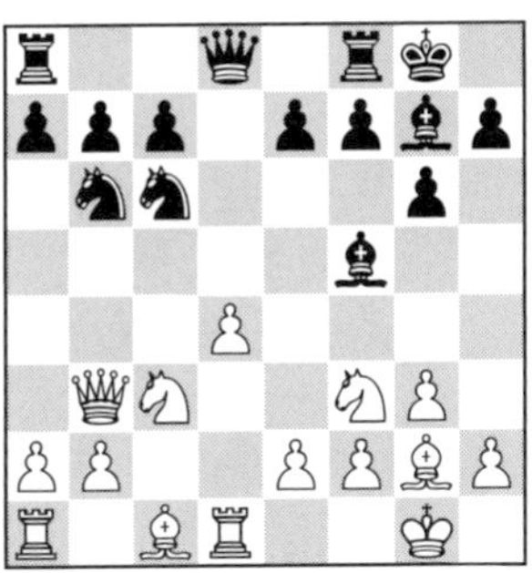

10...♕d7

10...a5!? is a very interesting alternative:

– 11.d5 a4! (an important intermediate move) 12.♘xa4 (12.♕a3 ♘e5 with an unclear position) 12...♘a5 13.♕b4 ♘c6! 14.♕e1 (14.♕b3 ♘a5 with a draw by repetition) 14...♘b4! (a crazy move!) 15.♕xb4 (15.♘xb6 ♘c2∓) 15...♖xa4 16.♕b3 ♖c4 17.♘e1 ♗d7 18.♖d2 ♕a8 and in spite of White's extra pawn, Black has a strong initiative.

– 11.e4 a4 12.♕c2 ♗g4 13.♘e2 (13.♘b5 ♖a5!) 13...e5!? with a double-egded position.

– 11.a4 ♘b4 (Black should be OK with such a square) 12.e4 ♗g4 13.♗f4 c6 14.♘a2 (14.♘e2 ♖c8=) 14...♗e6! 15.d5 ♘6xd5! (an important blow that gives Black a decent position) 16.♘g5 (16.exd5 ♗xd5 17.♕e3 ♘c2 18.♕c1 ♘xa1 19.♕xa1 ♕b6) 16...♘xf4 17.♘xe6 ♘xe6 18.♖xd8 ♖fxd8 with powerful compensation.

11.d5 ♘a5 12.♕b4 ♘ac4 13.♘d4 a5 14.♕b5 14.♕c5!? may be an improvement for White.

14...♘d6 15.♕xd7 ♗xd7 16.♗g5 ♖fe8

This position is equal, but as this was a blitz game the remainder is not so relevant. Black won on move 56.

CHAPTER 13

Max Illingworth

Sicilian: the Illingworth Gambit

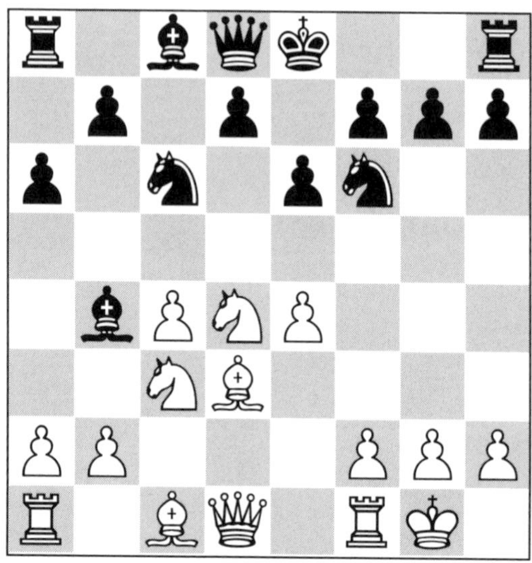

Sacrificing a piece with 8.0-0!

The Kan (or Paulsen) Sicilian has a well-deserved reputation of being solid yet very flexible, and it is far from easy to prove an advantage against it. The gambit I propose against the critical 5.c4 ♘f6 6.♘c3 ♗b4 (7.♗d3 ♘c6 8.0-0!) is not only very surprising, but also puts Black under immediate pressure and offers good chances of achieving an edge out of the opening. This means that the gambit can be effective even against an opponent who is aware of the line.

☐ **Max Illingworth**
■ **Yuan Zhao Zong**
Cammeray Australian Open 2011

1.e4 c5 2.♘f3 e6 3.d4 cxd4 4.♘xd4 a6 5.c4 ♘f6 6.♘c3 ♗b4

6...♕c7 is slightly more popular, but White's chances should be slightly preferable in the main line with 7.a3, and those looking for an SOS-style alternative should investigate 7.♕e2!?.

7.♗d3 ♘c6 8.0-0!

Astonishing! I have a confession to make at this point – I did not come up with this idea independently. It was proposed by 'brabo' on ChessPub Forum, and this gambit was discussed by some of the members of the Forum. However, as I am the first (and at the time of writing, only) person to play this gambit in a tournament game, I think it is fair to call 8.0-0 the 'Illingworth Gambit'.

8...♘xd4

A surprised opponent may decide to decline the sacrifice with 8...♛c7. I will consider this in the theoretical section.

9.e5

Now Black cannot retreat with 9...♘g8, because after 10.♛g4 White is threatening to win the h8 rook with ♛xg7 as well as regain the lost piece with ♛xd4, and after 10...♘e7 11.♛xd4 ♘c6 12.♛g4 White has a very pleasant position.

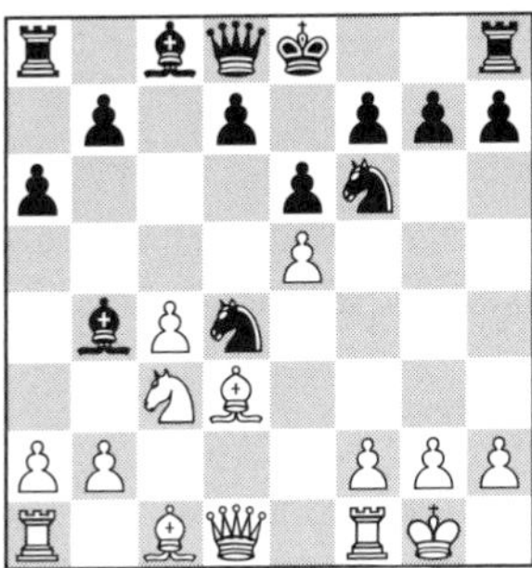

9...♗e7

A solid move, with the idea that after the bishop recaptures on f6, the d4-knight will be protected and Black's bishop will be well placed on the long diagonal.

Black's main alternatives are 9...♘c6 and 9...0-0, which I will analyse in the theoretical section.

10.exf6

10.♗e3!? ♘c6 will transpose to the game after 11.exf6 ♗xf6, but White has an interesting alternative in 11.♘a4!?, when 11...d6 (the computer line 11...0-0 12.♗b6 ♛e8 13.exf6 ♗xf6 feels unnatural to me: after 14.c5± Black's c8-bishop and a8-rook are entombed, and I would definitely prefer White's position) 12.exf6 ♗xf6 13.♘b6 ♖b8 14.♗e4 0-0 15.♛d2 gives White good long-term compensation for the pawn, as Black cannot easily complete his development and the d6-pawn is quite vulnerable. However, I think my choice in the game is more critical, intending to clamp down on the d6-square with ♘e4.

10...♗xf6

11.♗e3

This is not the only move, but this is certainly the most natural, continuing development and preventing castling due to the discovered attack with ♗xh7.

That said, 11.♘e4!? deserves attention, for example:

- 11...0-0 12.♛h5!? (12.♘xf6+ ♛xf6 13.♗e3 ♘f5 14.♗xf5 ♛xf5 15.c5 is better for White, who has succeeded in trapping the c8 bishop, but 13...♘c6!? with the idea of ...d5 is a better try. The tempting 12.c5?! allows the surprising 12...d5! 13.cxd6 ♗e5, when Black will get his pieces into the game, with good chances)

and now:
– 12...♘f5 13.♘xf6+ (13.g4 g6 14.♕h3 ♘d4 15.♗h6 ♖e8 16.♘d6 ♖e7 gives White an initiative, but this seems unnecessarily risky – if Black manages to complete his development after moves like ...b5 and ...♗b7 then White may regret playing g4) 13...♕xf6 14.g4 g6 15.♕g5! ♕xg5 16.♗xg5 ♘d4 17.♗f6 ♘c6 and White can force a drawish endgame if he wishes with 18.c5 b6! (otherwise Black is struggling) 19.♗e4! bxc5 20.♗xc6 dxc6 21.♖fc1 ♖b8 22.♖xc5 with equality. Black will have to return the extra pawn to bring his c8 bishop to life.
Of course, White can maintain the pressure with 18.♖fd1 d5 19.g5 with good compensation for the pawn even after the exchange of queens, but it is encouraging to know that the worst-case scenario for White after 11.♘e4 is an equal endgame.
– instead, 12...g6 13.♘xf6+ ♕xf6 14.♗g5 ♕e5 15.♕h4 gives White fantastic compensation in his bishop pair, lead in development, half-open d- and e-files for his rooks and a strong initiative.
● 11...♗e7 is more ambitious, keeping the bishop pair, but after 12.c5 d5 (12...0-0 13.♘d6 ♗xd6 14.cxd6 f5 15.♗e3 ♕f6 16.♗c4! ♘c6 17.♗b6 ♕xb2 18.♖b1 favours White) 13.cxd6 ♗xd6 14.♗e3 ♘c6 15.♘xd6+ ♕xd6 16.♖c1 only White can be better with Black's king stuck in the centre for some time.

11...♘c6

By moving the knight, Black prepares to castle.
11...d6 is the alternative, offering the extra pawn back to catch up in development, but White can keep the initiative with 12.♖e1! ♗e5 13.f4 ♗f6 14.♗xh7 and White will have the compensation without the pawn deficit.
Simply bad is 11...0-0? 12.♗xd4 ♗xd4 13.♗xh7+ ♔xh7 14.♕xd4±.

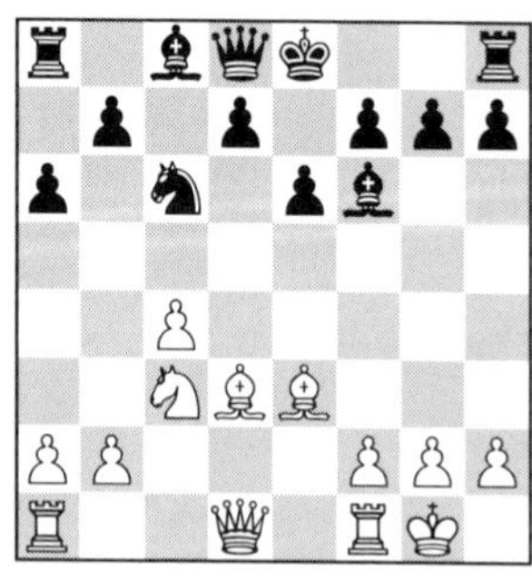

12.♘e4!?

On the ChessPub Forum 'brabo' gave 12.c5 an exclamation mark, but my over-the-board inspiration seems just as good.
● 12.♕h5!? was brabo's other idea (intending 12...♕a5 13.♕xa5 ♘xa5 14.c5 when White's compensation endures into the endgame):
– 12...d6 13.♖ad1 ♗e7 14.♖fe1 ♕a5 15.♕g4 g6 16.♗h6 and White is better as Black's king will remain vulnerable even if he castles queenside.
– The counter-sacrifice 12...b5 comes up short after 13.cxb5 axb5 14.♘xb5 d5 15.♗c5 ♗e7 16.♗xe7 ♕xe7 17.♖ac1 ♗b7 18.♖fe1 and with White threatening ♖xe6 – ...♕xe6 ♘c7 – Black will have to play ...♔f8 after which his position will be very unpleasant.
– It's not clear if 12...♕a5 13.♕xa5 ♘xa5 14.c5 is better for White after 14...d5! 15.cxd6 ♗d7, but 14.♗c5 looks like a good alternative.
● 12.c5 0-0 (12...♗e7 with the idea of ...d6 is inadvisable as this opens up the centre for White's better developed pieces: 13.♕e2 – 13.♘e4, see 12.♘e4 ♗e7 13.c5 – 13...d6 14.cxd6 ♗xd6 15.♖fd1 ♕c7 16.g3 0-0 17.♖ac1 ♖d8 18.♘a4 with an edge for White, as given by brabo on ChessPub Forum). Now 13.♘e4 will transpose to the main game, but brabo's 13.♘a4 is a good alternative:

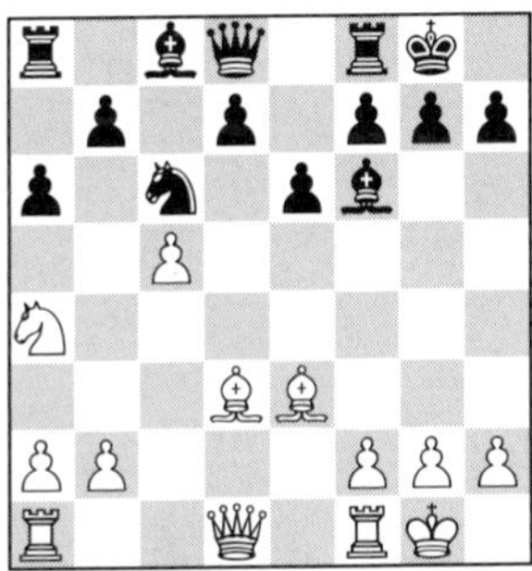

– 13...g6 looks strongest. 'Matemax' on ChessPub Forum suggested the idea of ...e5, ...♘d4 and ...d6, freeing Black's position, but this seems a bit too slow by Black. 14.♕b3 (or 14.♕d2 ♗e7 15.♖ad1 d5 16.cxd6 ♕xd6 17.♘b6 ♖b8 18.♘c4 ♕d5 19.♕c3 with a complicated position where I would rather be White) 14...d5 (14...♘d4!?) 15.cxd6 b5! 16.♘c5 (16.♗e4 ♖b8!) 16...♕xd6 17.♘e4 ♕d8 18.♘xf6+ ♕xf6 19.a4 with sufficient compensation for the pawn.

– After 13...♗e5 'brabo' recommended 14.f4, but I would prefer the computer's 14.♘b6! ♖b8 15.♘c4 ♗c7 (forfeiting the bishop pair can't be in Black's best interests) 16.♕d2 f5 17.♗g5 ♕e8 18.♖fe1 and White has the better chances, as Black cannot complete his development easily. White can later play ♗f4 to ensure complete control over the d6-square.

– 13...e5 was also suggested by Matemax, but runs into 14.♘b6 ♖b8 15.♗f5 ♘d4 16.♗xd4 exd4 17.♕d3 with a clearly better position for White – ♕g3 will win the exchange – as given by 'brabo'.

12...0-0

This is not the only move, but it seems best to get castled as soon as possible.

– 12...♗xb2?! is too greedy to be good: 13.♘d6+ ♔f8 14.♖b1 ♗e5 15.♗c5 and Black may be up two pawns, but his king is precariously placed and he still has the problem of developing his queenside.

– 12...♗e7 is the computer's suggestion, when the position after 13.c5 (rather than 13.♕g4 g6 14.♘g5 d5 which is pretty solid for Black, who is still a pawn up) 13...f5 14.♘d6+ ♗xd6 15.cxd6 0-0 is not clear at all. For example, play could continue 16.a4 b6 17.♕d2 ♗b7 18.♖fc1 ♖c8 19.♗f1 with a complex struggle ahead.

13.c5!?

This move is quite interesting, sacrificing a second pawn to clamp down on the d6-square, but I don't think it gives White an advantage.

Perhaps I should have grabbed the bishop pair with 13.♘xf6+ ♕xf6, but even here it is far from clear whether White has an advantage or only sufficient compensation: 14.♗c5 (14.♕c2 g6 15.♕b3 is also possible, for instance 15...d5 16.cxd5 exd5 17.♗c5 ♖d8 18.♖fe1 with 'only' sufficient compensation for the pawn; 14.♕d2!? d5 15.♗g5 ♕d4 16.♖ac1 is similar) 14...♖e8 15.♗d6! ♕xb2 16.c5

and I'd rather be White in this unclear position, though he does need to start an attack on the kingside before Black can consolidate with moves like ...b5 or ...b6.

13...♗xb2

Zhao correctly grabs the pawn as otherwise

White has achieved the very useful c5 for free.

13...d5 14.cxd6 ♗xb2 15.♖b1 ♗d4 16.♗c4 favours White, as the d6 pawn is more likely to be a strength than a weakness.

14.♖b1 ♗d4

14...♗e5 15.f4 ♗c7 16.a4 f5 17.♘d6 ♗xd6 18.cxd6 b5 19.axb5 axb5 20.♗xb5 is not clear either: Black has consolidated his position but White retains long-term compensation due to his superior minor pieces and the d6-pawn wedged in Black's position.

15.♗xd4 ♘xd4 16.♘d6

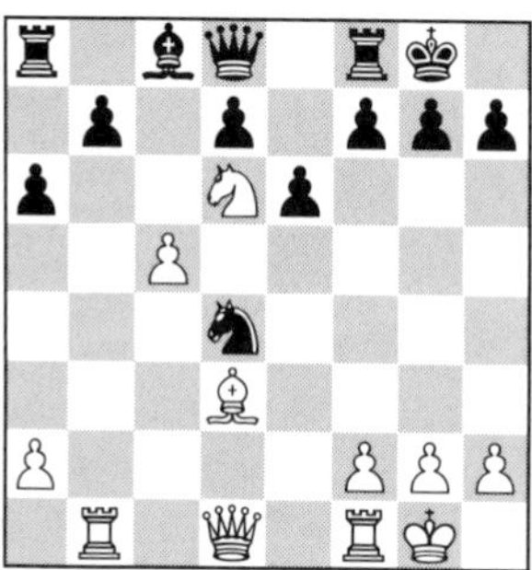

It looks bizarre to exchange the dark-squared bishops in this manner, but Zhao had a clever tactical idea in mind.

16...♘b5!

Now White has to either allow Black to exchange on d6 or open the a-file for Black's rook. My choice is probably the lesser evil.

17.♗xb5 axb5 18.♖xb5

18.♕d2 b6 19.cxb6 ♕xb6 20.♖xb5 gives White one more pawn than in the game, but setting the c8-bishop free isn't worth it.

18...♖xa2 19.♕b3 ♖a6

I wasn't sure what was going on in the position at this stage. Black is essentially down a piece, but the c8-bishop defends Black's b7- and d7-pawns. The game continuation suggests that the position is balanced.

20.♖b6

20.♖d1 may be marginally more accurate, since Black isn't threatening ...b6 in the near future.

20...♕g5!

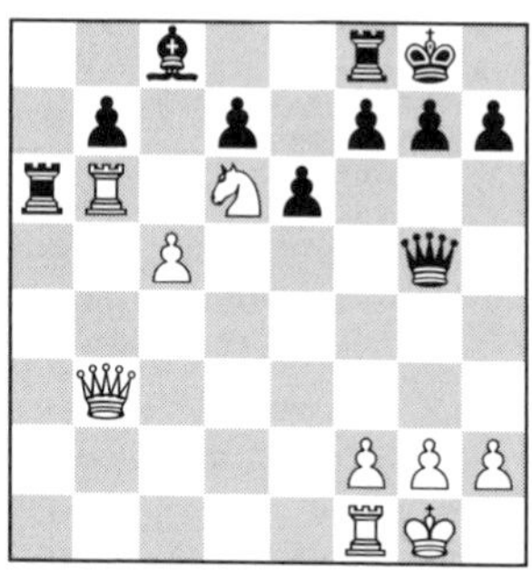

Active defence – in the game Zhao is able to create just enough counterplay to maintain the balance.

21.♕b4 ♕d5 22.h3 ♖a2 23.♕c3 f5

My last few moves were not the most accurate, and now Black may even be a little better, since I have to be careful with my king, and if my b6 rook moves then ...b6 becomes a serious possibility.

24.♖e1

With this move, I unintentionally set up a sneaky threat.

24...h6?!

A good move, except that it doesn't stop White's threat of ♘e8!.

25.♕e5?!

Now Black is doing well again.

25.♘e8! ♖xe8 26.♖d6 wins the queen, however it's hard to imagine Black losing after 26...♕c6 27.♖xc6 bxc6.

25...♕xe5 26.♖xe5

White should be able to draw this endgame, but he has to display a bit of care.

26...♖a5

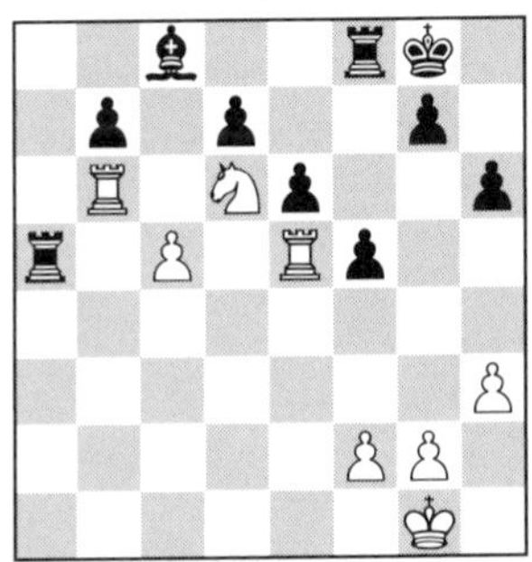

27.f4!

Stopping Black from playing ...g5 easily; perhaps Black should have played ...g5 a move earlier.

27...g5 28.fxg5 hxg5 29.g4!

Now all of the pawns will be liquidated with gxf5, and ...f4 doesn't come close to a win either.

29...♖a1+ 30.♔h2 ♖a2+ 31.♔g1 ♖a1+ 32.♔h2

And drawn.

I was very pleased that my opening held out against Australia's number one player.

Theoretical Section

Now we will consider Black's other answers to 8.0-0.

1.e4 c5 2.♘f3 e6 3.d4 cxd4 4.♘xd4 a6 5.c4 ♘f6 6.♘c3 ♗b4 7.♗d3 ♘c6 8.0-0 ♘xd4

● 8...♗xc3?! 9.bxc3 would leave White a full tempo ahead on the 8.a3 ♗xc3 9.bxc3 variation, which can only be favourable for White.

● Allowing e5 with 8...0-0?! 9.♘xc6 dxc6 10.e5 gives White a risk-free edge due to his space advantage after 10...♘d7 11.♖e1 ♘c5 12.♗c2.

● 8...d6 is a safe alternative: 9.♗e3 (the tempting 9.♘xc6 bxc6 10.♕a4 isn't so good after 10...♖b8! 11.e5 ♘g4 12.♕xc6+ ♗d7 followed by ...♘xe5, with superb counterplay for Black) 9...0-0 10.♘xc6 bxc6 and Black is solid but White can claim a pull after 11.♘a4! (a typical plan in this pawn structure) 11...♗a5 12.c5 d5 13.e5 ♘d7 14.f4 due to his space advantage and more active pieces.

● 8...♕c7

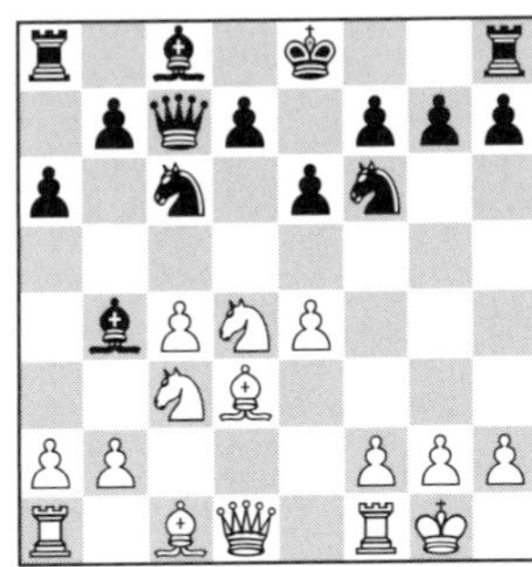

was suggested by 'drkodos' on ChessPub Forum, but this in fact transposes to 7...♕c7 8. 0-0 ♘c6, which is known to favour White slightly based on the game Karpov-Miles, Brussels 1986: 9.♘f3 (if White for some reason wishes to avoid 9.♘f3 then 9.♘xc6 dxc6 10.♗e3 e5 11.♘a4 or 9.♗e3 with the idea of 9...♘e5 10.♘f3!N ♘xc4 11.♗xc4 ♕xc4 12.♘a4! as mentioned by 'sssthepro' on ChessPub Forum also offer good chances of an advantage) 9...0-0 10.♗d2 b6 (this looks best even though Karpov went on to win) 11.♖c1 ♕b8 (11...♘g4!? offered more chances of equality) 12.♕e2 ♗d6 13.♔h1 ♗c7 14.♗b1 ♗b7 15.♖cd1 h6 16.b3 ♖e8 17.♖de1 d6 18.♗e3 ♘g4 19.♗c1 ♘ge5 20.♗b2 ♗d8 21.♖d1 ♗f6 22.♘e1 and White had a small edge.

9.e5

We covered 9...♗e7 in Illingworth-Zhao, which leaves the moves 9...0-0 and 9...♘c6 to consider, as 9...♗xc3 10.bxc3 ♘c6 11.exf6 ♕xf6 will transpose to 9...♘c6.

Variation A

9...0-0

Castling was suggested by 'JudgeMeek' on ChessPub Forum. Now 'brabo' analysed 10.♗e3, mentioning 10.exf6 and 10.♗g5 in passing.

10.♗e3!

Instead 10.exf6 ♕xf6 11.♘e4 is also interesting, but I don't think White is objectively better after 11...♕e5! 12.g3 (or 12.f4 ♕c7 when White can and probably should force a draw with 13.♘f6+ gxf6 14.♗xh7+ ♔xh7 15.♕h5+) 12...♗e7 13.♗f4 ♕a5 when it's not so easy to stop Black achieving counterplay with ...d5, ...e5 or ... f5.

Likewise, 10.♗g5 ♗e7 (Black cannot allow his kingside pawn structure to be damaged) 11.exf6 ♗xf6 12.♗xf6 ♕xf6 doesn't look worse for Black, for example 13.c5 (13.♕h5 h6 14.♕c5 isn't an improvement due to 14... d6! 15.♕xd6 ♖d8 16.♕g3 b5 when it is Black who gains the initiative) 13...♕e5 14.♘a4 d5 15.♘b6 ♖b8 16.♕d2 and the position is dynamically balanced, since Black still has problems completing development.

After 10.♗e3 the move 10...♘f5 transposes to A2 below after 11.♗xf5 exf5 12.exf6 ♗xc3 13.bxc3 ♕xf6. We will first investigate 10...♘c6.

Variation A1

10...♘c6 11.exf6 ♕xf6

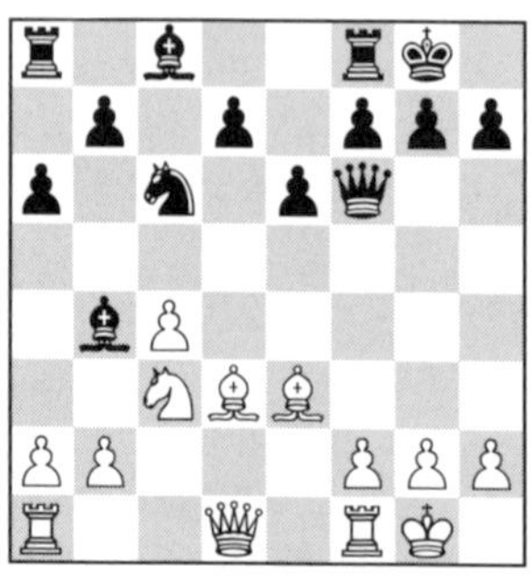

12.♕c2

This idea of brabo's is probably White's best try for an edge. I tried to make 12.c5!? work, but after 12...♕e5 (12...♗xc3 13.bxc3 ♕xc3 14.♖c1 ♕b2 15.♗f4! feels better for White) unlike in the illustrative game, Black can't get his a8 rook into play. 12...d5!? 13.cxd6 ♕d8 14.♘a4 ♗xd6 15.♘b6 ♖b8 16.♖c1 is dynamically balanced) 13.♘a4 f5 14.g3 f4! 15.♗xf4 ♖xf4 16.gxf4 ♕xf4 Black has sufficient compensation for the exchange.

12...♕h4! 12...h6 13.♖ad1 ♗e7 14.♘e4 ♕e5 15.f4 ♕c7 16.c5 is better for White as Black once again has problems developing his queenside. **13.g3 ♕h3 14.c5 f5 15.f4** With good long-term compensation but probably not enough for an edge after 15... d6 16.cxd6 ♗xd6 17.♖ad1 ♗e7.

Variation A2

10...♗xc3 11.bxc3 ♘f5 12.♗xf5 exf5 13.exf6 ♕xf6 is better for White after brabo's **14.c5!**

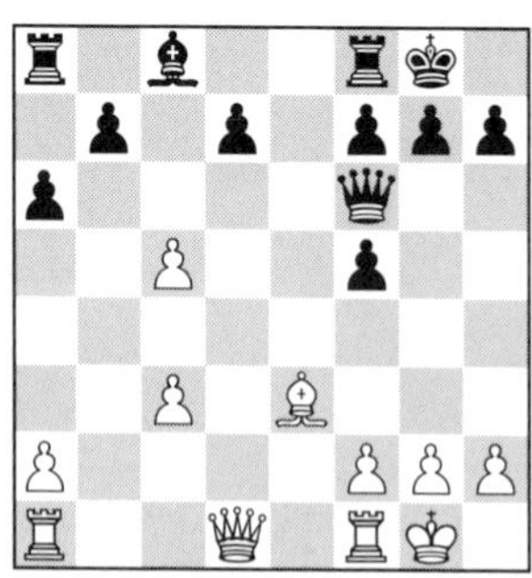

but Black should be able to hold, for instance:

– 14...d5! (suggested by JudgeDeath, aiming to liquidate to a drawn opposite-coloured bishop endgame) 15.cxd6 f4 (the computer prefers 15...♖d8, but 16.♗c5 ♗d7 17.♖e1 is also better for White) 16.♗c5 (16.♗b6!? ♗d7 17.♖e1 ♖fe8 18.♕d3 f3! is fine for Black) 16...♗d7 17.♖e1 (17.♗d4 ♕xd6

18.♗xg7 ♕xd1 19.♖axd1 ♔xg7 20.♖xd7 is a drawish endgame) 17...♖fe8 18.♖e7 ♗c6 19.f3 ♕xc3 20.♖c1 – here Brabo gives 'large compensation for the pawn', an assessment I agree with.

– 14...♕xc3 15.♖e1 (brabo) 15...♕c4 16.♕d2 d5 17.cxd6 ♗e6 18.♗b6 with wonderful compensation for the pawn.

– 14...♖e8 was also suggested by JudgeDeath: 15.♖e1 (15.♕d5!? ♕xc3 16.♗d4 ♕d2 17.♖ad1 ♕f4 18.♖fe1 may be even better – Black will have to eventually return one of the pawns to complete development, and White has a strong initiative) 15...♖e4 16.f3 ♖e6 17.♕d2 may well be tenable for Black, but White's position is clearly more pleasant.

Variation B

9...♘c6 10.exf6 ♕xf6

If Black inserts 10...♗xc3 11.bxc3 ♕xf6 then White has more than one route to an advantage:

– 12.♖b1 0-0 13.♗a3 (13.♕c2!? g6 14.♗a3 ♖e8 15.c5 ♘e5 – 15...d5? 16.cxd6 b5 17.c4± doesn't even give Black a pawn for his difficulties – 16.♗e2 ♘c6 17.♖fe1 ♕g7 18.♕b3 as given by 'brabo' also favours White, and 15.♗d6!? may be even better) 13...♖d8 (13...♖e8 could transpose to 13.♕c2 after 14. ♕c2 g6, though 14.♗d6!? ♕xc3 15.c5 may be even stronger) 14.♗d6! This idea is most effective when Black plays ...♖d8 as now the rook would be stronger on e8 (14.♕c2 d5! gives Black more activity than necessary): 14...♕xc3 (otherwise Black is just worse) 15.♖b3 ♕f6 16.♕b1 (the computer's 16.♖b6 also favours White – Black is essentially two pieces down) 16...g6 17.c5 ♘d4 18.♕b2 ♕g7 19.♖b6 (brabo) and once again White is definitely better – Black can hardly move.

– 12.♗a3 as played by 'Matemax' in two 3-minute games against an IM is also good: 12...♕xc3 13.♗d6 ♘e5 (13...♕d4 14.c5 b6 15.♖c1 is rather strong for White, as Black cannot evict the dark-squared bishop from the a3-f8 diagonal, meaning that the black king will be stuck in the centre for a long time) 14.♗e2 ♘xc4 15.♖c1 ♕xc1 16.♕xc1 ♘xd6 (sssthepro) and Black has got rid of the pesky dark-squared bishop, but White should keep an advantage as stated by ChessPub member 'MNb': 17.♕a3 ♘f5 18.♖c1 and Black's retarded development is a more significant factor than his material advantage.

11.♘e4

Sacrificing more material with 11.c5!? ♗xc5 12.♘e4 ♕e5 13.♘xc5 ♕xc5 14.♗e3 ♕e5 15.♖e1 0-0 16.♕c2 may appeal to some, but the more restrained 11.♘e4 is probably better.

The computer's 11.♗e3!?

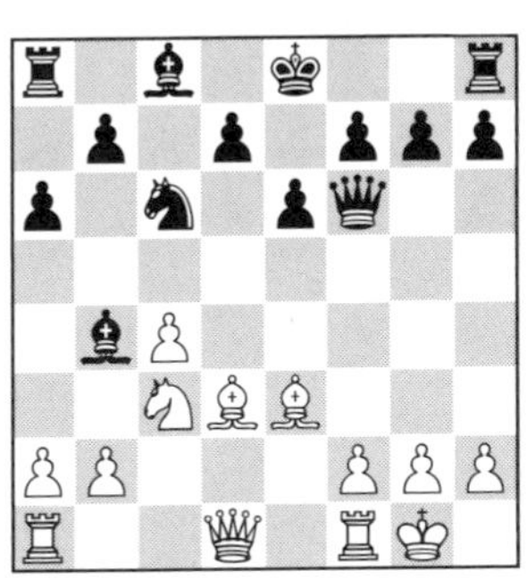

isn't a move I would have thought of, but it does seem quite logical, intending a quick c5. Note that the greedy 11...♗xc3 (11...0-0 transposes to 9...0-0 10.♗e3 ♘c6 11.exf6 ♕xf6) 12.bxc3 ♕xc3 13.♖c1 ♕a5 14.c5 gives White very nice compensation in view of his dark-square bind.

11...♕e5

Not 11...♕e7 12.a3 ♗c5 13.♗g5! ♕f8 (13...f6?! 14.♗xf6!) 14.b4± followed by c5 with a dreadful position for Black.

11...♕d4 is also bad, due to 12.♗e3! ♕xb2 13.♖b1 ♕e5 14.f4 ♕c7 15.c5 with a ferocious attack.

12.a3

Throwing in this move doesn't hurt White.

12.♘g5 deserves attention, improving the position of the knight. Play could continue 12...h6 13.♘f3 ♕c7 14.a3 ♗e7 15.♗e3 0-0 16.♕b3 with chances for both sides.

12...♗e7

12...f5 stops White from meeting ...f5 with ♘c3 as in our main line, but 13.axb4 (13.♘g5 ♗e7) 13...fxe4 14.b5! maintains White's initiative: 14...♘e7 (14...exd3 15.bxc6 bxc6 16.♕xd3 0-0 17.♗e3 is better for White. This isn't the first time in this line that White has achieved an opposite-coloured bishops position with the much stronger bishop) 15.♗c2 0-0 16.♗d2 d5 17.♗c3 and I think White can claim an edge here due to his domination of the dark squares.

13.♖e1!

13.♗d2 is too slow after 13...d5 14.cxd5 ♕xd5 15.♗f4 e5 and Black is starting to consolidate.

13...f5

Black has a few other moves, the most significant of which is 13...d5. If Black can get away with this then he will be doing very well, but after 14.f4! (14.♘c3 ♕d6 15.cxd5 exd5 is okay for Black) 14...♕c7 15.cxd5 exd5 16.♘c3 ♕d6 17.♕h5 ♗e6 18.f5 ♗d7 19.f6! ♕xf6 20.♘xd5 White has an inexorable initiative.

14.♘c3 ♕f6

This is not the only square for the queen: 14...♕d6!? is a typical computer move, but it's not so bad, e.g.:

– 15.♘a4!? 0-0 16.c5 ♕c7 17.g3 which is hard to assess after 17...♖b8 18.♗e3 d5 19.cxd6 ♗xd6

but if pressed I'd rather be White after 20.♗b6 ♕e7 21.♖c1.

– 15.g3 0-0 (15...♘e5 16.♗f4 ♕xd3 17.♗xe5 ♕xd1 18.♖axd1 is good for White, who has a pleasant dark-square bind that gains in importance as more pieces are exchanged) 16.♗f4 ♕d4 17.♘a4 with chances for both sides – White has typical compensation but Black is very solid.

– 15.♕h5+ g6 16.♕h3 0-0 17.♗h6 ♖f7 18.♖ad1 also gives White good play for the pawn.

15.♗f4

The alternative 15.♘a4 0-0 16.♘b6 ♖b8 17.♗f4 looks good, but Black has a strong reply in 17...♕d4! 18.♗xb8 ♕xb6 19.♗f4 ♕xb2, when Black has returned the extra material to curtail White's initiative and stands well.

15...0-0 16.♗f1

'brabo' stops here, stating 'White has excellent compensation for the pawn'. Objectively the position should be equal, but White's position does seem easier to play. If Black returns the pawn with

16...d6!? to complete development, then **17.♗xd6 ♖d8 18.♗xe7 ♕xe7 19.♕f3** gives White a tiny edge.

Conclusion: The Illingworth Gambit puts Black under immediate pressure, and can give White both strong short-term and long-term compensation, as we have seen in several variations where Black was unable to complete his development easily. My gambit doesn't guarantee an edge for White, but it looks like a better try than other eighth moves, and I've shown more than one way for White to fight for an advantage against each of Black's critical tries.

CHAPTER 14

Jeroen Bosch

Avoiding the King's Indian Sämisch

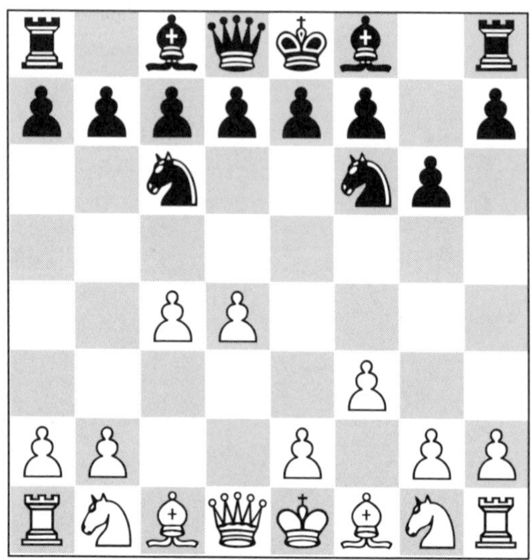

1.d4 ♘f6 2.c4 g6 3.f3 ♘c6!?

□ **Momchil Nikolov**
■ **Wang Yue**
Zurich 2010

1.d4 ♘f6 2.c4 g6 3.f3
An intriguing move that is employed by many players whose repertoire includes the Sämisch King's Indian. It is a move order weapon pur sang: the only idea is to avoid the Grünfeld proper, and to lure those Grünfeld-guys into unfamiliar territory. However, recently the adherents of Ernst Grünfeld are starting to strike back with a vengeance. For, the results of the surprising 3...♘c6!? are thoroughly encouraging.
3...♘c6
Before you condemn this move, please note that some players really like to 'tango' – they are happy to invite their queen's knight to the dance after 2.c4. Now, obviously the inclusion of 2...g6 3.f3 favours the second player: for even though the pawn on g6 takes away a square from the knight, things are worse for White, who can't develop his king's knight to its 'natural square'.

Before we embark on our investigation of the topical 3...♘c6!?, let's briefly discuss the points of 3.f3 and some alternative methods to combat 3.f3.
● First there is the natural 3...♗g7, when White is happy to reach a Sämisch after 4.e4 0-0 5.♘c3 (note that 5.♗e3 is a move

order weapon that holds some promise for the other side) and now 5...d6 leads to the position that White was hoping for all along. However, Black could try to muddy the waters with any of the following:

– 5...♘c6 – not as surprising as on move 3 but certainly an interesting option. After 6.♗e3 (6.d5 ♘b4!?) 6...e5! was a big success in Gheorghiu-W.Watson, London 1980. After some typical King's Indian tactics: 7.d5 ♘d4 8.♘ge2 c5! 9.dxc6 dxc6 10.♘xd4 exd4 11.♗xd4 (11.♕xd4 ♘d5 12.♕d2 ♘xe3 13.♕xe3 favours Black too) 11...♘xe4! 12.♗xg7 ♕h4+ 13.g3 ♘xg3 14.♗f6! ♖e8+ 15.♘e4 ♖xe4+! 16.fxe4 ♕xe4+ 17.♔f2 ♗g4! Black was winning.

– Also deserving of attention are 5...c6 6.♗e3 d5 7.e5 ♘e8, and

– the pawn sacrifice 5...c5 6.dxc5 b6.

● Secondly, White argues that 3...d5 4.cxd5 ♘xd5 5.e4 favours him, since Black cannot make the usual exchange on c3 to obtain typical Grünfeld counterplay with ...c5 later on. Still, the position after 5...♘b6 6.♘c3 ♗g7 7.♗e3 is highly theoretical, and also very popular among Grünfeld players.

● Moves like 3...c5 or 3...d6 are not particularly interesting, but 3...e5!? certainly is! This bold counter in the centre (an idea of Adorjan) owes much of its popularity to the game Kramnik-Leko, Tilburg 1998 (0-1 after 45 moves). The 'main' line goes: 4.dxe5 ♘h5 5.♘h3 ♘c6 6.♗g5 ♗e7 7.♗xe7 ♕xe7 8.♘c3 ♕xe5 and so on.

4.d5

White must pick up the gauntlet. Black's idea is reminiscent of Alekhine's Defence: White's central pawns are lured forwards, when Black reasons that they will provide him with some clear targets.

With 4.♘c3 White allows his opponent to get back into a Grünfeld set-up with 4...d5.

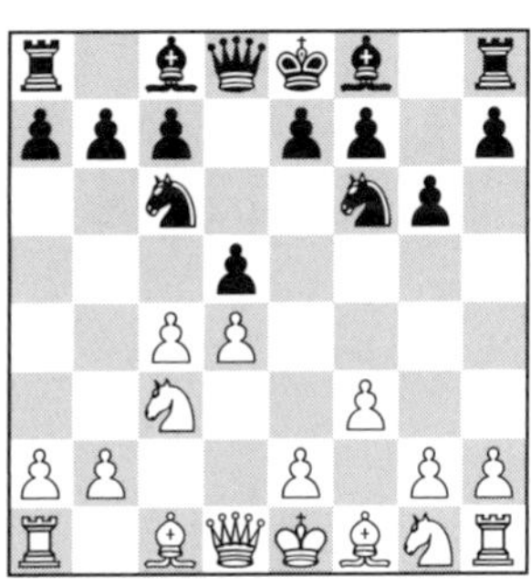

And now:

– 5.cxd5 ♘xd5 6.e4 ♘xc3 7.bxc3 e5! 8.♗b5 (8.d5 ♘a5 9.h4 ♗c5! 10.♗a3 ♕d6 already favoured Black in Zhang Ziyang-Ni Hua, Xinghua Jiangsu 2011) 8...♗d7 9.♘e2 ♗g7 10.♗e3 (here 10.♖b1 ♘a5 11.♗d3 ♕h4+!? 12.g3 ♕e7 13.0-0 0-0 14.♗e3 ♖ad8 15.♕c1 b6 16.♖f2 f5 17.♗g5 ended in a repetition after 17...♗f6 18.♗h6 ♗g7 19.♗g5, Kuzubov-Timofeev, Ohrid 2009) 10...0-0 11.d5 ♘a5 12.♗d3 b6 13.0-0 ♘b7! 14.c4 c5 15.dxc6 ♗xc6 16.♘c3 was equal in Anand-Carlsen, Linares 2009. Black has the better pawn structure, White has a stronghold on d5 for his knight.

– 5.e4!? dxe4 6.d5 ♘e5 7.fxe4 ♗g7 8.♘f3 ♘fd7 9.♗e3 0-0 should not unduly worry Black, after 10.♕d2 f5 11.♗h6 ♘xf3+ 12.gxf3 ♘e5 13.♗e2 ♗xh6 14.♕xh6 fxe4 (14...♕d6) 15.♘xe4 e6 he had no difficulty in equalizing in Caruana-Howell, Biel 2010.

– 5.♗g5 ♗g7 6.e3 e6 7.cxd5 exd5 8.♗b5 0-0 9.♘ge2 h6 10.♗h4 ♘e7 11.g4 b6 12.♕d2 c5 was the blindfold game Kramnik-Dominguez, Nice 2010. An exciting but balanced position.

Another point of 3...♘c6 is revealed after 4.e4, when Black can play 4...e5.

And now the lines fork:

– 5.d5 ♘d4 6.♘e2 ♗c5 (rather than taking up the typical fianchetto position the bishop controls the dark squares weakened by White's third move) 7.♘xd4 ♗xd4.

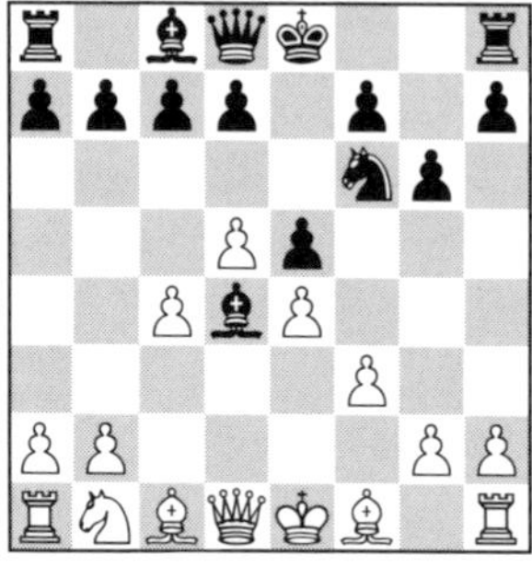

Black is doing well. For example: 8.♘c3 (8.♘a3 ♘h5!? 9.g3 d6 10.♘c2 ♗b6 11.♗e3 ♗xe3 – 11...0-0! – 12.♘xe3 0-0 13.♗d3 c5 draw, Michenka-Neubauer, Tatranske Zruby 2009) 8...♘h5 9.g3 d6 10.♗d3, Kuzmin-Kurnosov, St. Petersburg 2004, and now simply 10...0-0 is very comfortable for Black.

– After 5.♘e2 exd4 6.♘xd4 ♗g7 (6... ♗c5!?) it is telling that the natural 7.♗e3? blunders a pawn because of 7...♘xe4! 8.fxe4 ♕h4+.

– 5.dxe5 ♘xe5 6.♗e3 (6.♘c3 ♗c5) 6... ♗g7 7.♘c3 0-0 8.♕d2 d6 as in Laznicka-Dvoirys, Pardubice 2007, is a typical King's Indian, where Black is not doing badly in the development department.

4...♘e5 5.e4 d6

6.♘c3

The most natural move, although White does well to remember that after 6...♗g7, play has actually transposed to the Sämisch King's Indian (admittedly that was the point of 3.f3) in a version where he often prefers to postpone d4-d5: 1.d4 ♘f6 2.c4 g6 3.♘c3 ♗g7 4.e4 d6 5.f3 ♘c6!? 6.d5 (here 6.♗e3 and 6.♘e2 are far more popular!) 6...♘e5.

Black has done extremely well after the time-consuming 6.♘e2 ♗g7 7.♘ec3 (7.♘g3 h5!? was suggested by Svidler) 7...0-0 8.♗e2 e6 (immediately targeting the pawn – as explained earlier this is why Black has provoked d4-d5 in the first place) and now:

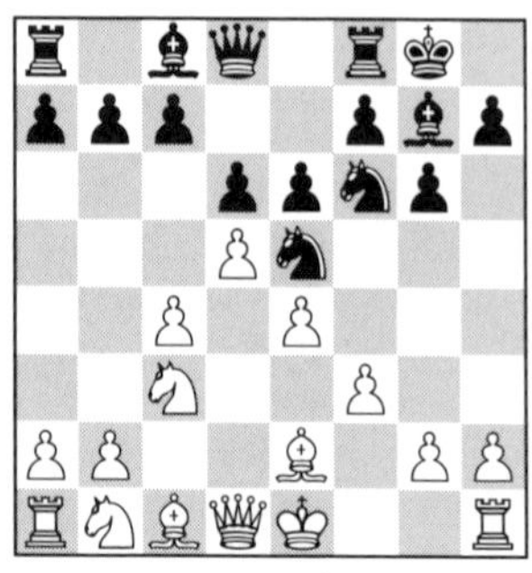

● 9.0-0 exd5 10.cxd5 c6. After one exchange on d5, Black targets the pawn again. This is essential to gain sufficient counterplay: 11.dxc6 (11.♗e3 cxd5 12.exd5 ♖e8 13.♕d2 ♗f5 14.♘a3 a6 15.♖ac1 ♖c8 was quite satisfactory for Black in Postny-Eljanov, Moscow 2006; White is clearly worse after 11.f4? ♕b6+ 12.♔h1 ♘eg4) 11...bxc6 12.♗e3 ♖e8 13.♘d2 d5 (Black has certainly solved all his opening problems) 14.♘b3 dxe4 15.♕xd8 ♖xd8 16.fxe4 ♗g4! 17.♗g5?! ♗xe2 18.♘xe2 ♖d6 19.♘c5?! ♘fd7 20.♘xd7 ♘xd7 and Black already won a pawn, and later the (blitz)game, in Mamedyarov-Carlsen, Moscow 2009.

● 9.f4 ♘ed7 10.0-0 (10.dxe6 fxe6 11.0-0 ♘c5 12.♕c2 b6 13.♗e3 ♗b7 14.♘d2 a5 is unclear according to Svidler – it looks pleasant enough for Black) 10...exd5 11.cxd5 ♖e8 12.♗f3 ♘c5 13.♖e1:

– Now after 13...h5 14.h3 b5 15.e5 dxe5 16.fxe5 ♘fd7 17.e6 ♘e5 Black won a complicated game in Nakamura-Svidler, Amsterdam 2009 (the game with extensive notes by Peter Svidler may be found in New In Chess 2009/7).

– However, according to Svidler it was even better to play the immediate 13...b5!, when similar complications as in the game occur without having weakened pawn g6.

6...♗g7

It makes sense to develop the bishop before attacking the centre.

Against Kramnik at the 2010 Olympiad in Khanty-Mansiysk, Navara tried the audacious 6...c6 7.f4 ♘ed7 8.♗e3 e5 9.dxe6 fxe6 10.♘h3 (Black's positional idea is 10.♘f3 e5 11.fxe5 ♘g4 12.♗g5 ♕b6) 10... e5 11.f5 (11.♗e2!?) 11...♕a5. The game eventually ended in a draw, but at present the position looks clearly preferable for White.

7.f4 ♘ed7 8.♘f3

It is not clear whether the knight is not better placed on f2. From this square it controls square g4 and protects the e-pawn. Play could continue 8.♘h3 0-0 9.♗e2 ♘c5 (in principle Black needs to play both ...e6 and ...c6. Therefore it was wrong to play 9...c6 10.♘f2 cxd5 11.cxd5 ♘b6?! for after 12.a4 ♗d7 13.a5 White had a substantial space advantage. He quickly gained the upper hand after 13...♘c8 14.0-0 e6 15.dxe6 fxe6 16.♕b3 in Kurnosov-Vokarev, Olginka 2011) 10.♘f2

10...e6 (I would prefer this plan over 10... ♖e8 11.0-0 e5 12.f5!? – this pawn sacrifice is more dangerous than 12.dxe6 ♗xe6 13.♕c2 ♗d7 14.♗f3 ♗c6 15.♗d2 a5 16.♖fe1± Grischuk-Kurnosov, Moscow 2010 – 12...gxf5 13.exf5 ♗xf5 14.♘g4 ♗xg4 15.♗xg4 ♘xg4 16.♕xg4 ♕d7 17.♖f5 and White is better despite being a pawn down. The Chinese champion quickly converted his positional edge in Ding Liren-Areschenko, Ningbo 2011) 11.0-0 exd5 12.cxd5 c6 (the principled approach, but play is very sharp of course) 13.dxc6 bxc6 14.♗f3 ♕e7!? 15.♗e3 d5!? (inviting great complications) 16.e5 ♘fd7 17.b4 (17. ♖c1 ♘e6 followed by ...♗b7 and ...f6 is the way to go when White plays more quietly) 17...♘e6 18.b5 This looks very strong, but Giri had calculated excellently:

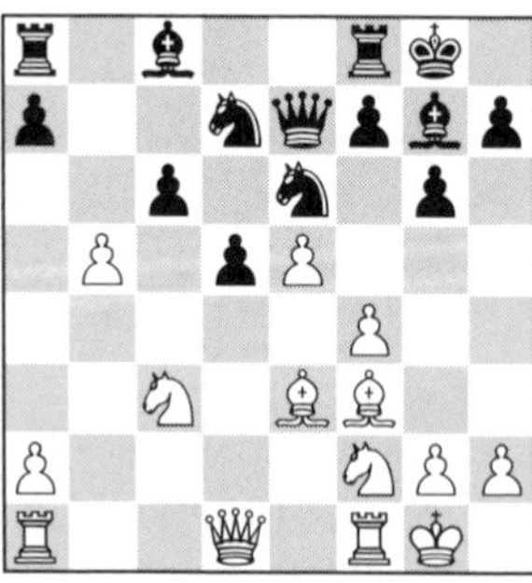

18...♘b6! 19.f5!? (19.bxc6 d4 20.♗xd4 ♖d8 21.♘b5 – 21.♘e2 ♗a6 22.c7 ♕xc7 23.♗xa8 ♘xa8∓ – 21...♗a6 22.♘d6 ♗xf1 23.♔xf1 and the engines will tell you that play is about equal!) 19...gxf5 20.♗xb6 axb6 21.bxc6 ♗xe5 22.♘xd5 and now 22...♕g5 was objectively better than 22...♕h4 23.g3 ♕g5 as in Grischuk-Giri, Wijk aan Zee 2011. Later in the game White missed a good chance, and then Giri missed an even better chance before it all ended in a draw...

8...0-0 9.♗d3

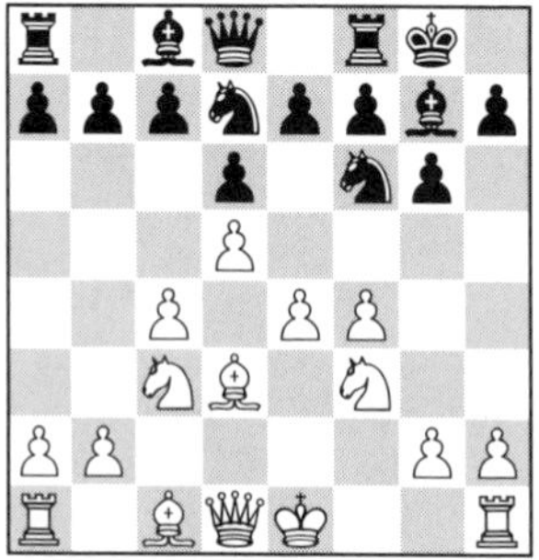

White has built up an impressive centre and has gained some space, yet Black has sufficient counterplay. He holds a (very) slight advantage in development, and he can attack the advanced d5-pawn easily. In the subsequent game extracts Black is almost always very OK, and it would appear that White has to find improvements earlier on.

9...e6

The other pawn move also comes into consideration: 9...c6 has the advantage of immediately opening up possibilities for the queen along the diagonal b6-g1: 10.0-0 ♘c5 (equally good looks 10...♕b6+ 11.♔h1 ♘c5 12.h3? – 12.♗c2 transposes below to the main line in this note after 12.♔h1 – 12...♕a6 – 12...♘h5! – 13.g4?! cxd5 14.exd5 ♘xd3 15.♕xd3 and now 15...h5 would have been even better than the game continuation 15...e6 Ward-Conquest, Scarborough 1999) 11.♗c2 and now:

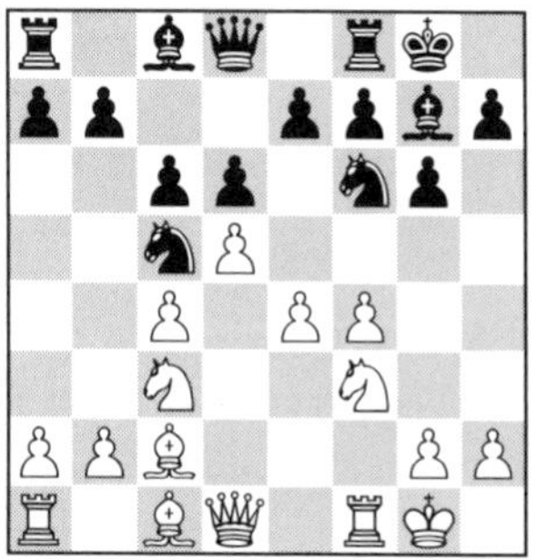

● 11...♕b6 12.♔h1 (12.♗e3? ♕xb2 13.♗d4 ♘xd5!) 12...♗g4 13.♖b1, and now:

– 13...cxd5 14.cxd5 ♖ac8 15.♗e3 ♕b4! 16.h3 ♘cxe4!? (16...♗xf3 17.♕xf3 ♘fd7) 17.♗xe4 ♖xc3! (17...♘xe4 18.hxg4 ♘g3+ 19.♔g1 ♘xf1 20.♕xf1±) 18.bxc3 and after this interesting exchange sacrifice the players agreed to a draw in Jussupow-Spassky, Linares 1983. The move order in this game was 5...♘c6 6.d5 ♘e5 and so on via a regular Sämisch King's Indian.

– 13...a5 is the most recent example from this position: 14.♗e3 ♘fd7 15.♕e2 ♕c7 draw, Vitiugov-Tomashevsky, Moscow 2011. There is of course a lot of play left in the position, although the chances are probably about equal.

● Bad is 11...e6? 12.dxc6 bxc6 13.e5 dxe5 14.♕xd8 ♖xd8 15.fxe5 ♘fd7 16.♗g5 ♖f8

17.♖fe1±, Yang-Bykhovsky, Lubbock 2011.
● Also quite reasonable is 11...cxd5 12.e5 (12.cxd5 ♕b6) 12...♘fd7! 13.♕xd5 (13.exd6 dxc4=; 13.♘xd5 e6∓) 13...♘b6 14.♕d4 ♗g4 which favoured Black in I.Sokolov-Martinovic, Cetinje 1991.

10.0-0 exd5 11.exd5

More ambitious is 11.cxd5 c6! 12.♗e3 (12.h3?! cxd5 13.exd5 ♕a5 14.♗c2 ♘b6 15.♗b3 ♖e8 clearly favoured Black in Mohota-S.Hansen, Pattaya 2011; 12.dxc6 bxc6 13.♔h1 ♘c5 is fine for Black) 12...♘g4 (12...cxd5) 13.♗d4 (a sacrifice, but if White has to give up this bishop for the knight he can never be better. Black's dark-squared bishop would be a monster) 13...♗xd4+ 14.♘xd4 ♘e3 15.♕d2 ♘xf1 16.♖xf1 ♖e8 17.♔h1 c5 18.♘db5 ♘f8 was a (too) optimistic exchange sacrifice in Bitan-Deepan, Bhubaneswar 2010.

11...c6 Also not bad is 11...♘c5 12.♗c2 ♖e8. **12.dxc6** Black is slightly better after 12.♔h1 cxd5 13.cxd5 ♘c5. **12...bxc6 13.♔h1**

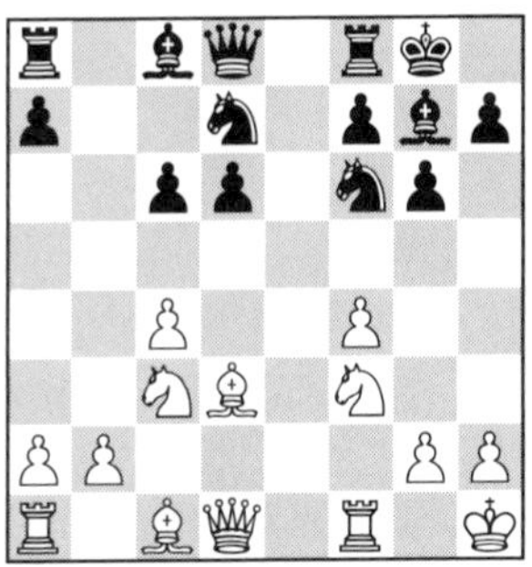

Black is already slightly more comfortable, and it is White who has to take care. The remainder of the game is not very interesting for our purposes, so I will restrict myself to a few short comments.

13...♘c5 14.♗e3 14.♗c2 ♗e6 gives Black the initiative. **14...♘g4** 14...♖b8 with the idea of 15.♖b1?? ♘xd3 16.♕xd3 ♗f5 was strong too. **15.♗g1** 15.♗xc5 dxc5∓. **15...♖b8 16.♘a4 ♖e8** 16...♘xd3 17.♕xd3 ♖b4!∓. **17.♘xc5 dxc5 18.♗xc5 ♖xb2 19.♘e5?**

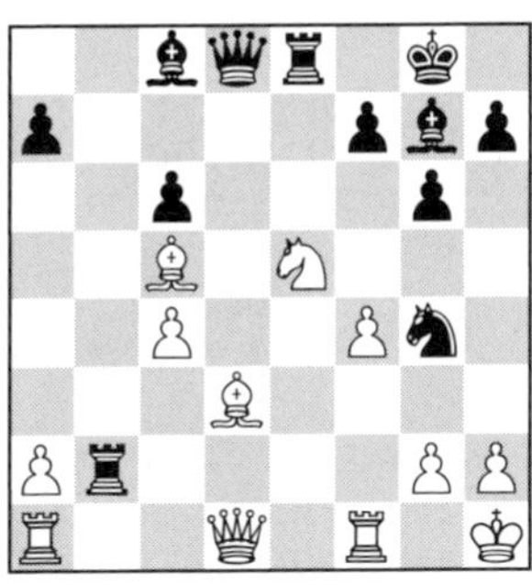

19...♗xe5 Also winning is 19...♖xe5 20.fxe5 ♕h4 21.♗g1 (21.h3 ♕g3–+) 21...♘xh2! 22.♕e1 (22.♗xh2 ♗xe5–+) 22...♕g5 23.♖f2 ♘g4!. **20.fxe5 ♘xe5?** Losing a substantial part of Black's advantage. 20...♘xh2! was winning in view of 21.♔xh2 ♕h4+ 22.♔g1 ♖xg2+ 23.♔xg2 ♗h3+. **21.♗c2 ♕xd1 22.♗xd1 ♘d3?! 23.♗d4 ♖d2 24.♗xa7 c5 25.♗f3 ♗e6 26.a4 ♗xc4 27.♖fb1** 27.♔g1 and White has drawing chances with his bishop pair and passed a-pawn. **27...♘e5 28.♖e1 f6? 29.♗xc5 ♖c8 30.♗e3 ♘xf3 31.gxf3 ♖c2** Now White should be able to draw without too many difficulties. Black later wins the game (again); probably because of the FIDE tempo. **32.♔g1 ♗d5 33.♖f1 ♖e2 34.♖ae1 ♖a2 35.♖a1 ♖cc2 36.♖xa2 ♖xa2 37.♗b6?** 37.♗d4! ♔f7 38.♖a1. **37...♖xa4∓ 38.♔g2 ♖a3 39.h4 ♔f7 40.♗c7 ♔e6 41.♔g3 ♔f5 42.♗d6 ♖b3 43.♗c5 h5 44.♔f2 g5** 44...♖xf3+ 45.♔g1 ♔g4 46.♖xf3 ♗xf3 47.♗d4 ♔xh4 48.♗xf6+ is a draw. **45.hxg5 fxg5 46.♗e3 ♖b2+ 47.♔g3 h4+ 48.♔h3 ♖b3 49.♗d2 ♗xf3–+ 50.♗e1 ♔g6 51.♔h2 ♖b2+ 52.♖f2 ♖b1 53.♖f1 ♔h5 54.♖xf3 ♖xe1** White resigned.

CHAPTER 15

Sinisa Drazic

Sicilian: the Bücker-Welling Variation

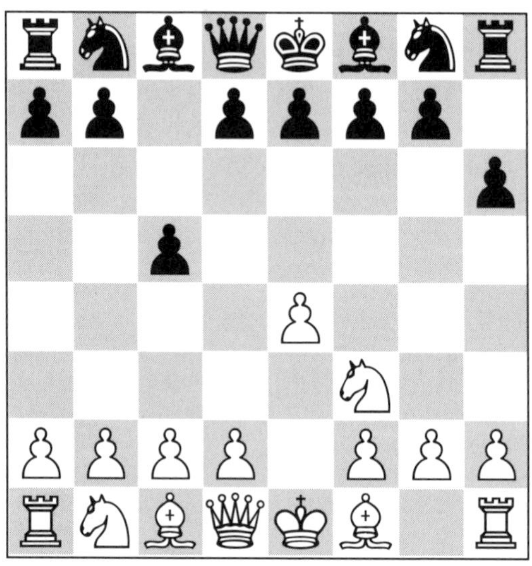

1.e4 c5 2.♘f3 h6!?

After playing chess for over a quarter of a century, I am more and more inclined to implement something new on the chess board. This is certainly inspired by the advance of modern chess technology and the activity of many chess 'parrots', who with their modern programs and notebooks in their hands, are ready to beat you in any corner of chess theory. The only way out of this situation is to move the boundaries and wrong-foot such opponents as early as possible.

In this article I will present you some of my recent efforts, with a surprise on the second move in the most popular chess opening: the Sicilian Defence!

As 2...h6!? is never played in high level games, I started very slowly and carefully with putting it in my practice, and until now with very decent results.

In this article, we will investigate the most popular and dangerous moves for White, and some active strategies for Black. You won't find much on 2...h6 in any of the current opening manuals. There is, however, one very good article written by Stefan Bücker more than twenty years ago, and published in New In Chess Yearbook 18.

He has dubbed 2...h6 the Bücker-Welling Variation.

☐ **Igor Malakhov**
■ **Sinisa Drazic**
Rijeka Ech 2010

1.e4 c5 2.♘f3 h6 3.d4

Just like in the O'Kelly Variation with 2...a6 (see SOS-7, Chapter 3, p.25) Black has prepared himself for 3.d4 and is therefore happy to see White 'fall' for it.

- 3.c3 is more quiet, White intends to build up his centre as usual, arguing that he has gained a useful tempo (why 2...h6). Black's best solution is to play some kind of French hybrid position with 3...e6 4.d4 d5 (see Doric-Drazic). For 3...g5 see Palac-Sulava below.
- 3.c4 similarly postpones d4. See Borgo-Drazic where I went for 3...d6 and 4...g5. The immediate 3...g5 is also possible.
- I do not think that 3.d3 poses a serious threat. Here 3...♘c6 4.g3 g5 is a Basman favourite.
- 3.♘c3 is a good move. Play may transpose into the Haberditz Variation.

3...cxd4

I have also played in 'Basman-style' with 3...g5 4.♗c4 (4.d5) 4...♗g7 5.♘e5 e6 6.♘xf7?! ♔xf7 7.♕h5+ ♔e7 8.e5 ♘c6 9.f4 ♕e8 10.♕g4 b5! 11.♗d3 cxd4 12.♘d2 ♔d8 13.0-0 ♘ge7 14.♘e4 ♘f5 and White had not nearly enough for his piece and lost in Sarcevic-Drazic, Pula 2010.

4.♘xd4

4...♘f6

Dubious is 4...e5?! when 5.♘b5 ♘f6 6.♘1c3 d6 transposes to the main game. However, 5.♘f5! is a strong reply. I give a sample line of what may happen after 5...d5: 6.♗b5+ ♘c6 7.exd5 ♗xf5 8.dxc6 ♕xd1+ 9.♔xd1 0-0-0+ 10.♘d2 b6 11.c3 ♗d3 12.a4 a6 13.♗xd3 ♖xd3 14.♔c2 ♖d5 15.♘c4 ♔c7 16.♗e3 ♗c5 17.b4 ♗xe3 18.♘xe3 ♖d8 19.b5 and White wins.

5.♘c3

Not 5.f3 e5 and Black is fine.

5...e5

Black wants to play the 'Lasker Sicilian', with good chances to confuse White in his plans. Indeed, ♗g5!? is no longer on the cards.

Alternatively, I have never tried 5...d6!?, but who knows?

6.♘db5

A serious reply is 6.♘f5, when after 6...d6 7.♘e3 ♗e6 8.♗c4 ♗e7 9.0-0 0-0 10.♘ed5 ♘bd7 11.♗e3 ♘g4 12.♕e2 ♘xe3 13.♘xe3 ♘b6 14.♖ad1 White held a slight edge in Kristensen-Jaksland, Denmark 1992.

More aggressive is 6...d5, which Bücker deems incorrect because of 7.♗b5 ♘c6 8.exd5 ♗xf5 9.dxc6 ♕xd1+ 10.♘xd1 0-0-0.

Instead 6.♘f3 ♘c6 (6...d6) is known from the Sveshnikov Variation, and does not really promise White anything. Play could continue 7.♗e3 ♗b4 8.♗c4 ♘xe4 9.♕d5 (9.♗xf7+ ♔xf7! 10.♕d5+ ♔f8 11.♕xe4 d5∓) 9...♘d6 10.♘xe5 ♕f6!! 11.f4 ♗xc3+ 12.bxc3 ♘xc4 13.♕xc4 (13.♘xc4 ♕xc3+ 14.♔f2 ♕xc2+ 15.♔f3 0-0 16.♘d6!?, with very interesting play!) 13...♘xe5 14.♕e4 d6 15.♗d4 0-0 16.fxe5 dxe5 and Black won in Poswiatowski-Prus, Grodzisk Mazowiecki 2007.

Naturally, White can also play 6.♘de2 and now 6...♘c6 7.♘g3 or 6...♗c5 7.♗e3!? as in Dekker-Welling, Eindhoven Dutch semi-finals 1988.

Bucker calls 6.♘b3 'solid and good'.

6...d6

Here is the point of 2...h6 if you like. Black has managed to play ...e5 without allowing White to fight for control over square d5 with ♗g5. Nor can White check on d6 as in the Haberditz Variation which arises after 6...♘c6 – we will examine this via the move order with 3.♘c3.

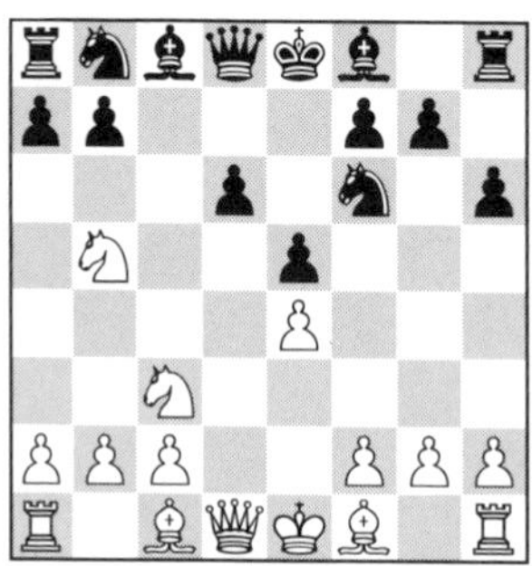

7.a4

● 7.♘d5 ♘xd5 8.♕xd5 (one of the critical positions in the main line with 3.d4. 8.exd5 a6 9.♘c3 ♗e7∓ 10.♗e2 0-0) 8...♘c6 9.♗e2 (this looks natural, but it's a losing move! When I first saw this game, I was shocked how Black could so quickly develop the initiative after a normal move like 9.♗e2; instead 9.♗e3 a6 10.♘c3 ♗e6 11.♕d2 ♖c8 12.a3 ♕a5 13.f3 ♕c7 14.♕f2 b5 15.♗d3 ♕b7 16.0-0 g5 17.♘d5 ♗xd5 18.exd5 ♘e7 19.♖fd1 ♗g7 20.♕e2 ♖a8 21.a4 0-0 22.axb5 axb5 23.♗xb5 ♘xd5 24.♗f2 ♘c7 25.♗c4 ♖xa1 26.♖xa1 ♕xb2 and Black won in Schneider-Stephan, Brakel 1967) 9...a6 10.♘c3 (10.♘a3 is the best move in this position, which means that White has done something wrong at an earlier point!) 10...♘d4! 11.♗d3 ♖b8 12.b4 (White actually creates square a5 to evacuate his queen! 12.♗e3 ♗e6) 12...b5! 13.a4

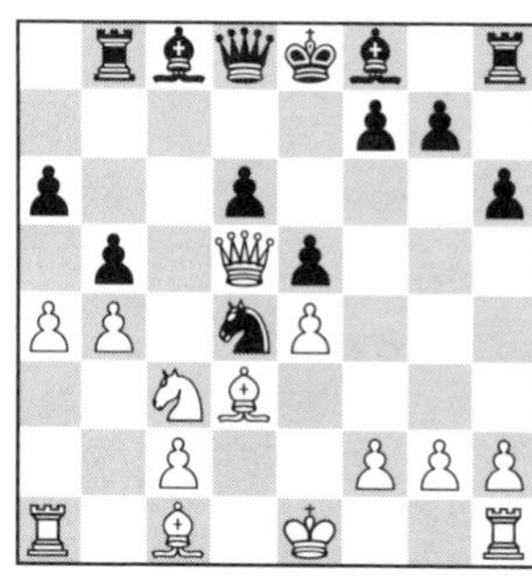

13...♗e6. No queen, no game! 0-1, Ridarcikova-Srienz, Bratislava 1991.

● A sample line after 7.♘a3 is 7...♗e6 8.♗c4 ♕c8 9.♗xe6 fxe6 10.0-0 ♗e7.

7...♗e6 8.f4 a6 9.f5!? ♗c8 10.♘a3 d5

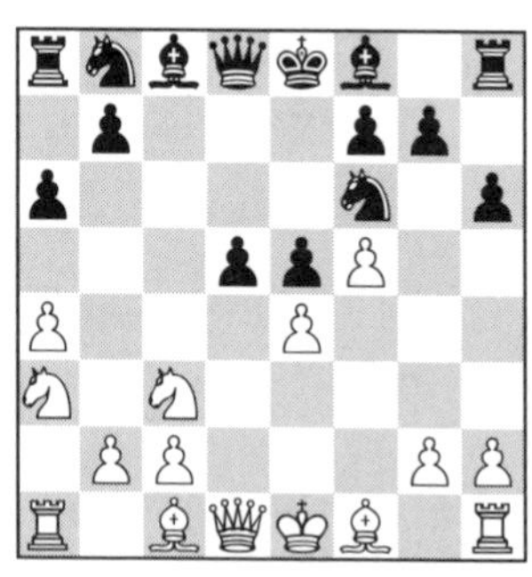

11.exd5

Or 11.♘xd5 when Black loses after 11... ♘xe4 12.♗e3 ♕h4+ (very romantic but wrong) 13.g3 ♘xg3 14.hxg3 ♕xh1 15.♘c7+ ♔e7 16.♗c5+ ♔f6 17.♕d8+ ♔xf5 18.♕xc8+.

Correct is 11... ♘xd5 which leads to unclear play after 12.exd5 ♗xf5 13.♘c4 ♗c5 14.♗e3 ♘d7.

11...♗xf5 12.♗e2 ♗c5 13.♘c4 ♘bd7

So material is equal and Black has all his light pieces developed; he can be happy with the outcome of the opening.

14.♗e3

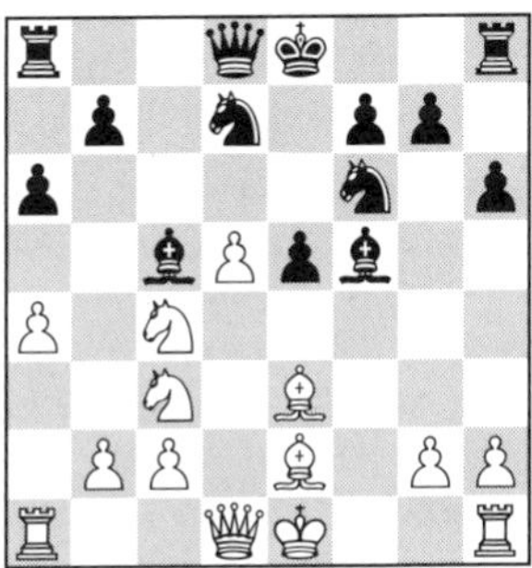

Of course White wants to go with his king to the safer side.

14...♗xe3 15.♘xe3 ♗g6 16.a5 0-0 17.0-0

Both sides have taken their safety precautions and now start setting the board on fire.

17...b5 18.♔h1 ♖c8 19.♗d3 ♗xd3 20.♕xd3 ♘c5 21.♕f5 b4 22.♘cd1 ♖e8

Black does not fully equalize after 22... ♘xd5 23.♕xe5 ♘xe3 24.♘xe3 ♖e8 25.♕f4 ♕c7 26.♕xc7 ♖xc7 27.♘d5 ♖b7 28.♖ae1 ♔f8 29.♖xe8+ ♔xe8 30.b3 (30.♖f4 b3) 30...♘e6 31.♔g1 ♖b5 32.♖d1 and White is slightly better.

23.♘f2 ♖c7 24.♖ad1 b3 25.cxb3 ♘xb3 26.♕d3

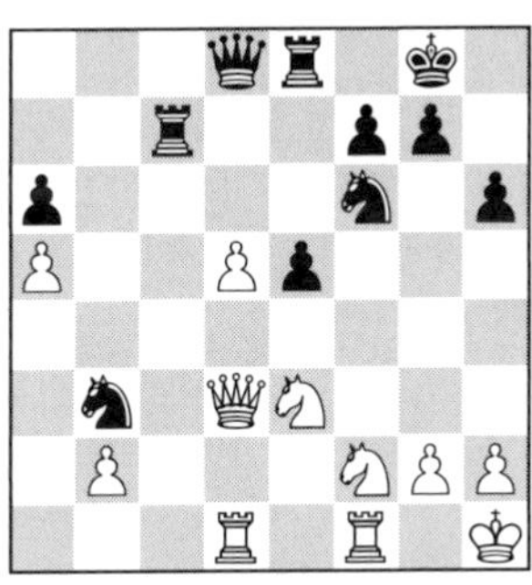

26...♘d4

26...♘c5 probably gives more chances for a longer fight: 27.♕a3 ♕b8 28.b4 ♘ce4 29.♘xe4 ♘xe4 30.♖c1 ♖ec8.

27.♕xa6 ♘xd5 28.♘fg4 ♘xe3 29.♘xe3 ♕b8 30.♕d6 ♖a7 31.♕a3 ♕b3 32.♕c5 ♖b7 33.♘c4 ♖b5 34.♕c7 ♖b7 35.♕c5 ♖b5 36.♕c7 ♖b7

Draw.

□ **Nenad Doric**
■ **Sinisa Drazic**
Rijeka Mediterranean Open 2010

1.e4 c5 2.♘f3 h6 3.c3 e6

For 3...g5!? see the next game.

4.d4 4.♗e2 d6 5.d3 b6 6.0-0 ♗b7 7.♘bd2 ♘f6 ½-½ was Fercec-Drazic, Rijeka 2010.

4...d5

5.exd5
White can also opt for the Advance Variation in the French Defence with 5.e5, when Black has played the unusual ...h6. If you don't like this then check out 3...g5!?.
5...exd5
5...♕xd5 6.♗d3 (6.♗e3 cxd4 7.cxd4 ♗b4+ 8.♘c3 ♘c6 9.a3 ♗xc3+ 10.bxc3 ♘f6 11.♗d3 0-0 12.0-0 ♖d8) 6...♘f6 7.0-0 ♘c6 8.♖e1 ♗e7 9.♗e3 cxd4 10.cxd4 0-0 11.♘c3 ♕d6 with a normal IQP position in Hartung-Schammo, Luxembourg 1997/98.
6.♗b5+ ♗d7 7.♕e2+
Alternatives are 7.♗xd7+ ♘xd7 8.0-0 ♗e7 and 7.a4.
7...♕e7 8.♗xd7+ ♘xd7 9.dxc5 ♕xe2+ 10.♔xe2 ♗xc5 11.♗e3
Black is also comfortable after 11.♖d1 ♘gf6 12.♗e3 ♗xe3 13.♔xe3 0-0-0 14.♔e2 ♖he8+ 15.♔f1 ♘c5.
11...♘gf6

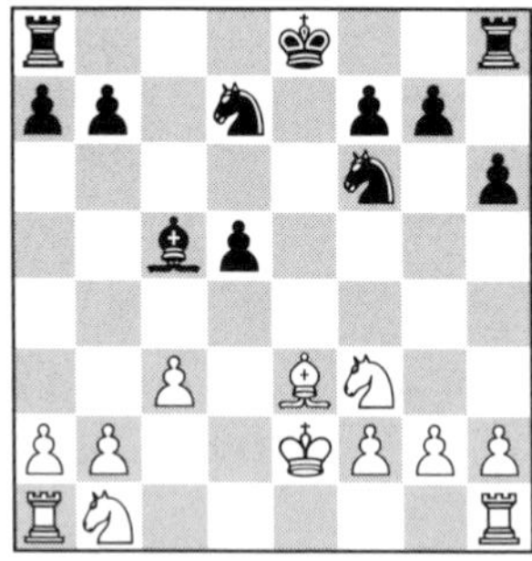

12.♘bd2
Or 12.♗xc5 ♘xc5 13.♖d1 0-0-0 14.♘a3 ♖he8+ 15.♔f1 ♘a4 16.♖ab1 ♖d7 with a balanced position.
12...0-0 13.♘b3
Or 13.♖hd1 ♖fe8 (13...♗xe3 14.fxe3 ♖fe8 15.h3) 14.♘f1.
13...♗xe3 14.♔xe3
White runs risks after 14.fxe3 ♖fe8 15.♖hd1 a5 16.a4 (16.h3 a4 17.♘bd4 ♘b6 18.♘d2 ♖e7 19.♔d3 ♖ae8 20.♖e1 unclear) 16...♘b6 17.♖d3 (17.♘bd4 ♘c4∓) 17...♘c4 18.♖a2 ♘g4 19.♖xd5 ♘cxe3 20.♖xa5 ♘xg2+ 21.♔f1 ♘2e3+ 22.♔g1 ♖ad8∓.
14...♘g4+ 15.♔e2 ♖fe8+ 16.♔f1 ♘b6

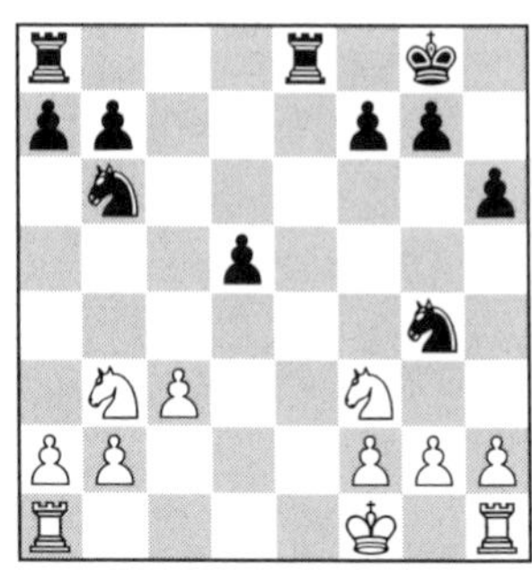

Black will now use the position of White's king to provoke some weaknesses in the opponent's pawn structure.
17.♘c5 ♘c4! 18.♘d3 a5 19.♘d4 ♘ge5 20.♘xe5 ♖xe5 21.♘f3 ♖e7 22.b3
A weakness is created!
22...♘a3 23.♘d4! ♖c8 24.♖c1 b5
Time is very important now!
24...g6 25.h4 ♔g7 26.♖h3
25.♘e2 ♖ce8 26.♘d4 ♖c7 27.♘e2 b4 28.cxb4 ♖xc1+ 29.♘xc1 ♘c2 30.g3
Bad is 30.♘e2? d4 31.g3 d3 32.♘c3 axb4 33.♘d1 ♖e1+ 34.♔g2 d2 35.f4 ♖xd1. But playable was 30.♘d3 axb4 31.h4.
30...axb4 31.♘d3 ♖a8 32.♘c1 ♖e8 33.♘d3 Black wins after 33.♔g2 ♘e1+ 34.♔f1 d4. **33...♖a8 34.♘c1 ♔f8 35.♔e2 ♔e7 36.♖d1** 36.♔d2. **36...♔d6 37.♖d2 ♘a3 38.♘d3 ♘b1 39.♖c2 ♘c3+ 40.♔d2 ♘xa2**
Black has won a pawn, but the win still involves a lot of hard work.
41.h4 g6 42.♖b2 ♖a7 43.♖c2 ♖a3 44.♖b2 g5 45.hxg5 hxg5 46.♖c2 ♘c3 47.♘xb4 ♘e4+ 48.♔e2 ♖xb3 49.♘d3 ♘c3+ 50.♔d2 d4

51.♖b2?

In such positions it is a cardinal sin to exchange rooks. Almost every knight endgame with a pawn up is winning!

51...♘e4+ 52.♔e2 ♖xb2+ 53.♘xb2 ♔d5 54.♔f3 f5 55.♔e2 ♔c5 56.♘a4+ ♔b5 57.♘b2 ♘c5 58.♔d2 ♔b4 59.f3 ♔b5 60.♔e2 ♔c6 61.♔d2 ♔d5 62.♔e2 ♘d7 63.♘d3 ♔c4 64.♔d2 ♔d5 65.♘b4+ ♔c5 66.♘d3+ ♔c4 67.♘b2+ ♔d5 68.♘d3 ♘e5 69.♘e1 g4 70.fxg4 fxg4 71.♘g2 ♔e4 72.♔e2 ♘d3 73.♘h4 ♘b2 74.♔d2 ♘c4+ 75.♔e2 d3+ 76.♔f2 ♘e3 77.♔e1 ♘f5 78.♘g6 ♘xg3 79.♔d2 ♘f1+ 80.♔e1 ♘e3 81.♔d2 g3 82.♘h4 g2

White resigned.

□ **Mladen Palac**
■ **Nenad Sulava**

Montecatini Terme 1995

The interesting fact is that I was present at the same tournament, and this game drew my serious attention, because both players were good friends of mine, and I felt a high tension between them. Sulava as a very original player surprised the theoretical expert Mladen Palac and there arose some kind of hybrid of the Panov Attack in the Caro-Kann, with a very unusual early ...g5!

1.e4 c5 2.♘f3 h6 3.c3 g5

Basman's move, and a main idea of 2...h6!?.

4.d4 cxd4

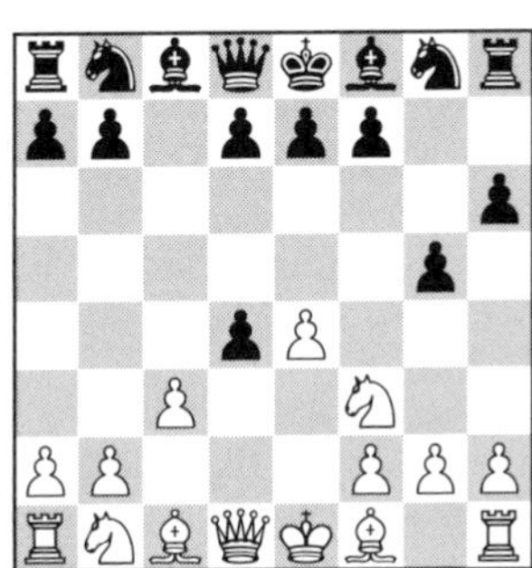

5.cxd4

Unusual but not necessarily bad is 5.♕xd4 ♘f6 6.e5 ♘c6 7.♕a4 ♘d5 8.h4!? gxh4 9.♕xh4 d6 10.♕e4 dxe5 11.♘xe5 ♕d6 12.♘xc6 bxc6 13.♘d2 Casper-Rechel, Germany Bundesliga 1994/95.

5...d5 6.exd5

6.e5 ♘c6 7.♘c3 ♗g4 8.♗e2 (8.♗b5 e6 9.♕a4 ♘e7; 8.♗e3) 8...e6 and this looks like a French, with the bishop on g4, and an 'slightly' exposed black kingside.

6...♘f6 7.♘c3 ♗g7 8.h4

Black has a difficult choice now, to take on h4 and to destroy his kingside, or to play 8...g4, with unclear consequences.

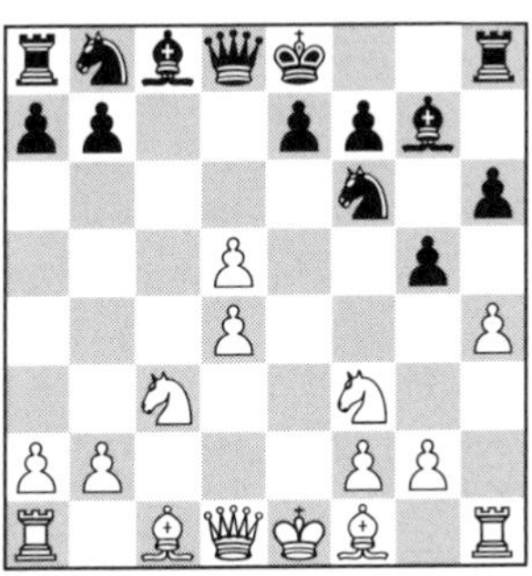

8...g4 9.♘e5 a6 10.♗e2 h5 11.0-0
Nothing is gained by 11.f3 ♘xd5 12.fxg4 ♘xc3 13.bxc3 ♗xe5 14.dxe5 ♕xd1+ 15.♗xd1 ♗xg4 16.♗xg4 hxg4 17.♖b1 b5. But it was also normal to play 11.♕b3 b5 (11...0-0 12.♗g5 ♘bd7) 12.a4.
11...♘bd7 12.♗g5 ♘b6 13.♕b3 0-0
Play favours White after either 13...♘fxd5 14.♘xd5 ♘xd5 15.♗c4, or 13...♘bxd5? 14.♗xf6 exf6 15.♘xf7 ♔xf7 16.♗c4.
14.♖fe1 ♘h7!?
Inviting complications.
15.♗xe7 ♕xe7 16.♕xb6 ♕xh4 17.g3 ♕d8 18.♕xd8 ♖xd8 19.♗f1 Perhaps 19.♘a4!?. **19...♘g5 20.♗g2 ♗f5 21.♘e2 ♖d6 22.♘f4 ♖h6**
Black has found a very interesting way to attack in the middlegame without queens. White is a pawn up, but this doesn't help so much, because he has no dynamic potential in his position. On the other hand, Black is a pawn up on the kingside, an active rook and bishop pair.
23.♖ac1 h4 24.gxh4 ♖xh4 25.d6
Now White has his own trump, but Black is ready to strike.

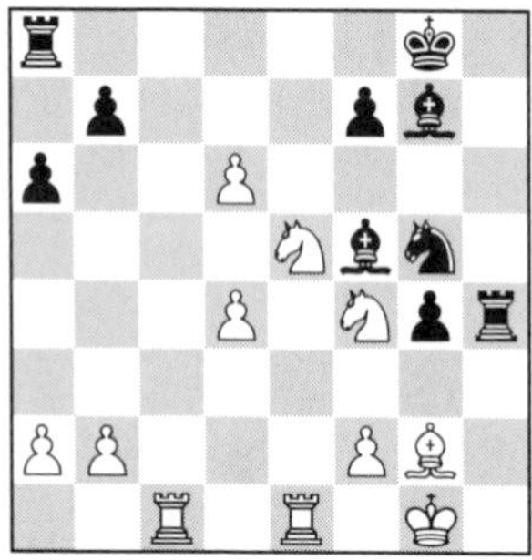

25...♘f3+! 26.♗xf3 gxf3 27.♘d5 ♔h7
Preventing the check on e7, and freeing the g-file for the other rook.
28.♘e7 ♗e6 29.♘xf3 ♖g4+ 30.♔f1 ♖d8 31.d5 31.♖c3 ♖xd6 32.♔e2 ♗xd4 33.♘xd4 ♖dxd4∓. **31...♗d7 32.♖e3 ♗h6 33.♖c7 ♗b5+ 34.♔e1 ♗xe3 35.fxe3 ♖xd6 36.♖xb7? ♖g2 37.a4 ♖h6! 38.♘g5+ ♖xg5 39.axb5 ♖g2 40.♔f1 ♖xb2 41.bxa6 ♖h1** Mate.

□ **Giulio Borgo**
■ **Sinisa Drazic**
Milan 2010

1.e4 c5 2.♘f3 h6 3.c4
The critical 3.c4, perhaps the move which made me most nervous, before the decision to play the risky move 2..h6!?.
3...d6
Black will play for dark-square control a la the Myers Defence (1.c4 g5) as all normal Sicilian lines will lead to bad Maroczy's. The immediate 3...g5 is also playable.
3...♘c6 makes no sense, because after pushing d2-d4, Black has no time to push g7-g5, which was already prepared by ...h6! – 4.d4 g5 5.d5 g4 (5...♘a5 6.h4 g4 7.♘e5 – or 6...gxh4 7.♗d2 ♗g7 8.♗c3±) 6.dxc6 gxf3 7.cxd7+ ♗xd7 8.♕xf3 ♗g7 9.♘c3.
Just bad is 3...e6 4.d4 cxd4 5.♘xd4 ♘f6 6.♘c3.
4.d4 g5 4...cxd4 5.♘xd4 ♘f6 6.♘c3 is not tested yet! **5.♗e3** If 5.♘c3 then 5...♗g7 6.d5 ♗xc3+ 7.bxc3 ♘d7.
5...♗g7 6.♘c3 ♘d7
I decided to keep the tension in the centre at any cost.

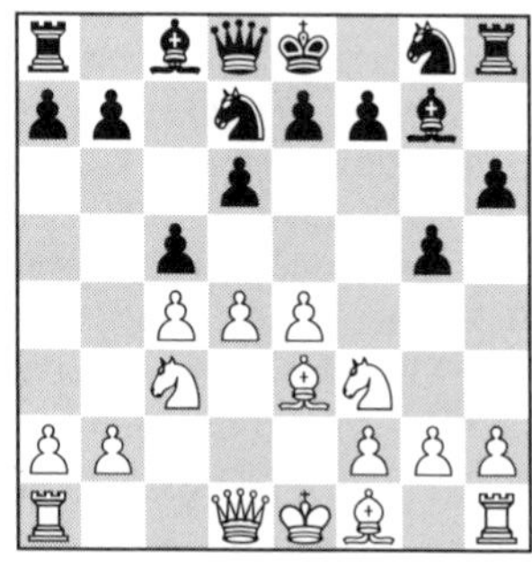

7.h3?!

This move made me very happy. It seems that White does not have a clear idea how to undermine Black's strategy. Besides, he will lose a tempo if he decides to play h3-h4 later on.

7...a6 8.Qd2 e6 9.0-0-0 Qa5 10.Kb1 Ne7 11.Be2

The remaining time for White was 44 minutes, which means half his time has already been consumed after only 11 moves. The surprise is working well!

11...Ng6 12.h4

Only five moves before h2-h3 was played!

12...g4 13.Ne1 h5 14.f4

White should keep the tension in the centre with 14.Nc2!.

14...gxf3

This move takes me almost 15 minutes, because of the change of the pawn structure, and estimating the consequences of opening the g-file.

15.gxf3 b5

Heightening the tension. Chess can be fun!

16.e5

Or 16.cxb5 axb5 17.Bxb5 0-0 18.dxc5 dxc5 19.Bxd7 Rd8. Defintely not 16.Nc2? b4.

16...cxd4

Here White had left himself with 21 minutes against my 51.

17.Ne4 Qxd2 18.Nxd6+ Ke7 19.Bxd2 Bxe5 20.Nxc8+ Rhxc8 21.cxb5 axb5 22.Bxb5 Nb6

Almost by force, a position similar to a Meran has arisen, with the 'small' difference that the white king is on the other side of the board. White has a weakness on h4, and his passed pawns are almost blocked, due to the activity of the black pieces, especially the rooks.

23.Bb4+ Kf6 24.Nd3 Nd5 25.Nxe5 Kxe5 26.Rhe1+ Ne3 27.a4 Nxh4

28.Bd6+

Black is also clearly better after 28.Bc3 dxc3 29.Rxe3+ Kf6 30.bxc3 Ng2 31.Re2 (31.Red3 Nf4 32.Re3 Nd5) 31...Nf4 32.Rc2 Rc5.

28...Kf6 29.Rxd4 Nhf5

White was in time-trouble, Black had 36 minutes left.

30.Rd3 Nxd6 31.Rxd6 Nf5

31...Nd5 32.Bc6 Ra6 33.Bb7 (33.Rxd5 exd5 34.Bb7 Rca8 35.Rh1 Kg5) 33...Rxd6 34.Bxc8 Nb6 35.Bb7 Nxa4.

32.Rd2 h4 33.Rh2 Rg8 34.Bc6 Ra6! 35.Bb5 Rd6 36.Rc1 Rg3 37.Bc6 Nd4 38.Be4 Kg5 39.Rch1 f5 40.Bb7 Rb6 41.f4+ Kf6 42.Rd1 Nb3

The bishop is dominated.

43.Bc8 h3 44.Rdh1 Nc5 45.Rxh3 Rxh3 46.Rxh3

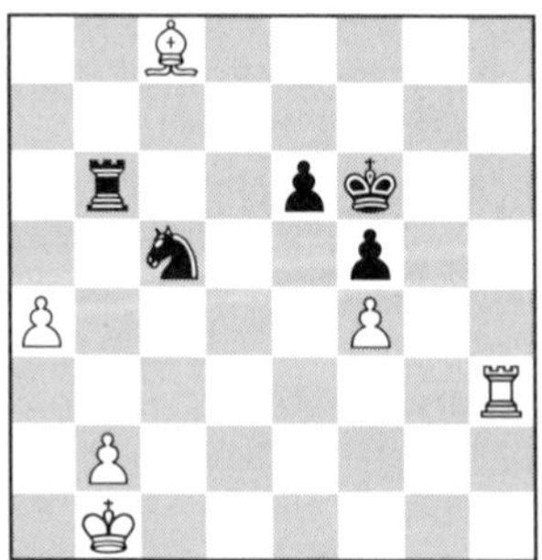

46...♘xa4

Black would win after 46...♖c6 47.♖c3 ♖xc8 48.b4 ♖b8 49.♖xc5 ♖xb4+ 50.♔c2 ♖xa4. Unfortunately White has 47.b4!! ♘xa4 48.♗d7 ♖a6 49.♗xa4 ♖xa4 50.♖b3.

47.b3 ♘c5 48.♔c2 ♔e7

48...♖c6.

49.♖e3 ♔d6 50.♖e5 ♖c6 51.♗xe6 ♘xe6+ 52.♔d3

52.♔b2 ♖c5.

52...♘xf4+

White resigned.

3.♘c3 – Transposing to the Haberditz Variation

1.e4 c5 2.♘f3 h6 3.♘c3

A clever move order in my opinion.

3...♘c6

Alternatively, there is 3...g5 4.d4 ♗g7, or 4...g4 5.♘g1 cxd4 6.♕xd4 ♘f6 7.h3 ♘c6 8.♕d3 d6 with a slight advantage for White according to Bücker in Yearbook 18. It seems strange to go for a 'normal' Sicilian with ...h6 included: 3...e6 4.d4 cxd4 5.♘xd4 d6, or 3...d6 4.d4 cxd4 5.♘xd4 ♘f6 6.♗c4.

4.d4 cxd4 5.♘xd4 e5

Again 5...♘f6 6.♗c4 d6 is a strange Sicilian with ...h6. A blunder is 6...♘xe4?? 7.♘xe4 d5 8.♘xc6 bxc6 9.♗b3 dxe4 10.♗xf7+.

6.♘db5 ♘f6

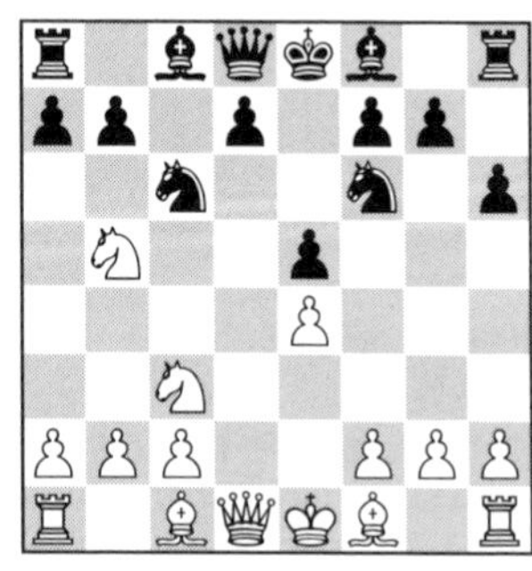

7.♘d5!?

This is the Haberditz Variation. In SOS-2 (Chapter 10, p.78) Dimitri Reinderman wrote on this line. See also the SOS Files of volume 4.

7.♘d6+ looks like the best move in this position if you ask me. After 7...♗xd6 8.♕xd6 ♕e7 9.♘b5 the star move is 9...♖b8 as reported by Reinderman. Instead 9.♕xe7+ ♘xe7 10.♗e3 d6 is a slight edge for White.

7...♘xd5 8.exd5 a6

8...♘b8 9.d6±.

9.dxc6 axb5 10.cxd7+ ♗xd7

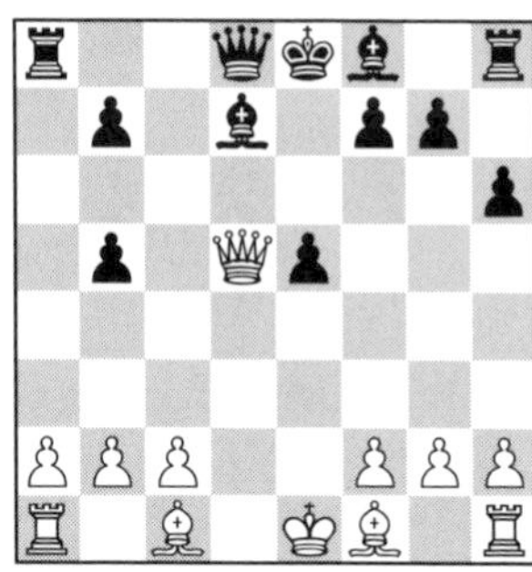

White has a slightly better pawn structure, but Black has free development and a central pawn as Reinderman pointed out. Chances are about equal.

□ **Giuseppe Fabriano**
■ **Michael Basman**
London 1993

1.e4 h6 2.Nf3 c5

Via a small transposition we have arrived in our favourite Sicilian. Probably this is one of the more 'theoretical' positions of the highly original player Michael Basman, who always plays wild and original chess. This game is no exception, and he shows that if you want to beat strange openings, you should play more directly and accurately than White does in this game!

3.d3 d6 4.g3 Nc6 5.Bg2 Nf6 6.0-0

A sample line of what could happen after 6.Nbd2 is 6...e5 7.0-0 Be7 8.Nh4 g6 9.c3 Nh5 10.Ndf3 Bg4.

6...g5

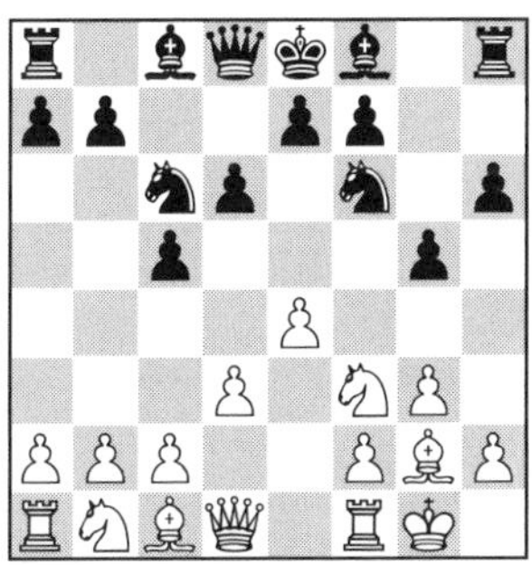

The move ...g5 is much stronger after White has castled of course.

7.Nbd2

Play would be unclear after 7.h4 gxh4!? 8.Nxh4 e6 9.Be3 Be7 10.Nd2 h5 11.Bg5 Ng4 12.Bxe7 Qxe7 13.c3 Bd7.

7...Bg7 8.c3 Bg4 9.Re1 Qd7 10.Qc2 Bh3 11.Bh1

Better was 11.Nf1 Bxg2 12.Kxg2, or 11...Nh5 12.Ne3 Bxg2 13.Kxg2 e6 14.Qd1 0-0-0 15.d4 cxd4 16.cxd4 Kb8.

11...Nh5 12.Nc4

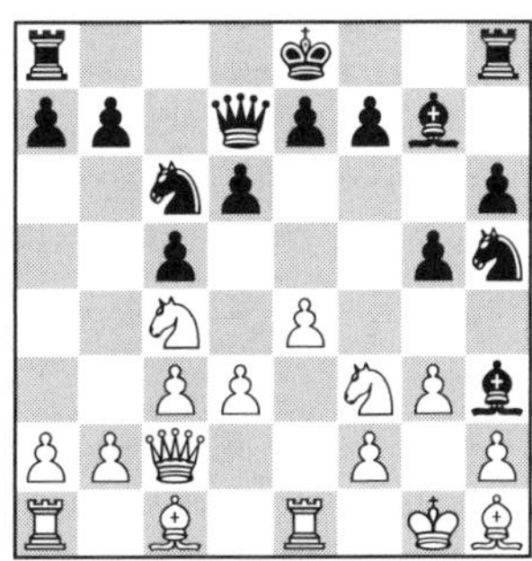

12...f5!?

I don't know many players who would play such move in this position!

13.a4 f4 14.e5 0-0-0

Black's attack is already underway, while White is getting nowhere fast on the queenside.

15.d4 Bf5 16.Qd2 d5 17.Na3 Rhf8 18.dxc5 Be4 19.e6 Qxe6 20.Nb5 fxg3 21.hxg3

21...Nxg3!! 22.fxg3 Qg4 23.Rxe4 dxe4 24.Nfd4 Qxg3+ 25.Bg2 Be5

White resigned.

CHAPTER 16

Jeroen Bosch

Fianchetto in the Alekhine Four Pawns

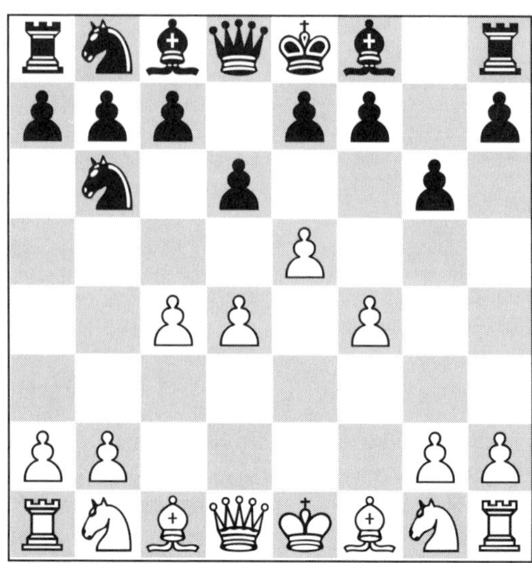

The less explored 5...g6!?

☐ **Ivan Denisov**
■ **Alexander Khalifman**
Aix-les-Bains ch-EUR 2011

1.e4 ♘f6 2.e5 ♘d5 3.c4 ♘b6 4.d4 d6 5.f4

The famous Four Pawns Attack. With a little help from his Alekhine-opponent White is setting up the most impressive pawn centre imaginable. Now if Black doesn't watch out, he will be 'crushed like a bug' as Alburt and Schiller have crudely expressed it in their old book on the Alekhine (Batsford, 1985). Having said that, I feel that most Alekhine players ought to welcome 5.f4. Indeed, the Modern Variation 4.♘f3 is the way to claim a theoretical edge, and White's space advantage may easily turn against him when Black gets in his levers ...c5 or ...f6, or makes use of the loose squares surrounding White's king, or simply develops forcing White to protect his far-advanced pawns. A legitimate question is: Hasn't White simply fallen for Black's provocative first move, and walked right into it? Well, it's not nearly that simple either. I fully agree with John Cox who formulated Black's predicament when talking about the main line as follows: 'Black has to tread a narrow path, and for a rare line like the Four Pawns Attack a reply which leads to less explored play might be preferable. Moreover there are a couple of virtually forced draws lurking in the main line'. (John Cox, *Starting Out: Alekhine's Defence*, Everyman 2004, p.127). In a recent Everyman publication (Timothy Taylor, *Alekhine Alert!*, 2010) the same sentiment is expressed. It should surprise no one that we advocate a line which leads to less explored play in this SOS chapter!

5...g6

Fully playable is 5...dxe5 6.fxe5 and now:

– 6...♘c6 7.♗e3 ♗f5 8.♘c3 e6 9.♘f3 when 9...♗e7 is the sound main line (the following alternatives also occur: 9...♗b4, 9...♗g4, 9...♕d7 and 9...♘b4). However, things do get hairy after the sharp 10.d5 unless you have fully memorized the theory (and repeated the complex lines ever so often) and are not averse to a draw.

– The even sharper 6...c5 7.d5 e6 8.♘c3 exd5 9.cxd5 c4 was rehabilitated by Alexander Shabalov owing to 10.♘f3 ♗b4 11.♗xc4 ♗xc3+! 12.bxc3 ♘xc4 13.♕a4+ ♘d7 and so on. However, the problem is 10.d6 when I would prefer White – although there is a full battle ahead of course.

– 6...g6 looks similar to our line, but has the disadvantage that the diagonal for White's dark-squared bishop is opened too soon.

6.♘c3

The most demanding reply.

● Less accurate is 6.♘f3, mainly because White loses out on early h4-h5 options when Black castles too soon (Black obtains the option of ...♗g4, rendering the attack harmless). Anyway, it is hard to believe that White can do without ♘c3, for options with ♘bd2 do not look very threatening. 6...♗g7 7.♘c3 (7.♗e3 0-0 8.♗e2 dxe5 transposes to 6.♗e2 ♗g7 7.♘f3 0-0 8.♗e3 dxe5 below) 7...0-0 8.♗e3 ♗e6 transposes to the note to White's 8th move in our main game after 8.♘f3 0-0.

● 6.h3?! – White understandably wants to prevent a pin on his king's knight, but a tempo is still a tempo (although Alekhine players have their own personal outlook on opening rules like don't play twice with the same piece in the opening of course): 6...♗g7?! (slightly inflexible perhaps, Black could have taken advantage of the weakening of the e1-h4 diagonal. 6...dxe5 7.fxe5 c5 8.d5 e6 is much stronger and looks like the refutation of 6.h3 in my opinion) 7.♘f3 0-0 8.♗e2 ♗e6! (this is the star move in the fianchetto system. Protecting the c4 pawn would be very annoying for White, while d4-d5 has the drawback of 'overreaching'. The Ukrainian grandmaster Vladimir Sergeev is the main proponent of this system) 9.d5 ♗c8 10.♘c3 c6 (taking advantage of the outpost on d5) 11.0-0 cxd5 12.cxd5 ♘6d7 (more natural is developing with 12...♘8d7, but Black's Alekhine knight will be harrassed with 13.a4, forcing the weakening 13...a5 – 13...dxe5?! 14.a5 – when White is a little better after 14.♕d4 ♘c5 15.♗e3) 13.♕d4?! (13.exd6 exd6 14.♗e3 is stronger and preserves a slight edge; 13.e6 fxe6 14.♘g5 ♘c5 is sharp and unclear) 13...dxe5 14.fxe5

14...♘xe5! (the point of his 12th move) 15.♘xe5 ♘c6 16.♕h4 (16.♘xc6 ♗xd4+ 17.♘xd4 ♕b6 and while it is nice to have a lot of pieces, White's position is rather loose here) 16...♘xe5 gave Black an extra pawn in Mrva-Sergeev, Bardejov 1996.

● The slightly subtle 6.♗e2 is an alternative. Still, can White really do without ♘c3? However, Black should take care as in these lines the wonder move ...♗e6 is hardly ever strong; because of the absence of the knight on c3 Black does better to react immediately in the centre. 6...♗g7 7.♘f3 0-0

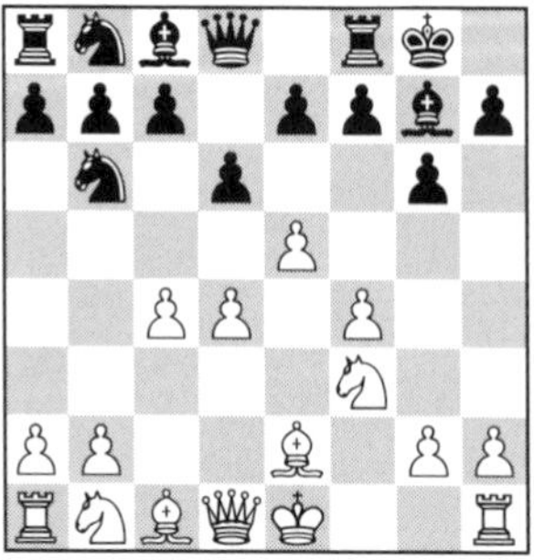

and now after 8.♗e3 dxe5 (now 8...♗e6 is inaccurate in view of 9.♘bd2) there is:

– 9.fxe5 ♗g4 10.♘bd2. This is the point of delaying the development of the queen's knight. White will now be able to take back on f3 with the knight defending d4. Black, however, will obtain counterplay with ...c5.

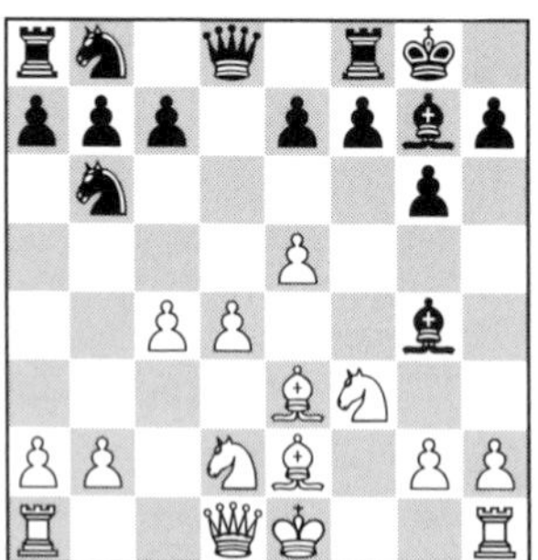

10...c5 (10...e6 11.0-0 ♘8d7 12.h3 ♗xf3 13.♘xf3 ♕e7 is too slow, although Black eventually won in Nagy-Sergeev, Szombathely 2003) 11.dxc5 (Black's play is straightforward after 11.d5 ♘8d7 12.0-0 ♕c7 13.♗f4 ♗xf3 14.♘xf3 ♘xe5) 11...♘6d7 12.0-0 ♕c7 was sharp but OK for Black in the old game Quinones-Darga, Amsterdam 1964.

– 9.♘xe5 also deserves to be investigated: 9...c5 10.d5 (Black is alright after 10.dxc5 ♘6d7 – 10...♕xd1+ 11.♔xd1 ♘a4 12.♔c2 ♘d7 is also good enough for equal chances in a sharp queenless middlegame – 11.♘xd7 ♘xd7 12.♘c3 ♕a5 13.♕d2 ♘xc5 14.♘d5 ♕xd2+ 15.♔xd2 and the ending is equal after 15...♘a4!, since 16.♘xe7+?! ♔h8 17.b3 is well-met by 17...♖d8+!, but not 17...♗xa1? 18.♖xa1±) 10...♘8d7 11.♘xd7 ♗xd7 12.♘c3 ♕c7 13.0-0 ♘c8 (the knight is moved to the ideal d6-square) 14.♖c1 ♕a5 15.♕d2 ♘d6 16.♗d3 ♖ac8 17.♕e2 a6 and Black was already slightly better in Gretarsson-Polaczek, Reykjavik 1990.

You should know what to do against 8.0-0 too: 8...dxe5! (I don't like 8...♗e6 for two reasons: 9.d5 ♗g4 10.♘g5!? looks dangerous, and surely White is better after 9.b3 c5 10.d5 ♗g4 11.♗b2) 9.fxe5 ♗g4 (the correct move order; not 9...c5 10.d5 ♗g4 11.♗f4 – again correct is 11.♘g5!, when White is better – 11...♘8d7 12.♘bd2 ♕b8! and Black gained the upper hand in Nedela-Velicka, Filseck 1999) 10.♘bd2 (10.♘c3 c5) 10...c5 11.♘b3 (11.dxc5 ♘6d7; 11.d5 ♘8d7) 11...cxd4 12.♘fxd4 ♗xe2 13.♕xe2 ♕c7! 14.c5 ♘d5 15.e6 f5 16.♘b5 ♕c6 and White's pawn weaknesses are more important than his slight initiative, Bernardo-Szmetan, Mar del Plata 1996.

- 6.h4? dxe5! 7.fxe5 c5 (7...♘c6)

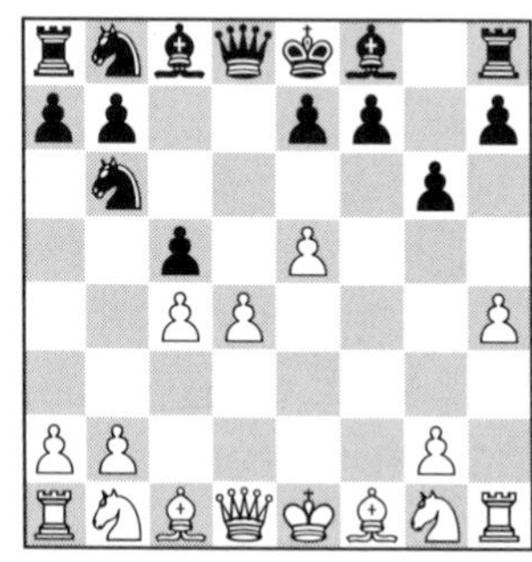

8.d5 and after eight consecutive pawn moves White is over-extended. Black soon won after 8...♗g7 9.♗f4 e6 10.♘c3 exd5 11.cxd5 0-0 12.h5 ♘8d7 13.♘f3 ♘xe5! and so on in Asensio Linan-Narciso Dublan, Montcada i Reixac 2011.

6...♗g7 7.♗e3

Developing the queenside first is White's most accurate move order.

– If White has no ambitions whatsoever, then he can play 7.c5?! dxc5 8.dxc5 ♕xd1+ 9.♔xd1 ♗g4+ when 10.♗e2 looks equal, but 10.♔e1 ♘6d7 11.♗e3 ♘c6 12.♗c4 g5! saw Black slowly seize the initiative in Gikas-Haakert, Germany Bundesliga 1987/88.

– 7.♘f3 0-0 8.♗e3 ♗e6 transposes to the comments on the next move after 8.♘f3.

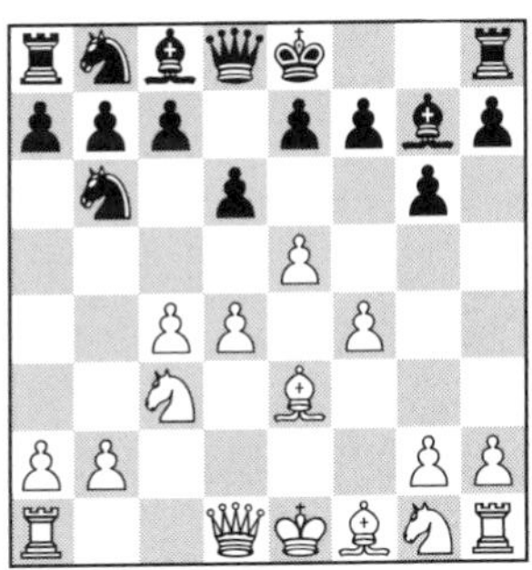

7...♗e6!

White's move order makes this move essential. You should really keep this finesse in mind when you want to adopt this system as Black.

Too slow is 7...0-0?! 8.c5 ♘6d7 and now either 9.h4 with a dangerous attack, or 9.♘f3 with a positional edge.

8.d5

Valentin Bogdanov provides this move with an exclam in his book on the Alekhine (Gambit, 2009), and it must indeed be crucial to the evaluation of 7...♗e6.

- With the bishop on e6 8.c5 is of course nothing because of 8...♘d5 when Black has an easy game.
- 8.♕b3 is well-met by 8...a5, when in order to prevent ...a5-a4 White has to weaken the b4-square: 9.a4 ♘a6 10.♖d1 ♘b4 11.♘f3 d5 12.cxd5 (12.c5 ♘c4) 12...♘4xd5 13.♘xd5 ♗xd5 14.♕c2 ♗xf3 15.gxf3 ♘d5 and Black has a clear strucutral edge, Kotek-Sergeev, Czechia 1997/98.
- 8.♘f3 0-0 (an important position that may also be reached via 6.♘f3)

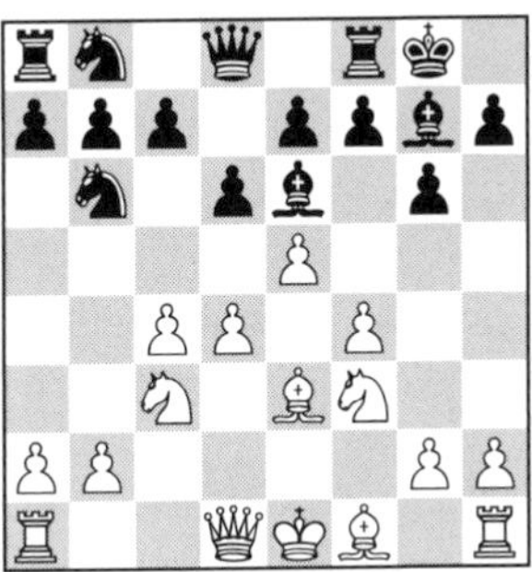

and now:

9.♕b3 a5 10.♘g5! (10.a4 is met by 10...♘a6 when the knight will be excellently placed on b4) 10...a4 11.♘xe6 axb3!? (stronger is 11...fxe6 12.♕d1 ♘c6 for in the ending 13.c5 below is a problem) 12.♘xd8 ♖xd8 13.a3 ♘c6 is rightly given as equal by Cox. 14.0-0-0?! ♘a5 15.c5 dxc5 16.dxc5 ♖xd1+ 17.♘xd1 ♘bc4∓ Brener-Pushkin, Soviet Union 1988. However, White should investigate the immediate 13.c5 which seems to favour him and is neglected by other sources.

Too passive is **9.♘d2?!** dxe5 10.fxe5 c5 11.d5 (11.dxc5 ♘6d7 is excellent for Black of course. White's centre has crumbled to dust) 11...♗f5 12.♗f4 (not 12.♗xc5 ♘8d7; 12.g4 is rather loosening after 12...♗c8) 12...e6! 13.d6 ♘c6 14.♘f3 ♘d7 (14...♗g4) 15.h3? ♘dxe5 16.♗xe5 ♗xe5 (or

16...♘xe5) 17.g4 ♗xc3+ 18.bxc3 ♗e4 and Black was winning in S.Schmidt-Haakert, Germany tt 1988/89.

9.b3 is the normal move, but by means of a tactical trick Black can now make use of the unprotected knight on c3. 9...c5! and now:

– 10.dxc5 ♘6d7! (this is the point of 9...c5, the move 9.b3 has left the c3 knight unprotected)

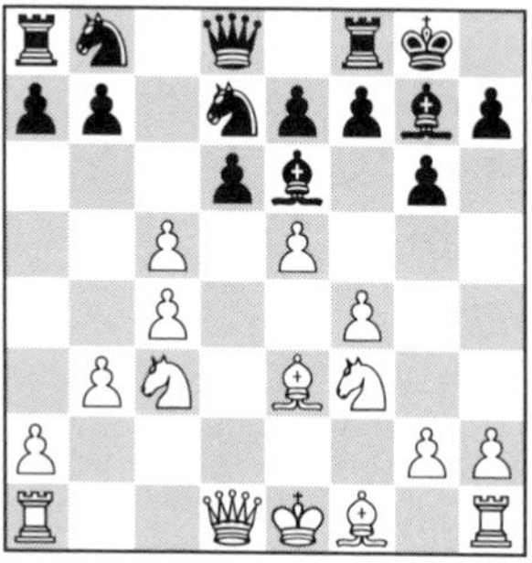

11.cxd6 (11.♖c1 dxe5∓, Fedorov-Sergeev, Warsaw rapid 2004) 11...exd6 12.♕xd6 (12.♗e2 dxe5 13.♕d2 ♘c6 14.♖c1 exf4 15.♗xf4 ♘c5 leaves White with a slight disadvantage just after the opening, Sevian-Taylor, Los Angeles 2011) 12...♘xe5! 13.♕xd8 (13.fxe5 ♕xd6 14.exd6 ♗xc3+ is the trick I mentioned above) 13...♘xf3+ 14.gxf3 ♖xd8 15.♖c1 ♘c6

Black is fully developed, with a sound pawn structure. He has more than enough for the pawn: 16.♘e4 (16.♔f2 ♘e7 17.♗e2 ♘f5 18.♖hd1 ♖xd1 19.♗xd1 ♘xe3 20.♔xe3 ♖e8 was a slightly better ending for Black in Stopa-Narciso Dublan, Montcada i Reixac 2011) 16...♘b4 17.♘c5 Grabher-Ager, Austria 2002/03, and now simply 17...♘xa2 is troublesome for the first player.

– 10.♗e2 cxd4 11.♗xd4? (11.♘xd4 dxe5 12.♘xe6 fxe6 13.♕xd8 ♖xd8 14.♖c1 was a better chance) 11...♘c6 12.exd6? ♘xd4 13.♘xd4 ♕xd6 and Black is completely winning, Lefebr-Korostelev, Cheliabinsk 2008.

– While 10.d5 ♗g4 also favours Black.

9.d5 ♗g4 clearly favours Black compared to the main line, where after White's more accurate move order Black is forced to return to c8 with the bishop after d5. 10.♕d2 (10.♗e2 ♗xf3; perhaps White should have considered muddying the waters with 10.h3 ♗xf3 11.♕xf3 dxe5 12.f5) 10...c6! (not 10...♗xf3 11.gxf3 dxe5 12.f5 and White will castle queenside with unclear play) 11.c5!? (11.0-0-0 cxd5 12.cxd5 dxe5 13.fxe5 ♘8d7 14.e6 leaves Black a pleasant choice between 14...fxe6 15.dxe6 ♘e5 16.♕xd8 ♖axd8 17.♖xd8 ♖xd8 18.♘xe5 ♗xe5 with a superior ending, and 14...♘e5 15.exf7+ ♖xf7 16.♘xe5 ♗xe5 17.♗e2 ♗xe2 18.♕xe2 ♗xc3 19.bxc3 ♘a4 20.♗d4 ♕xd5 with a pawn up but with the queens still on) 11...♘xd5 12.♘xd5 cxd5 13.♕xd5 ♘c6 Black is fully developed and we can conclude that White has let himself be provoked by the typical Alekhine strategy. 14.cxd6 ♗xf3 15.gxf3 exd6 16.♗b5? ♕h4+ 17.♔e2 dxe5 with a winning attack in J. Bauer-Sergeev, Sala 1993.

● 8.b3!? is better played immediately, rather than with the inclusion of 8.♘f3 0-0 as we saw above: 8...0-0 when best is

9.♕d2 and now:
– 9...dxe5 10.fxe5 c5 11.d5 ♗f5 12.♘f3 ♘8d7 is fine for Black.
– Here too Black should not play 9...c5?! for, after 10.dxc5 ♘6d7 11.cxd6 exd6 12.♕xd6 ♘xe5? (12...♘c6 13.♗e2 ♖e8 14.♕d2 f6 15.♘f3 fxe5 16.0-0! exf4 17.♗xf4 ♘de5 18.♘g5?! ♗f5 – 18...♕xd2 19.♗xd2 ♗f5= – 19.♘d5± Fercec-Kostrun, Pula 2002) there is no intermediate check on f3 as there was after 8.♘f3 0-0 9.b3 above. Interestingly, it favours White to lose a tempo with 9.♕d2!.
– 9...a5!? 10.♘f3 a4 is another way to seek counterplay.

We already investigated 9.♘f3?! c5 10.dxc5 ♘6d7!.

Note that 9.♖c1 should be met by 9...dxe5 (with c3 protected it is a mistake to play 9...c5?! 10.dxc5 ♘6d7? 11.cxd6 exd6 12.♕xd6 and with no tricks along the diagonal, Black has insufficient compensation for the pawn, Dabo Peranic-Kostrun, Pula 2002) 10.fxe5 c5 11.d5 ♗f5.

● After 8.♗e2 Black can play 8...♘xc4!? (8...0-0 9.d5 ♗c8 – 9...♗f5 – 10.♘f3 ♗g4 could still be a little better for White) 9.♗xc4 ♗xc4 10.♕a4+ b5 11.♘xb5 ♗xb5 12.♕xb5+ ♘d7 and this has not been tested in practice, but it looks quite OK for Black.

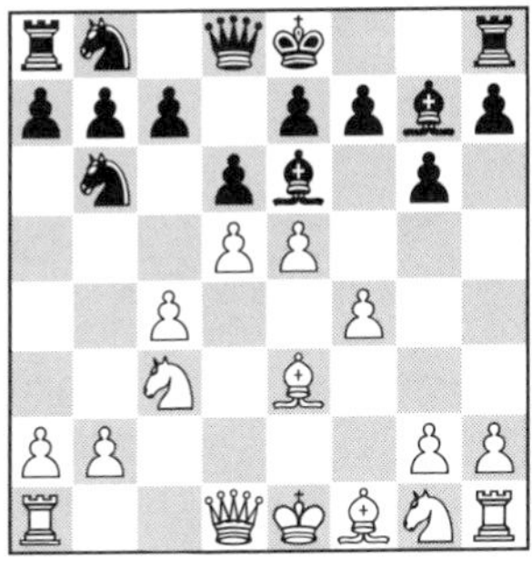

8...♗c8

It may look strange to undevelop the bishop, but in combination with Khalifman's 10th move it may well be best.

Riskier is 8...♗f5, as the bishop sometimes provides White with a target: 9.♘f3 (9.♗e2 0-0 10.♘f3 e6 11.dxe6 ♗xe6 12.c5!?) 9...e6?! (9...0-0! 10.♗e2) 10.exd6 cxd6 11.♗d4 ♗xd4, Mazyrin-Korostelev, Cheliabinsk 2008, and now 12.♘xd4±.

9.♘f3

White should think about his development, and he should not fear ...♗g4 (Black has already moved his bishop twice).
– Too sharp is 9.e6 fxe6 10.h4 exd5 11.cxd5 e6 12.♗d4 ♕e7 13.♗xg7 ♕xg7 14.dxe6 ♘c6 15.♘f3 ♗xe6, Flores-Llanos, Buenos Aires 1998.
– The same goes for 9.c5 ♘6d7 10.cxd6 exd6 11.e6 fxe6 12.dxe6 ♘f6 13.♕b3 ♕e7 14.0-0-0 ♕xe6 15.♕xe6+ ♗xe6 16.♖e1 ♘c6 17.♘f3 ♔d7 18.♘g5 ♗f5∓, Arribas Lopez-Navarro Cia, Pamplona 2008.

9...0-0

● Sergeev has played the immediate 9...c6, when 10.♗e2 0-0 11.0-0 ♗g4 looks somewhat better for White:
– 12.♕d2 ♗xf3 13.♖xf3 cxd5 14.cxd5 dxe5 15.fxe5 ♗xe5 16.♗h6 and now Sergeev sacrificed the exchange and held on to the draw rather easily: 16...♘8d7 (16...♗g7? 17.♖h3!) 17.♗xf8 ♕xf8 18.♘e4 ♕g7 19.♖af1 ♘f6 20.♘xf6+ exf6 21.d6 ♖d8 22.♖d3 ♘c4 23.♕b4 ♘xd6 24.♖fd1 ♕h6 25.g3 ♕f8 26.♗f3 ♕e7 27.♔g2 ♔g7 28.a4 b6 29.b3 h5 30.♕d2 draw, Petr-Sergeev, Usti nad Orlici 2006.
– 12.exd6! exd6 13.♗d4 (13.dxc6 ♘xc6 and Black has sufficient activity for the weak pawn on d6) is slightly better for White.
– 12.e6 fxe6 13.♘g5 is met by 13...♘xc4!

● 9...♗g4 10.h3 ♗xf3 11.♕xf3 dxe5 12.c5 exf4 13.♗b5+ (13.♗xf4 ♘6d7 14.d6 is also interesting) 13...♘6d7 14.♕xf4 0-0 15.0-0 c6! 16.♗c4 with compensation for the pawn in Zvara-Stocek, Czechia 2009.

10.♗d3

Ambitious, but Khalifman comes up with a good reply.

Simply 10.♗e2 can be met by any of the standard replies, but then White should be a little better. The computer rather likes the piece sacrifice following 10...♘8d7!? (10... c6, 10...♗g4, 10...e6), but this looks too dangerous: 11.0-0 (11.♗d4!?) 11...dxe5 12.c5 (12.fxe5 ♘xe5 13.♘xe5 ♗xe5∓) 12... exf4 13.♗d4 (13.♗f2! ♗xc3 14.bxc3 ♘xc5 15.♗xc5 ♕xd5 favours White) 13...♘xd5 14.♘xd5 e5 15.♗f2 (15.♗c3 c6 16.♘b4 a5 17.♘c2 ♖e8∓) 15...e4 16.♗h4 ♘f6 17.♘xf6+ ♗xf6 18.♗xf6 ♕xf6.

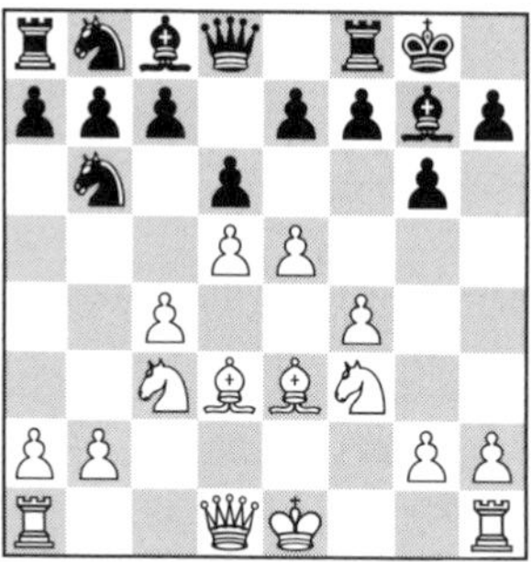

10...e6!

Both of White's central pawns have advanced and they are easy targets.

10...♗g4!? 11.0-0!? dxe5 12.fxe5 and if Black now takes the pawn, White will obtain enough piece play. However, Black can also continue to attack White's centre with 12...c6 or 12...e6 (12...♘8d7 13.c5 ♘c8 14.♕b3; 12...♗xe5 13.♗h6; 12...♗xf3 13.♕xf3 ♗xe5 14.♗h6).

11.0-0 ♘a6

Black would be more flexible after 11... exd5!?.

12.♗e2

Now that White is moving back and forth with the bishop, Black may do the same:

12...exd5 13.cxd5 ♗g4

Black has counterplay against White's centre.

14.♗d4

The alternatives do not pose Black any real problems either: 14.♕b3 ♗xf3 15.♗xf3 dxe5 or 14.♗xa6 bxa6 15.h3 ♗xf3.

14...♘b4

Black equalizes with 14...dxe5.

15.♕b3

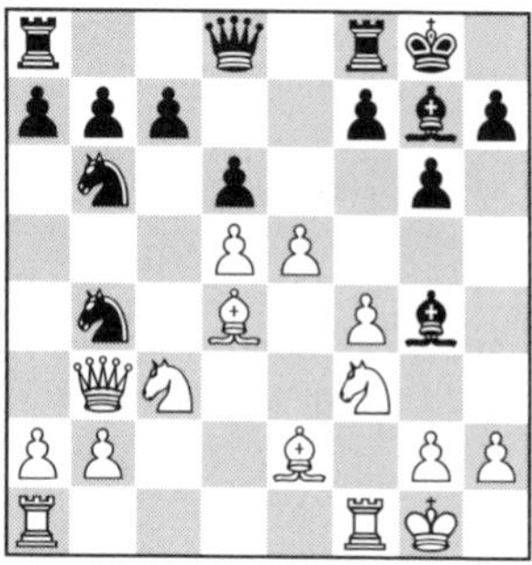

15...c5 16.dxc6

16.♗e3 ♗f5! with counterplay. For example: 17.♖ac1 ♗d3! 18.♗xd3?! ♘xd3 19.♖cd1 c4.

16...♘xc6 17.♗xb6

This exchange does not promise anything.

17...♕xb6+ 18.♕xb6 axb6 19.exd6 ♖fd8

Black will retrieve the pawn with even chances.

20.♖fd1 ♗f8 21.h3

The safest way to the draw against his stronger opponent.

21...♗xf3 22.♗xf3 ♗xd6 23.g3 ♗c5+ 24.♔g2 ♗d4 25.a3 ♗xc3 26.bxc3 ♔f8 27.♔f2 ♖xd1 28.♗xd1 ♖d8 29.♗e2 ♘a5

And the players agreed to a draw.

CHAPTER 17

Arthur Kogan

King's Gambit – a Patzer Check

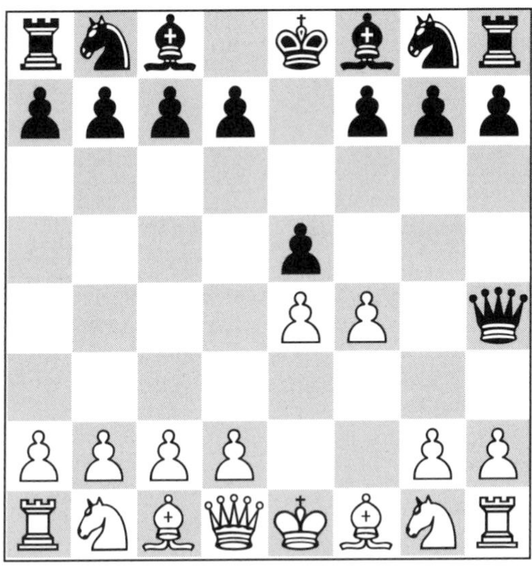

1.e4 e5 2.f4 ♕h4+!?

1.e4 e5 2.f4!?

The King's Gambit! My students often think that the idea behind this gambit is to create attacking positions. However, I teach them that in reality the main idea in nearly all gambits is first of all to try to surprise (not with the Queen's Gambit!), and secondly to obtain maximum control of the centre and more space for the pieces to smile, and only then to attack the king! The King's Gambit is a romantic way of playing, that many have thought to refute after long analysis, but do you have enough time or enough motivation to memorize it all? I guess that by buying this SOS book you and I both think in the same way: we both like fun in chess and we both like to make our opponents shake their heads in surprise!

The King's Gambit is not that common anymore, but there still are many aggressive players who like to use it from time to time. One example from 2010 was the fantastic win of Polgar against Topalov! In that game she played the 3.♗c4 line, allowing ...♕h4 to hide her king on f1, and then win time versus the black queen, making her pieces smile thanks to her central pawns! However we will not allow something like this to happen!

2...♕h4+!

The exlamation mark is for the surprise effect! If a patzer sees a check... is what our opponent will surely think. However, in reality I first saw this funny looking move in a game of GM Murey as White in which the result of the opening was completely against the usual aggressive spirit of the King's Gambit! The problem with playing a main line versus the King's Gambit is that there is so much analysis that you need to memorize (and keep up-to-date). Just ask yourself: is all that work worth it for the few King's Gambit games that you will encounter in your life? I think 2...♕h4 check is a good practical choice, and in analysing it I found it a cool SOS-weapon which I successfully played myself.

Just for fun I give you the game J.Polgar-Topalov, Mexico City rapid 2010, that I mentioned above:

2...exf4 3.♗c4 d5 4.exd5 ♕h4+ 5.♔f1 ♗d6 6.♘f3 ♕h5 7.♘c3 ♘e7 8.d4 0-0 9.♔f2 ♘d7 10.♖e1 ♘b6 11.♗b3 ♘exd5 12.♘xd5 ♘xd5 13.c4 ♘e3 14.♗xe3 fxe3+ 15.♖xe3 ♗f5 16.c5 ♗f4 17.♖e7 ♗g4 18.♖e4 ♕f5 19.♗c2 ♗h5 20.♖e5 ♗xf3 21.♔xf3! ♕f6 22.♖f5 ♕h6 23.♖xf4 ♖ae8 24.♕d3 f5 25.h4 ♖e4 26.♕d2 ♖e7 27.♖e1 1-0.

3.g3

Although we now have to move our lady again, the weakening of White's kingside may well be worth it! This is a very important psychological point as well, for the main danger in the King's Gambit is the attack on f7 with a bishop on c4, and an open f-file and crazy sacrificial ideas. However, can you imagine a bishop on c4 ignoring the white square weaknesses made by g3? Needless to say that we don't fear a bishop fianchetto, but that doesn't mean that the case is closed. No! Black has lost time with his queen and White will try to use his advantage in development. So let's continue to prove our case that 2...♕h4 was correct!

3.♔e2? is in the spirit of Steinitz, but such things must not be exaggerated! Funnily, it was tried by a few players, probably because they prepared the line 2...exf4 3.d4?! ♕h4+ 4.♔e2. However, here Black still didn't lose the centre and he can get a clear edge in more than one way, for example: 3...d5!, a counter gambit in the Olala spirit, opening files and diagonals and making the black pieces smile! (3...♕xf4 4.♘c3 ♘c6 5.♘f3 ♘d4+∓ is also good, Schmitt-Anders, Bad Homburg 2009) 4.♘f3 ♗g4 5.d3? dxe4 6.dxe4 ♘c6 7.c3 ♘f6 8.♕e1 ♕h5 9.♘d2 exf4 10.♔d1 0-0-0 led to a simple win in Tejada-Padros, Spain cr 1985.

3...♕e7!

This may look strange, but the idea is to keep control of the centre, and to keep an eye on the unprotected pawn on e4. From this position we will investigate 4.fxe5 and 4. ♘c3, as well as the witty 4.♕e2.

□ **Dirk van Dooren**
■ **Rikard Medancic**
Schwarzach 2009

1.e4 e5 2.f4 ♕h4+ 3.g3 ♕e7 4.fxe5

This is a critical line, as is 4.♘c3! which we will investigate later on (Leignel-C.Foisor, Bethune 1997).

4...d6!

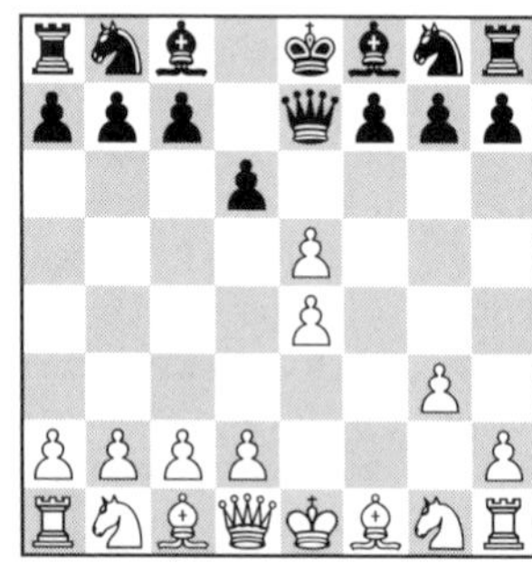

Another surprise! This is the main point of 3...♕e7 and the reason why I liked this line so much.

Instead, 4...♕xe5? will just help White to gain some tempi for development and central control. For some reason it was played a few times by the expert Christina Foisor. I guess she simply likes to dance with her queen? 5.♘c3:

– 5...♘c6 6.♘f3 ♕e7 and now 7.d4! (7.♗c4 d6 8.d3 ♗g4 9.♘d5 ♕d7 10.c3 ♗xf3 11.♕xf3 ♘e5∓ Cabello Fernandez-C.Foisor, Oviedo rapid 1993) is strong, when 7...d5 (or 7...d6 8.♗g5) 8.♘xd5 ♕xe4+ 9.♕e2 is a better endgame for White.

– Or 5...♘f6 6.d4 ♕a5 7.♗d2 ♗b4 and now 8.e5! is a logical novelty – 8.a3 ♗xc3 9.♗xc3 ♕b6 10.♕f3 d5 gave Black counterplay in Cantero Martin-Mora, Barcelona 2001 – 8...♘d5 9.a3±.

5.♘c3

5.exd6 leads to an endgame that we will encounter in the next game (Borner-Kogan, Biel 1991).

After 5.♘f3 dxe5 6.♗g2 ♗g4 7.0-0 ♘d7 8.d3 ♘gf6 9.♔h1 ♕e6! 10.♕e1 ♗c5 11.♘bd2 0-0 12.♘c4 ♖fe8 13.b4 ♗f8 14.♗b2 ♗xf3 15.♖xf3 b5 16.♘e3 ♘b6 17.♖f5 ♘fd7 18.♗c3 c5 19.a3 ♖ac8 Black had nice counterplay in Sluka-Mokry, Czech tt 1996/97.

5...dxe5 6.♘f3

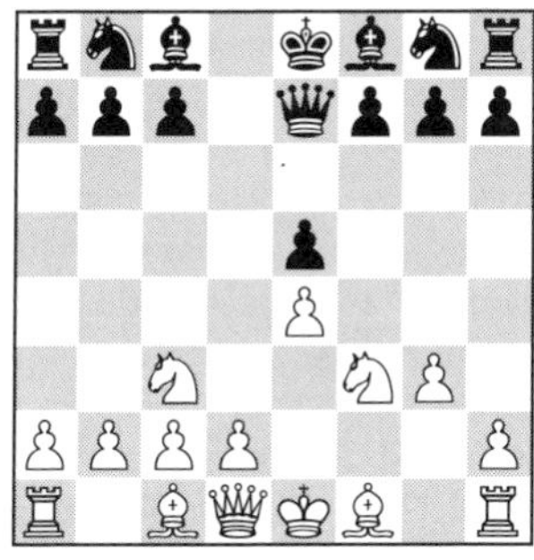

6...♘f6!

This is the most flexible move. It is better to wait for White to commit his kingside bishop before playing ...c6, as a quick ...♘c6 (with the idea of ...♘d4 or ...♘a5) can be a good reply when White develops the bishop to c4.

Therefore 6...c6?! seems worse even though Black managed to win in a game between two GMs: 7.♗c4 ♗g4 (7...♗h3 8.d4) 8.d3 ♘d7 9.0-0 ♘gf6 10.♔g2 b5 11.♗b3 ♘c5 12.h3 ♗xf3+ 13.♕xf3 a5 14.d4! (this is very strong) 14...a4 15.♗g5 (and now 15.♗xf7+! would have been the correct follow-up: 15...♔xf7 16.dxc5 ♕xc5 17.g4 h6 18.h4 with a very nice initiative) 15...axb3 16.axb3 (16.dxc5) 16...♖xa1 17.♖xa1 ♘e6 18.dxe5 ♕b7! 19.♗xf6 gxf6 20.exf6 ♗d6 (Black is taking over the attack) 21.♘e2 ♖g8∓ and Black later won in Rodriguez-Spangenberg, Mar del Plata 1999.

7.♗c4

7.d3 ♘c6 8.♗g5 ♕b4! 9.♖b1 and now 9...♗e6! intending to castle queenside is stronger than 9...h6?! 10.♗xf6 gxf6 11.♘d2 ♗e6 12.♘d5 which was played in Obukhov-Solovjov, Alushta 2002.

7...♘c6!

This is the reason why Black should postpone ...c6. The knight is very active and can annoy the bishop.

8.d3

8.0-0?? blunders a piece after 8...♕c5+.

8.a4 ♗h3! looks great for Black! Again, queenside castling is up next.

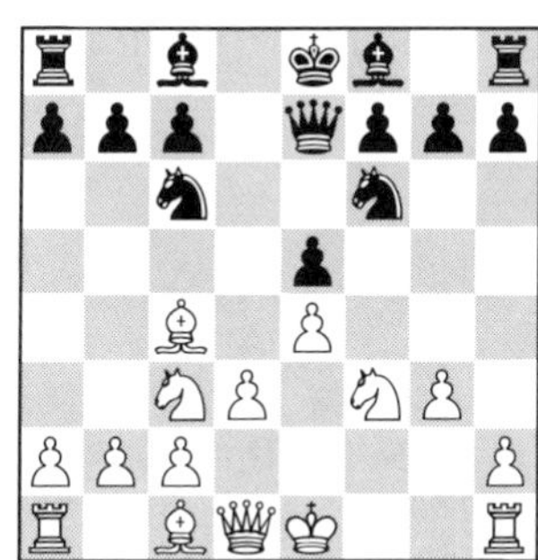

8...♘a5!

Black is getting rid of the most dangerous piece that White has.

9.♗b3 ♘xb3 10.axb3 h6!?

Also interesting is 10...♗h3.

11.h3 c6

11...♕e6 is another option.

12.♗e3 a6 13.♖a5 ♘d7 14.0-0 ♕e6 15.♔g2 ♗b4 16.♖a4 ♗e7 17.d4?

Missing the hidden threat!

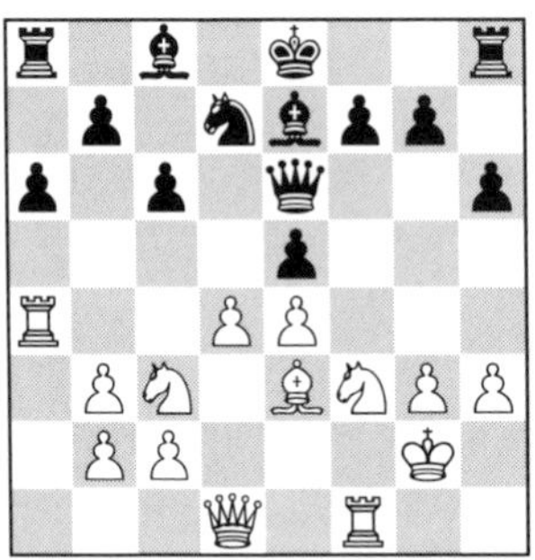

17...♘b6

Black has a huge edge after this discovered attack.

The remainder is no longer relevant for our analysis of the opening of course.

18.♖a5 ♕xh3+ 19.♔f2 ♘d7 20.♘xe5? ♕h2+

20...♘xe5 21.♖xe5 ♗g4!.

21.♔e1 ♘xe5 22.♖xe5 ♕xg3+ 23.♗f2 ♕g4 24.♕d3 ♕d7 25.♖g1 f6 26.♖h5 ♗b4 27.♕g3 g5 28.♖gh1 ♕g7 29.♗e3 ♗e6 30.♔d1 0-0-0

Now Black's king is safe and the outcome is no longer in doubt.

31.♘a4?

Threatening mate, but Black has a simple and strong reply.

31...♗d6 32.♕f3 ♔b8 33.♖f1 ♕f7 34.♔c1 ♖df8 35.♖fh1 ♕g6 36.d5? cxd5 37.exd5 ♗f5 38.♕d1 ♖e8 39.♗g1 ♗xc2

And White resigned. (39...♗f4+! 40.♔b1 ♗xc2+ 41.♕xc2 ♖e1+–+.)

□ **Daniel Borner**
■ **Artur Kogan**
Biel 1991

1.e4 e5 2.f4 ♕h4+ 3.g3 ♕e7 4.fxe5 d6 5.exd6

Instead of 5.♘c3 as in the previous game.

5...♕xe4+ 6.♕e2 ♕xe2+ 7.♘xe2 ♗xd6

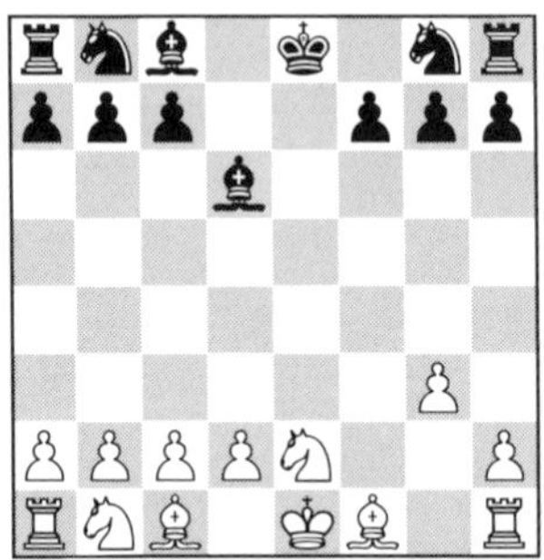

When I was young I discussed this position with GM Murey (who often played the King's Gambit). I was more in Black's favour here, while he took the white side. According to my practice and my analysis the ending is most probably about equal, but Black has good chances to seize the initiative! All we need from an SOS line, right?

8.♗g2

- 8.d3 was played in the stem game of the 2...♕h4 line (at least according to my database). A game between two famous GMs! I guess you will be surprised to learn that the strategist Ulf Andersson was once a fan of gambits! Yes, we all get old within time... 8...♗d7 9.♗g2 ♗c6 10.♗xc6+ ♘xc6 11.♗f4 ♗xf4 12.♘xf4 ♘f6 and now the players agreed a draw, Andersson-Keene, Nice ol 1974.
- 8.♘bc3 c6! (not 8...♘c6 9.♘b5) and now:

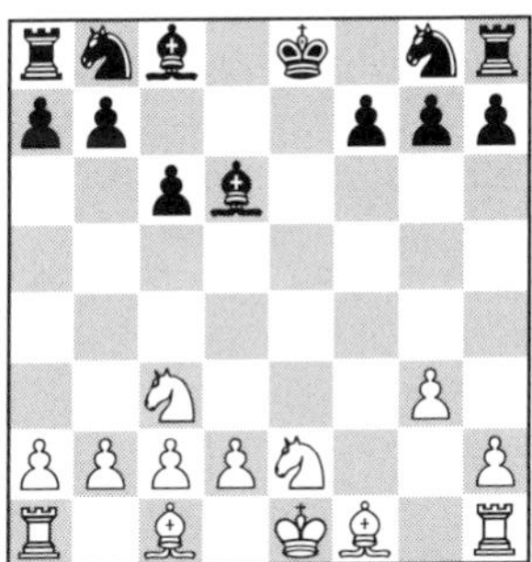

– 9.♗g2 ♘e7 (9...♘a6!?) 10.d3 0-0 11.♖b1 ♗c5 (11...♘a6) 12.♘a4 ♗b4+ 13.♗d2 ♘a6 14.a3 ♗d6 15.b4 ♘c7 was unclear in Olesen-Shvidler, Tel Aviv 1995.

– 9.b3 ♘f6 10.♗b2 ♗g4 (here 10...0-0 11.♗g2 ♖e8 12.0-0-0 ♗g4 13.♖de1 ♘bd7 is OK for Black) 11.♗g2 ♘bd7 12.h3 and here 12...♗xe2 (12...♗f5 13.0-0-0 0-0-0 14.♖hf1 ♗g6 15.♘f4 was slightly better for White in Murey-Eng, Beer-Sheva 1985) 13.♘xe2 h5!? is decent enough, as is 13...0-0 planning ...♖e8 and ....a5.

8...h5!?

An interesting practical choice to disturb my opponent.

No worse is 8...♘c6 9.d4 ♗g4 10.c3 0-0-0 11.h3 ♗xe2 12.♔xe2 ♗xg3 13.♗g5 f6 14.♔f3 ♗d6 15.♗e3 f5, Moskovets-Korobov, Alushta 2002.

9.d4 h4 10.♗f4 ♗xf4 11.♘xf4 ♘f6 12.♘d2 hxg3 13.hxg3 ♖xh1+ 14.♗xh1 ♘c6 15.c3 ♗g4 16.♔f2 0-0-0

Black should have sufficient counterplay to compensate for White's stable centre.

17.♖e1 g5!? 17...♖h8. **18.♘d3 ♗f5 19.♗xc6**

19.♘c5 is best met by 19...b6!.

19...♗xd3 20.♗f3 ♖h8 21.♖h1 ♖xh1 22.♗xh1 ♘g4+ 23.♔f3 f5

And I went on to win this slightly more comfortable endgame for Black:

24.♗g2 ♔d7 25.♗h3 ♘f6 26.♔e3 ♗c2 27.♗g2 b6 28.c4 a5 29.♗f3 ♔e6 30.♗e2 ♘e4 31.♘xe4 ♗xe4 32.a3 c5 33.♗d1 ♗b1 34.♗e2 ♔d6

35.♗d3??

This is a huge mistake, White could keep the draw with 35.♗h5.

35...cxd4+ 36.♔xd4 ♗xd3 37.♔xd3 a4! Fixing White's structure and winning the game. **38.♔d4 f4 39.gxf4 gxf4** And White resigned as the pawn ending is lost.

□ **Nicolas Leignel**
■ **Christina Foisor**
Bethune 1997

1.e4 e5 2.f4 ♕h4+ 3.g3 ♕e7 4.♘c3!

Developing and planning ♘d5 is also very logical of course.

Witty and interesting is 4.♕e2!?

– A very creative SOS-like reply with the queen! It even led to a win of an amateur player (2060) versus GM Mitkov! So, we should not underestimate it: 4...♘f6 5.fxe5 ♕xe5 6.♘c3 ♗b4 7.♘f3 ♕c5 8.e5 ♘g4 9.♘e4 ♕d5 (9...♕e3 is funny, but not good enough 10.♕xe3 ♘xe3 11.♗d3±) 10.c3± and with d4 and ♗g2 coming White is dominating! Luco-Mitkov, Metz 1992.

– A stronger reply is 4...♘c6!, with ...♘d4 in mind: 5.c3?! was played in the only game in my database, but here I would recommend a counter King's Gambit surprise with 5.♘f3 d6 with ...♗g4 coming. Black is fighting for control over square d4, he could even castle queenside, and ...g6 and ...♗g7 are also on. Black is OK!.

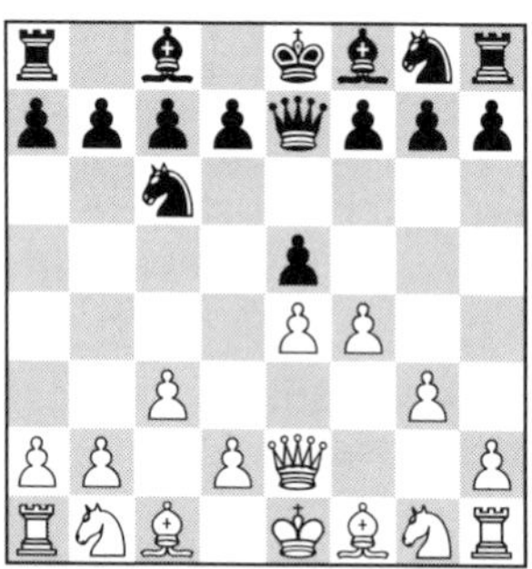

5...f5!! (I prefer White after 5...♘f6 6.d3 – 6.fxe5 ♕xe5 7.♗g2± – 6...d5 7.exd5 ♘xd5 – 7...♗g4 – 8.♗g2 ♕e6 9.♘h3 Bengtson-Mukharji, USA 1995) 6.exf5 (6.d3 fxe4 7.dxe4 ♘f6∓; 6.fxe5 fxe4! 7.♕xe4 ♘f6∓ and Black is the one with a clear edge in development!) 6...d5 7.♗h3 ♘h6 with the initiative. Also good is 7...e4 8.♕h5+ ♔d8 and Black has central control and will win tempi on White's queen.

4...d6!

The best reply in my opinion. After 4... exf4?, which was once the usual choice of Christina Foisor, White is better: 5.d4 (5.d3!? fxg3 6.hxg3 c6 7.♕e2 ♘a6 8.♘f3 d6 9.♗g5 ♕c7 10.0-0-0 also gave White a superior position in Pautrot-C.Foisor, Montpellier 1997) 5...fxg3 6.♗f4 (6.♘f3 d6 7.♗g5 f6 8.♗f4 ♘c6 9.♕d3 ♕f7 10.0-0-0 and White won in Stocek-Vokac, Prerov 2001) 6...c6 7.♕d2 b5 8.0-0-0 f6 9.e5± and this led to another disaster for Black in Chaderon-C.Foisor, France 1998.

5.♗c4

Or 5.♕f3!? ♘f6 6.b3 ♘c6 7.♗b5 ♗d7 8.♘ge2 ♘b4! 9.♗d3 d5! 10.exd5 0-0-0! 11.♗b2 ♗g4! and Black had achieved a killing attack and won in Olala style (as played by my Spanish student Juan Luis Ramiro), Ramon-Ramiro, La Puebla de Alfinden 2010. After the attacking 5.♘d5 Black has 5...♕d8 6.♘f3

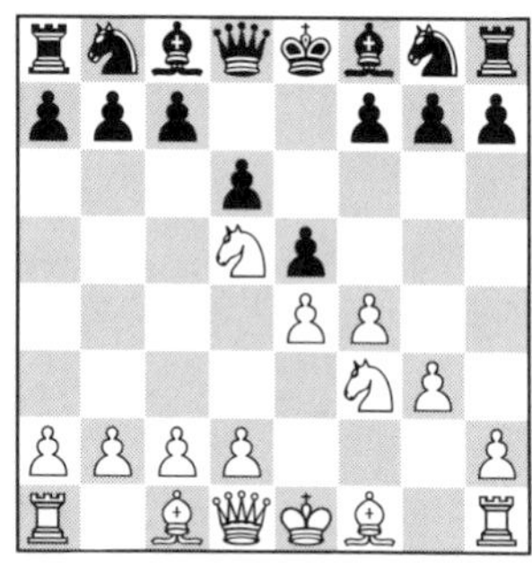

6...c6! (6...♘f6!? is also playable, as after 7.♗c4 ♗e6 8.d4 ♗xd5 9.exd5 exf4 10.♗xf4 ♗e7 11.0-0 0-0 12.♗b3 ♘bd7 White is a little better, but Black held in Vouldis-Plachetka, Bled 2002) 7.♘e3 (7.♘c3 ♘f6!? – or 7...exf4 8.gxf4 d5! with unclear play – 8.fxe5 – 8.d3 ♘bd7 with ...b5 ideas is a good Philidor! The light-squared bishop will be passive on e2 or g2 – 8...dxe5 9.♘xe5 ♗c5 is a good gambit, as the black king will feel much safer than his opponent's, right? 10.♗g2 – 10.♘a4?! is met by 10...♗d4! 11.♘f3 ♘xe4 – 10...0-0? 11.♘e2 ♖e8 12.d4 ♗b6 13.c3 c5! with obvious compensation) 7...exf4 8.gxf4 ♘f6 9.d3 d5

10.e5 ♘h5! looks good for Black, as 11.f5 is met by 11...d4.

5...c6 6.fxe5 dxe5 7.d3 ♘f6

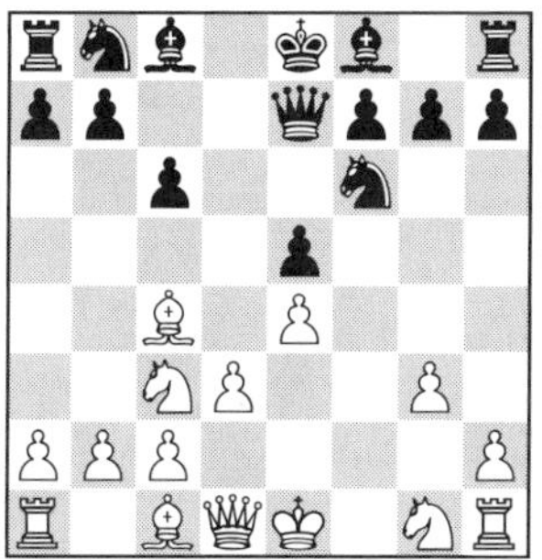

8.♘ge2?!

Against the stronger 8.♘f3 my choice would be the prophylactic 8...h6!, to prevent ♘g5 or ♗g5 (8...b5!? 9.♗b3 ♘a6 10.♘g5 ♗g4! 11.♘e2 ♗h5 is another option. But I don't like 8...♗g4?! 9.h3 ♗h5 10.g4 ♗g6 11.♗e3 and while Black went on to win in Carbonnel-Dobrev, France 2008, this is not a dream bishop on g6) 9.0-0 (9.a4 ♗h3) 9...♗h3 10.♖e1 b5 11.♗b3 ♘g4 looks more to the point.

8...♗h3!

This emphasizes the point of 2...♕h4+!. Having provoked g3 Black takes advantage of the weakened light squares.

9.♗g5 ♘bd7 10.♕d2 h6 11.♗e3 ♘g4

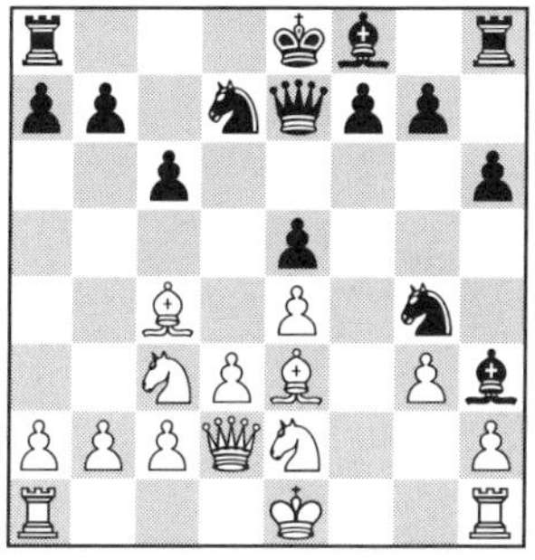

Black already has a very comfortable edge.

12.0-0-0 Black is also much better after 12.♘g1 ♘xe3 13.♘xh3 ♘xc4 14.dxc4 ♘b6.

12...♘xe3 13.♕xe3 b5 14.♗b3 a5!

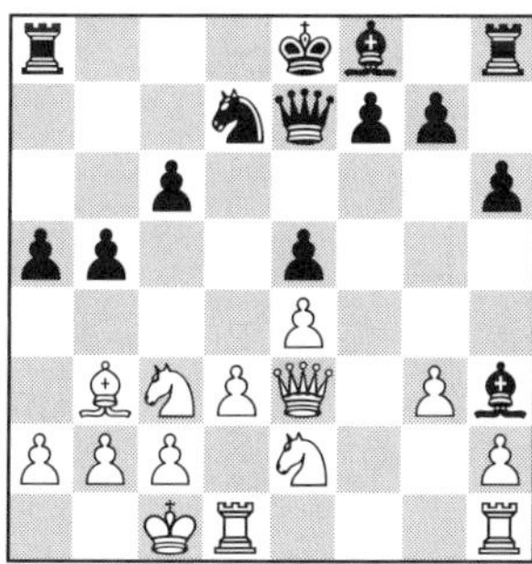

Gaining more and more space, and annoying White's pieces!

15.a4 b4 16.♘b1 ♕g5!

What could be better than solving the problem of the queen by exchanging into a clearly better endgame, owing to the weakness on h2 and the two Olala Bishops!

17.♕xg5 hxg5 18.d4 ♗g2 19.♖he1 ♖xh2 20.♘d2 ♗e7 21.d5 c5 22.♗c4

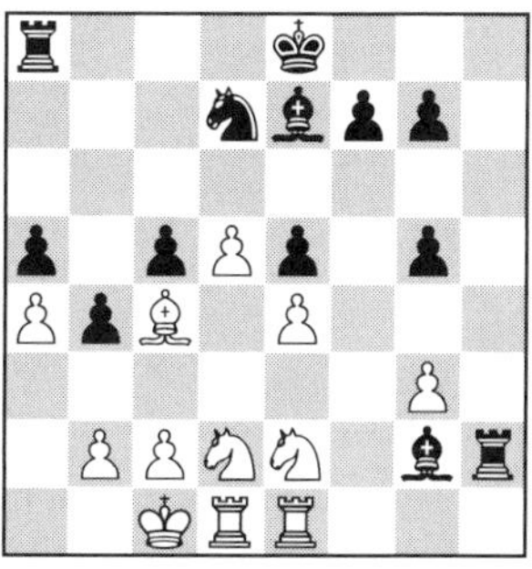

22...g4! 23.♗b5 ♗g5 24.♗c6 0-0-0!

Always nice to castle this late into the game. Christina went confidently on to win the game:

25.♘g1 ♗h1! 26.♗b5 ♘f6 27.♗d3 c4! 28.♗xc4 ♘xe4 29.♖e2 ♖xe2 30.♘xe2 ♗xd2+ 31.♖xd2 ♘xd2 32.♔xd2

And White stopped the clock.